GANGĀDEVĪ'S MADHURĀVIJAYAṀ

A Literary Study

GAṄGĀDEVĪ'S MADHURĀVIJAYAṀ

A Literary Study

B.A. Dodamani

SHARADA

Sharada Publishing House

Delhi

2008

First Published : 2008

ISBN : 978-81-88934-51-5

SHARADA ₹ 750/-

Published by
Anjana Bansal
SHARADA PUBLISHING HOUSE
(Publishers on India's Past and Present)
111, Vidya Vihar Apartment
Sector-9, Rohini, Delhi-110 085 (INDIA)
Ph. : +91-11-3292 1560, 2755 2102
Email : bansal_sph@rediffmail.com

Printed at
Salasar Imaging Systems
Delhi

Preface

The aim of this work is to draw upon the fulness of the epic poem Madhurāvijayaṁ. An attempt to analyse the writings of Gaṅgādevī carefully and systematically, shows that these writings are rich in historical accounts of Vijayanagar empire. There is, of course, no dearth of research papers or book-lets on this epic poem; but a single and systematic study of the Madhurāvijayaṁ in its literary and historical perspectives, has, to my knowledge, not yet been undertaken. With this in view, I have taken up in this work a literary study of the Madhurāvijayaṁ.

Indeed, Gaṅgādevī stands out among the poetesses in the field of Sanskrit literature. Intelligible in itself, Gaṅgādevī's writings need no further elucidation for the learned to understand and appreciate them. But, for further clarification of Alaṅkāras, Rasa-delineation etc., the Sanskrit commentary "Bhāvaprakāśikā" by Subrahmanya Shastri has been frequently referred to in this work.

This work attempts to show how Gaṅgādevī's reinforces the historical facts and restores literary aspects. This is what may be considered to be the contribution of Gaṅgādevī to the world of secular Sanskrit literature. It is hoped, the References given at the end of each chapter will add to the usefulness of the work.

It has been my privilege to mention the name of my bosom friend, Dr. K.B. Archak, Reader in Sanskrit, Karnatak University, Dharwad. Without his constant guidance and prompt corrections, this work would not have been possible. It is thus a great pleasure for me to express my deep sense of honour and heartfelt thanks to him.

I extend my deep respectful sense of honour to my teacher Dr. D.N. Shanbhag, Professor of Sanskrit (Retd.), Karnatak University Dharwad, and recipient of prestigious award from the President of India, for having given many useful suggestions for the improvement of this work.

It is my pleasant duty to record my most hearty thanks to Anjana Bansal, Sharada Publishing House for accepting this work as its publication and accomplishing the same neatly with meticulous care as well as magnificient co-operation.

Dharwad **B.A. Dodamani**

Contents

Preface v

Chapter-1

Introduction
(Life, Date and Works of Gaṅgādevī) 1

Chapter-2

History in the Madhurāvijayaṁ 28

Chapter-3

The Art of Narration 39

Chapter-4

Description in the Madhurāvijayaṁ 73

Chapter-5

Alaṅkāras in the Madhurāvijayaṁ 105

Chapter-6

Rasa Delineation in the Madhurāvijayaṁ 143

Chapter-7

Gaṅgādevī's Scholarship 163

Chapter-8

Conclusion 185

Bibliography 191

Index 199

Chapter-1

Introduction

(Life, Date and Works of Gaṅgādevī)

There are many more Sanskrit scholars who have displayed their skill in various ways, in the world of Sanskrit literature, in particular, the poetic literature. Like the poets, poetesses too have been very popular with their charming and comprehensive compositions. Thus, Rājaśekhara says—

पुरुषवत् योषितोऽपि कवी भवेयुः संस्कारो-
ह्यात्मनि समवैति, न स्त्रैणं पौरुषं वा विभागमपेक्षते।
श्रूयन्ते दृश्यन्ते च राजपुत्र्यः महामावदुहितरो-
गणिकाः कौतुकिभार्याश्च शास्त्रप्रहतबुद्धयः कवयश्च।।[1]

काव्यमीमांसा, अ०10

It is here suggested that even during the time of Rājaśekhara, poetesses existed. Even the wife of Rājaśekhara, Avantisundarī, was a great poetess, as can be seen from the following statement:

बाहुणकुलमौलिमालिका राजशेखर कवीन्द्रगोहिवी।
भर्तुःकृतिमवन्तिसुन्दरी सा प्रयोजयितुमेतदिच्छति।।[2]

कर्पूरमञ्जरी, I-11

(*Cf.* Kannada Kāvyamimamśa of K. Krishnamoorthy Sharada Mandira Mysore 1964, p. XVI)

Unfortunately, the number of works written by the poetess have been lost in the fast flow of time.

In the later period, *i.e.*, from 16th century to the 18th century, poetesses by name, Bhāratī, Vijjhatā, Mohanāṅgī, Varadāmbikā, Rāmabhadrāmbā etc., adorned the world of Sanskrit literature. Another poetess called Tirumalāmbā in her work entitled, Varadāmbikāpariṇaya describes the marriage story of the King Achutadevarāya and his wife Varadāmbikā. Another poetess–Rāmambikā has translated into Sanskrit, the entire Telagu-Rāmāyaṇa of Raghunāthārāya. Similarly, another female Sanskrit scholar Nachamamba having acquired the knowledge of Sanskrit, won many Paṇḍits in the royal assembly of Rajasthan. Incorporating all these incidents, she composed a Sanskrit drama. In this manner, poetesses too have contributed a lot to the development of Sanskrit studies, hence they have been equally honoured by the Sahṛdayas.

Gaṅgādevī of the Madhurāvijayaṁ, chief queen of Kampaṇa, has been one of such important poetesses. She is believed to be of Kākatīya race. Ekaśilānagara of Andhra is the native place of Gaṅgādevī.

In the course of the following pages the date, life and works of Gaṅgādevī, have been examined with reference to other historical works, in some detail. The Madhurāvijayaṁ, as the title indicates, deals with the story of the, conquest of Madhurai by the King Kampaṇa, the hero of the poem. However, this Mahākāvya consists of certain aspects which are free from its purely historical nature. The sixth and the seventh cantos of the poem describe only the amors of the prince Kampaṇa and his sports with the queens. Perhaps, it might be the intention of the poetess to make us known that after the conquest of Kāñcī as described in the fourth canto, Kampaṇa gained the hearts of his subjects by his just and benevolent rule. The fact that he could enjoy his life in Kāñcī without any fear, shows that his rule was very popular, and he had full support of the people of Tondaimandalam when he started on his compaign against Madhurai.

Just as, in the Nāgānandam of Harṣa, there is the episode of a goddess presenting a sword to Jimūtavāhana, in the eighth canto of the Madhurāvijayaṁ a goddess telling a plightful condition of Tamil country after the Muslim occupation,—is a poetic convention. It may be considered as the personification of Dharma. Also this introduction of the supernatural element in the poem does not affect the accuracy of the main details. There could be some defects considered according to the principles of modern historiography in this poem. Yet, such minor things need not be taken with very serious notice of in the poem, since it has been the only historical work for the history of South India, before the fifteenth century.

No doubt, the writing of India's past history in the frame of literature, is not an easy task. The literature sprinkles some ideas of meagre history which many substantiate the basis of a preconceived history. Therefore, a need was to develop an objective outlook on the part of historians. It is the Madhurāvijayaṁ, that has fulfilled the need; as such, it has been a very important work as a hand-mind to Archaeology, Epigraphy and Numismatics.

In fact, there are such historical works like Kalhaṇa's Rājataraṅgiṇī–telling the story of the Kings of Kashmir, Bāṇa's Harṣacaritaṁ–narrating the story of the king Harṣa, Daṇḍin's Daśakumāracaritaṁ–dealing with the story of the ten royal youths. But, there is good deal in all such works which does not partake of the nature of correct history. In this respect, the Madhurāvijayaṁ has been regarded as an important literary source in the reconstruction of the past history of India.

At this juncture, it is appropriate to look into the historic background of the glory of Kampaṇa's rule:

"On the banks of Tuṅgabhadrā river, Hari Hara Rayalu

built the city of Vijayanagar after the fall of the kingdom of Kampile, made it his capital, and founded the Vijayanagara empire. In the first half of the 14th century A.D. the southern India became disintegrated into pieces unable to withstand the Muslim armies and the entire south upto Rameswaram bounded by the sea fell into Muslim hands. The fort of Devagiri in the hegemony of Rāmachandra Deva, king of Sevuna, fell into the hands of Alauddin of the Khilji dynasty in 1295 A.D. and in 1314 A.D., after the death of Rāmachandra merged and became the stronghold of the Delhi Empire."

"Malik Kaffar's armies, raided the kingdoms of Dwarasamudram, Warangal and Madhura. Though disabled and devoid of independence, these kingdoms somehow pulled on until the collapse of the Khilji dynasty. But with the emergence of the Tugalak Rāj, for south India, again evil days had commenced. Muslim invasions increased. Hindu kingdoms were eventually wiped out and led to the establishment of the Tuglak empire. The Warangal fort of Kakathīyas fell in 1323 A.D. Later, all the seashore forts of the Andhras were annexed by the Mohammadans. Even Mabar and Madhura were snatched away from the Pāṇḍyas and were merged in the Delhi Empire."

Even then invasions did not cease. In the Karnatak, Hoyisala and Kampile kingdoms had yet to be subdued. Without conquering them, the emperors of Delhi could not have suzerainty over the entire South India.

"Kampila the founder of the Kampili kingdom having been originally in the service of Yadava Rāmachandra I gained vast experience in the battle between Hoyisalas and his king, and on the capture of Rāmachandra by Malik Kaffar and removal to Delhi revolted against the Muslims. He waged war incessantly against the Muslims, refused to yield, established his kingdom and even extended it, by conquering a portion of it from the adjacent kingdom of Ballāla."

"So Malik Kaffar, the commander of Alauddin of the Khilji dynasty, came upon Kampilaraya in vain and returned discomfited. Thence, the Kampila kingdom continued to be independent."

"Kampilirāya gave shelter to Harihara and Bukka" ministers, of Prataparudra after the fall of the Kakathīya dynasty, and employed them in his own service. Bahuddin, a relative of Sultan Mohammad-Bin-Tuglak rebelled against the Delhi Empire at Gutasp Sagar but was unfortunately defeated by the Delhi armies. So, he sought refuge under Kampilirāya. Thus, Kampila became a target to the wrath of the Delhi Padushah. In spite of several invasions against Kampila, the latter successfully resisted and defeated the armies from Delhi. But in the end, during the siege of the fort of Hosa in 1327 A.D. Kampilarāya died. His sons, and the ministers Harihara and Bukka were taken as captives and were converted into Islam."

"At the fall of Kampila, Bahauddin Gustasp sought the shelter of Ballala of the Hoyisala kingdom. The armies of Delhi, pursued Gustasp and entered the Hoyisala kingdom. Ballala was incapable of resisting the Delhi forces. So, he arrested Gustasp and surrendered him to the Delhi Sultan. Mohammad-Bin-Tuglak, rejoiced over it and returned to Delhi without invading the Hoyisala kingdom of Ballala."

"By this, Tuglak became the Emperor of the entire (Akhand) Hindu India. With the conquest of the south, his empire, extended from Peshawar on the west, to Bay of Bengal on the east and from the Himālayas on the north to Setu Bandha and Rameswar on the south. But soon after, even his vast empire became disintegrated into pieces. After the fall of the kingdom of Kampila, the Sultan stayed for two years in the south, to set right and consolidate or stabilise the administration, but, in 1329 A.D. he had to go back on account of the revolt in the Punjab. Taking advantage of this, the leaders of Telangana under the leadership of Musunuri Prolayanayak, rebelled against muslim the administrators, set up by the Sultan. Prolayanayak was soon crowned with success. The entire coastal area of Andhra went into the control of Prolayanayak. Seeing this, Soma Deva the great descendent of the dynasty of Araveedu, raised a revolt in the western part of the Andhra. Many local Hindu nāyakas assisted him. With the assistance of Ballala Deva and others, Somadeva confronted and defied the Sayab Mohammad set up at Kampila by the Sultan and snatched away from him the forts at Anegondi, Rayachuru, and Mudgalu etc., and annexed a portion of the empire. The ruler of Kampila town was subjected to several privations. Neither paddy nor other commodities were allowed to reach that town. Hindu nāyakas stopped paying tributes to him and put him to manifold difficulties. Unable to bear all this, the ruler sought the help of the Sultan at Delhi. The Sultan sent Harihara and Bukka the ministers of Kampilarāya, then in his captivity, for administering the Kampila Deśa. They came to the south. But as they were converts. into Islam and came on behalf of the Sultan, Ballala and Somadeva did not accept their authority. They were defeated in the fight with Ballāla and fled to the woods nearby. But, by the grace of Vidyaranya Yateendra, then stationed near the Pampapathi temple near Hampi, they were converted into Hindu fold, and resolved to drive out the Muslims and protect and revitalise Vedic Dharma. With the help of Vidyaranya, they subdued Ballala and Somadeva and with Anegondi as the capital, began to rule."

"At this juncture, all the vigorous efforts made by the Delhi Emperor to subdue the revolt of Jalaluddin, Governor of Mabar, having failed, the prestige of the emperor waned and the trials to revive the Hindu Rāja gathered strength and momentum. Soon after the departure of the Sultan from the South, Kapayanayakudu who succeeded Prolaya sought and obtained military help from Ballala, and defeated Malik Makbul the ruler of Telangana in 1336 A.D. and captured Warangal. Makbul fled to Delhi. Kapayanayakudu assisted by Ballala, entered Tondaimandalam, drove away the Muslim armies belonging to Mabar, from there and entrusted that province to Sambuvaraya."

"Thus, the suzerainty of the Sultan ended in the south. In the Telugu land, not only the kingdom of Kapayanayaka but also some other Hindu kingdoms sprang up. Koppulanayakulu, with Pithapur as capital, ruled over the Krishna and Godavari regions. The Reddy kings of Kondaveedu held sway over the region between Srisailam and the sea to its east, while the Velama kings began to reign in the Nalgonda Area. In Tamilnadu, the Tondaimandalam (or region) under Sambuvaraya, Chola and Pāṇḍya regions under the governor of Mabar became independent and defied the Sultan.

Without letting loose this opportunity, Hari Hara Rayalu and Bukkarayalu began to expand their kingdoms with a view to revive and rehabilitate Hindu Religion. At the behest of Vidyaranya, they built Vijayanagar in 1336 A.D., as capital and while Hari Hara Rāya was effectively administering the kingdom, Bukkaraya under the able guidance of his minister Madhava extended the kingdom as far as the sea on the east. This expansion has furnished sufficient power and financial stability. By then, on the west, the Hoyisala kingdom under the 3rd Ballala became an impediment to the growth of the Vijayanagar empire on account of its stability and expansion. So, Bukkaraya gradually began to invade the Hoyisala kingdom. In 1340 A.D., he could annex the Kukkalanadu region, to his Rāja. But Ballala reconquered it and protected his kingdom till 1342 A.D. When in the war he waged against the Sultan of Madhura, Ballala III died at the hands of Ghiyajuddin during his raid against Tiruchirapalli. Being aware of this unprotected state of the Hoyisala Rāja, Bukkarayalu, then ruling over Udayagiri and Gutti invaded and conqured the fort at Panugonda. Gradually even by the next year, he subdued Hosapatnam and Dwara Samudram and the Mulbagal region in the Kolar district and also drove away Ballala IV from the Hoyisala and annexed it to the Vijayanagar empire."[3]

Despite all this victory of Harihararayalu and Bukkarāyalu, Hindu religion was destroyed by the Sultan of Delhi and the Muslim rulers of Madhura. All Hindus were subjected to series of miseries. Many temples were destroyed. All people were reduced to slavery. There was no scope for the development of Fine arts, Culture and Vedic Dharma, as all these were suppressed ruthlessly beyond recognition.

In such critical time, Kampaṇa, the son of Bukka came on the scene, salvaged Hindu Religions, gave protection to the people and strove for the prosperity of the country.

A perusal of the Madhurāvijayaṁ makes it evident that Kampaṇa's talents were not restricted to war and to the rejuvenation of Hindu religion only but also seen in the fields of Music and Literature. He had the titles like Saṅgītai-kanidhi", "Saṅgīta-Sahityarnava", Guṇaparama maheśvara etc. These notes suggest that Kampaṇa had abundant depth of Hindu culture, Music and Poetry. It is here, therefore, an opportunity to recall the history of such a great hero.

Sanskrit scholars of ancient period do not usually give any information about their personal life which would facilitate the work of compilation of their biography or to get a glimpse of the social life of their time. Therefore, whenever a student proposes to write on the life and date of any Sanskrit author, many questions concerning the author remain unanswered. It is true that a few Sanskrit authors such as Bāṇa, Rājaśekhara and Bilhaṇa, have provided some information about themselves in their works. But these works contain more of poetry than of contemporary history and as such any account concerning the personal life of the author recorded in them can hardly satisty the curiosity of modern students. Under such circumstances, it has been difficult to ascertain details with regard to the personal life of any author. In spite of these handicaps, many modern research scholars –Western as well as Indian–have made efforts to bring to light several bits of information with the help of which the biography of any author can be compiled with authenticity.

An Account of Gaṅgādevī's Life

From time immemorial, many scholars in the field of

Sanskrit literature have written a number of works which have become more popular. There are many eminent women of learning in Sanskrit literature who have written epic poems and become famous on par with Kālidāsa, Bhavabhūti etc. In 950 A.D., Rājaśekhara praises by extracting a few stanzas of each, introduces some poetesses in Sanskrit literature who have been important figures in the history of poetry. He praises some poetesses like Sītā, Vijjanaka or Vijjā or Vijjallā, Subhadrā, Prabhudevī, Vikṭanitambī.[4] Ballala's Bhojacarita mentions some poetesses too, but it is doubtful whether these were not fictitious names. Historical evidence also proves this excepting some. The history also affirms the same-barring the few poems so extracted the rest of their poetry became extinct now. A study of the available secular Sanskrit kāvyas, makes it clear that amongst all such poetesses Gaṅgādevī occupies the foremost place.[5] The great Sanskrit scholar, K. Raghavacharya states that this great poetess occupies the first and foremost position amongst all the South Indian poetesses.[6]

The peculiar interest of this biographical poem is that its author. Gaṅgādevī is known to be the wife of Kamparāja whom it eulogises and that in all probability she accompanied her husband in his sojourns in the south.[7] She was the chief queen of Kampaṇa II, and though nothing is known about her lineage, it may be said that she must have come from a noble family as the suffix Devī would imply. She is described as being very highly accomplished and endowed with all charms and grace; as such Kampaṇa has lavished all his love and attention on her though he had other wives.[8]

M. Krishnamachariar mentions about Gaṅgādevī in his work "History of Classical Sanskrit Literature." Gaṅgādevī was the consort of Kampaṇa or Kamparāya, the second son of Bukka I (1343-1379 A.D.).[9]

Gaṅgādevī the poetess is described as a concubine of Kampaṇa by Jayanh Rāmayyapantulu.[10] The Madhurāvijayaṁ refers to her as a wife of Kampaṇa For these ślokas:

अथ कम्पनृपोऽपि कृत्यवित् कृतसन्ध्यासमयोचितक्रियः।
अवदत् सविधे स्मितां प्रियां भुवि गंगेत्यभिनन्दिताह्वयाम्।।
कमलाक्षि! कटाक्ष्यतामयं समयो वर्णनया रसार्द्रया।
जन एष वचस्तवामृतं श्रवसा वारयितुं कुतूहली।।
इति सा दयितेन भाषिता दरनम्रं दधती मुखाम्बुजम्।
वदति स्म शनैः शुचिस्मिता सरसोदारपदां सरस्वतीम्।।

VII-39-42

The ending lines of these verses lay much emphasis on Gaṅgādevī's being the queen of Kampaṇa, rather than his concubine.

N. Lakshminarayan Rao with regard to this opines as follows: Among the ladies of the first Vijayanagar dynasty, there was a famous poetess named Gaṅgādevī who wrote a great Sanskrit kāvya called Madhurāvijayaṁ. In this work, she has described the conquests of her husband, Kampaṇa, the son of Bukka I.[11]

M. Winternitz, when dealing with the life of Gaṅgādevī remarks that she was the queen of King Kampaṇa of Kanchivaram.[12] V. Raghavan too concurs with Winternitz. Moreover, Renupant Lucknow has given his opinion regarding Gaṅgādevī in the following words:

"The poetess who incidentally was the queen of Kamparāja describes in detail. Two important compaigns of her husband.[14]

According to R.S. Mugali, Gaṅgādevī the daughter-in-law of Bukkarāya, wrote the Madhurāvijayaṁ in excellent Sanskrit.[15] Extolling the exploits of her heroic husband the task of conquering the Tamil country was entrusted by Bukka to his son Vīra Kumāra Kampaṇa, the husband of the famous royal-poetess Gaṅgādevī.[16] All these references emphasize that Gaṅgādevī definitely was the wife of Kumāra Kampaṇa.

She was the queen of Kamparāja the son of Bukka who conquered the Cola territory for Vijayanagara and in her charming poem Madhurāvijayaṁ. She eulogises the conquest of by her husband.[17]

M.B. Paraddi also mentions that Gaṅgādevī was the wife of Kamparāja, the hero of the Madhurāvijayaṁ.[18]

B.A. Saletore states about women status in Hindu society. During the Vijayanagara times woman occupied a prominent place in literature. We have had some occasions of mentioning the learned Gaṅgādevī, wife of Kampaṇa who wrote the Madhurāvijayaṁ or Vīra Kamparaya Caritaṁ.[19]

In the description of Kampaṇa's marriage with Princess as mentioned in the third canto of the Madhurāvijayaṁ, she says like Śaśī to Śākra (Indra), Ramā (Lakṣmī) to Śārṅgin (Viṣṇu) and Satī (Pārvatī) to Śambhu (Śiva). Possibly, the name of the poetess who was his principal consort is introduced).[20] This description clearly shows that she was the queen of Kampaṇa. Further, it is described that she allowed when he attained prime youth to marry several princes; and the unions partook the grandeur of the ocean receiving the rivers at the advent of the rainy season.[21] It shows Gaṅgādevī was one of the queens of Kampaṇa.

She may have been called Gaṅgā before her marriage. And after her marriage with Kampaṇa, the suffix 'devī' may have been added indicating her being in an exalted position. We can find out all these things in the description of day and night which was described by Gaṅgādevī before her husband, the dutiful king Kampaṇa duly performed the worship of Sandhyā and afterwards addressed his queen who was near and whom the world was delighted to call Gaṅgā, thus.

अथ कम्पनृपोऽपि कृत्यवित्
कृतसन्ध्यासमयोचितक्रियः।
अवदत् सविधे स्थितां प्रियां
भुवि गंगेत्यभिनन्दिताह्वयाम्।।

MV. VII-39

Once again it may be said, though repetition, it lays much stress on Gaṅgādevī's being the queen of Kampaṇa rather than his concubine.

When one proposes to write something on the life, date and works of any Sanskrit author the first problem one encounters is lack of sufficient biographical material. One of the Western sanskrit scholar, W.D. Whitney states.[22] All dates given in Indian literary history are pins set up to be bowled down again. Winternitz also gives a similar opinion in these words : we can often say this or that Book this or that class of literature is older than a certain other. However, with regard to its real age it is only possible to offer hypotheses as the surest marks of differentiation for, this relative chronology still lies in the language.[23]

Arabian traveller Albereine who flourished during 1030 A.D. wrote a book on India, which is very important for us to identify the weakness of Indian scholars. Unfortunately the Hindus do not pay much attention to the historical order of things. They are very careless in relating the chronological succession of their kings and when they are pressed for information and are at a loss not knowing what to say, they invariably take to romancing.[24]

If this were to be the status of history of the ruling dynasties, one can well imagine what it must be in the case of poets, dramatists, philosophers, and artists, patronized by them. We have to cull out information about their date, life and social conditions bit by bit from all possible sources, and scrutinise it in the light of available evidences.

Gaṅgādevī is an exception to this general rule. Unlike several other Sanskrit authors, she has indeed given us considerable information about her ancestors, her original home, learning and the date of her work Madhurāvijayaṁ.

Gaṅgādevī was an Andhra princess born in a place near Orugal in or about 1340 A.D. She had the privilege of being the queen of Vīrakampaṇa, king of Karnataka.[25] As has been said before, Gaṅgādevī has been accepted as a contemporary of Viśvanātha who lived during the period 1294 to 1325 A.D. He was the court poet of king Pratāpa Rudradeva who lived during 1296 to 1325 A.D.[26] On the basis of this, we can say that Gaṅgādevī must have lived in the period from 1301 to 1400 A.D.[27] Gaṅgādevī mentions the name of Gaṅgādhara who flourished during 1250-1350 A.D. She mentions the name of Agastya who lived during the period from 1275 to 1325 A.D.[28] She also mentions the, name of Tikkaya who lived in the period 1290 to 1350.[29] It shows that Gaṅgādevī must have lived during this period and she was influenced by all these poets.

V. Raghavan supplies some material life accounts of poetess Gaṅgādevī and date with regard to the Madhurā-vijayaṁ. According to him she was the queen of King Kampaṇa who ruled Kāñcī about A.D. 1367.[30] N. Lakshmi-narayan also has mentioned about the date of Gaṅgādevī and her work, Madhurāvijayaṁ. "It is well known that Vijayanagara kings were great patrons of learning, men of letters and of the fine arts like poetry and music. Gaṅgādevī has written Madhurāvijayaṁ in the year 1360 A.D."[31]

On the basis of all these evidences, it may be said that Gaṅgādevī was the queen of Karnataka king, Kampaṇa and the daughter-in-law of Bukka who ruled over Vijayanagar,[32] the poetess Gaṅgādevī flourished during the period from 1301 to 1400 A.D.

Nelson gives a description as found on a native manuscript of the excesses of the troops of Malikkaar in the Madhurā town, he says Kumāra Kampaṇa's conquest of Tamil country within 1365 A.D. It is also mentioned in the inscription alike on the Mīnākṣī temple that shrine 48 years before the conquest of Kumāra Kampaṇa. If we take into account the view of Nelson the clause of the Mīnākṣī shrine might have happened around 1317 A.D. But during 1317-18 A.D. the Second Muslim conquest took place which was described to be uneventual one. On accepting the view of other scholar: who hold 1374 A.D. as the year of Kumāra Kampaṇa conquest, it can be said that Gaṅgādevī has written the Madhurāvijayaṁ after the conquest of Madhurā by her husband Kampaṇa.[33] May be taken note, the opinion of N. Anantarangachar that the Madhurāvijayaṁ has been composed by Gaṅgādevī during A.D. 1380.[34]

About the Work

The Madhurāvijayaṁ of Gaṅgādevī runs into the hundred and twenty one verses which have been divided nine cantos. The total number of verses in Madhurāvijayaṁ may differ from edition to edition, as some verses have been found added and some dropped. All the nine cantos have been set with beautiful and lucid words, as well as robust thoughts. A brief summary of the poem may be as below:

I Canto

The poetess Gaṅgādevī at the outset pays homage to her favourite gods and elderly poets preceded her. The section of benediction itself runs into sixteen verses. At the first step, she offers Salutation to the elephant faced God *i.e.*, Gaṇapati, Lord Śiva, and Goddess Sarasvatī, among the divinities. Then, the poetess pays respectful compliments to the well known poets who influenced her. These are Kriyāśakti (her preceptor), Vālmīki, Vyāsa, Kālidāsa, Bāṇa, Bhāravi, Daṇḍin, Bhavabhūti, Tikkayya, Agastya, Gaṅgādhara and Viśvanātha.

Then, Gaṅgādevī speaks on literary criticism. As the crow shows a preference to nimba fruit without caring for the mango in the forest, a vile man searches for faults in a poetic composition, in disregard of its merits (I-20). A good composition of a poet promotes fame, serves for wealth, destroys baseness and awakens delight. Thus, what is there that a good poetry does not yield? The Sahṛdayas need no invitation to taste the sweetness of poetry, who argues with the bee to suck the sweet juice of a flower (I-23-24). Likewise, it may be said here that the Madhurāvijayaṁ is just Madhu or honey and many a Sahṛdaya do honour this work with respect and get themselves immersed in reading the poem.

Then follows the description of the greatness of Bukka, the father of Kampaṇa. He is said to have been reigning at Vijayanagara. He was a brave and a courageous king. His vassals and generals were very respectful and loving. They were loyal to the king. He possessed good qualities of head and heart and generous minded kings from different countries had come and pay their homage to him. His fame had spread in all the four corners of the world. His Chief Queen is Devāyī.

Next, the poetess devotes a few verses to the description of the city of Vijayanagara. It is said as situated on the bank of the river Tuṅgabhadrā. In its suburb there is a temple of Virūpākṣa. The city of Vijayanagara was full-fledged in all respects. It was surrounded by ramparts on all sides. It had lofty and gemset towers, pleasure-groves, sporting lakes inhabited by beautiful swans, and high built palaces. The people were happy with what they had—In toto, the city was a playground of all good fortune. Prosperity in all its aspects delighted to live in its saloons. The city looked like a garland of precious stones on the shores of the sea of virtue. The city of Vijayanagara thus shone as Indra's Amarāvatī.

Thus, ends the first canto of the Madhurāvijayaṁ.

II Canto

This canto expresses that the Chief Queen Devāyī conceived by the king and bore the seed of royal race in her womb. Then follows the description of her longings during pregnancy. She expresses her desire to eat particles of earth, which are very tasty to her. Gaṅgādevī imagined that she was the beloved consort of the Lord of this earth and indulged in tasting particles of it as if to teach the responsibility of reigning over the world to the infant in her womb. Then she says she takes bath in the Tāmraparṇī even though she has the opportunity to take the bath in river Tuṅgabhadrā which is flowing near the city. The King celebrated the ceremony of Puṁsavana Saṁskāra (II-13) at a proper time on a scale befitting his royal rank. On an auspicious day, the queen presented her lord with a boy as Goddess Pārvatī bore to Śiva, Subrahmaṇya.

On an auspicious day, the Jātakarma rites of the child were performed as directed by the priest. The child grew in splendour like the god of fire (II-33). The king named his child Kampaṇa as he clearly foresaw in his mind that his son would become a matchless warrior and was sure to make his enemies in the battle (II-39) field quake with fear. In course of time the queen gave birth to two other sons called Kampaṇa and Saṅgama who were like Pārijāta and Cintāmaṇi that sprang from the milky ocean (II-40). Thus, the three sons began to grow day by day and shone like Śiva with his three eyes, the Moon, the Sun and the Fire. Thus, ends the second canto of the Madhurāvijayaṁ.

III Canto

It begins with the description of the extra-ordinary qualities and lustre of Kampaṇa, seen in his childhood. In a very short time he obtains knowledge of all the sciences. He becomes quite proficient in all the branches of learning. He is said to be well trained in the military science. When Kampaṇa is yet young, his father Bukka discourses to him on the evils of indulgence in women, gambling, hunting, drinking and so on, he advises him to avoid giving a thought to such things. Bukka advises him on the duties of the royal princes and putout to him the work that lie before him. Kampaṇa's marriage with Gaṅgādevī and other princesses is described. He asks Kampaṇa to march against Campana the ruler of the Tundiramandalam and reduce Kāñcī to subjugation. When in a good position, he should subdue the several forest chiefs and then proceed. against the king of the Turaskas who was made his head-quarters at Madhurā.

After this advice, Kampaṇa resolves to lead an expedition to the south.

IV Canto

On the instruction of his father Bukkarāya, Kampaṇa proceeded with a huge army of elephants, horses, and infantry to defeat the rebel Chieftain led by Champarāja. He took five or six days to cross the country of Karnataka and reached the town of Kantakanana (Mulbagil) stayed few days in that place then he attacked Champarāja. The dust which was raised by the march of Kampaṇa's army made the waters of the river Palar black and in colour it looked like a signal for the defeat of the Sambuvarāya ruler. Then Kampaṇa stationed his camp at Virincipuram from there he laid seige to his hill fortress of Sambuvarāya kings, which appear to be the Padaividu fortress. He entered the country of the Dramiḍa king and a fierce fight took place between Kamparāya and Sambuvarāya. Forces of Sambuvarāya were defeated and he was killed by the Kampaṇa, then he established a firm rule over Karachi. Thus, the here ends the fourth canto.

V Canto

After vanquishing the king of Dravida, Kampaṇa made Maratakanagaral (Kāñcī), the capital of his newly acquired province and rules in such a way as to be loved by all. Kings from various countries approache-him with different kinds of presents. King of Magadha, Mālava, Sevuna, Siṁhaḷa, Dramila, Kerala and Gauḍa waited at his gates for their turn to pay their homage.

Kampaṇa had much interest in listening to the compositions of good poets in his court, which were sweet like the sounding of Sarasvatī's anklets as she practised graceful walking.

Further, poetess gives the description at length, of different seasons, in the context of Kampaṇa's hunting expeditions. The song of the seasons begins (15-23) with Summer Season (*Grīṣmaṛtu*).

"The elephant cupid, getting scorched in the sun found shelter in the breasts of beautiful ladies which were wet with pastes of sandal and had the cooling contact of pearl strings."

Then continues (24-37) the description of the rainy season (*Varṣā-Ṛtu*)—"The rain-bow with its colours–green, red and white, shone like girdle, set with emerald, coral and pearl of the Beauty Goddess of Sky."

Then continues (38-50) the description of the Autumn season (*Śarad Ṛtu*)—"Autumn like a beautiful lady with lotus eyes, desired as it were to see her face every now and then in the mirror of the Sun whom she, therefore, frequently drew out from his wrapper of white clouds."

Then commences (51-55) the description of the Winter Season (*Hemanta Ṛtu*).

"Lotus clusters were hit by snow and the moon became pale in colour. Only the faces of the kings' beloved consorts gained unmatched charm."

Then commences (56-61) the description of the cold season (*Śiśira Ṛtu*).

"The breasts of his ladies warm with blossoming youthfulness drove away the cold of the season when the king cast longing looks on them."

Then comes (62-67) the description of the Spring Season (*Vasanta Ṛtu*).

"In the Spring festival ladies wanted to paint a form of Cupid on picture-boards. But they ended by painting the form of king Kampaṇa who was always in their heart."

In this manner the King Kampaṇa rendered the third goal of life *i.e.,* Kāma fruitful. Here ends the fifth Canto.

VI & VII Cantos

Though both the cantos sixth and seventh, contain no

historical information provide beautiful description of the water sports of the prince, description of day and night.

"Sporting in the waters made the ladies look as if they just had their sexual satisfaction. Their lips were colour-free, their eyes devoid of collyrium and their foreheads without their decorating mark. And such a sight pleased the king immensely." (VI-62).

"The goddess of Day sealed, as it were, the closed lotuses with the lac of black-bees sitting close on their surface, with a view to guarding the fragrance-treasure of honey within." (VII-18)

"Lady darkness decking her plait of hair with flowers of stars waited for a short time for her lover, the moon, smiling, as it were, with the blossoms of the white lily."

VIII Canto

The mysterious lady who appeared before Kampaṇa while he was at Kāñcī was said to have described the pathetic condition of the Tamil country owing to the tyrannical rule of the Sultans of Madhurā. Gaṅgādevī has described the political and social conditions in such a way that it looks like a faithful portrait of the actual state of affairs. She describes the disastrous consequences of the Mohammedon invasion of the Southern and the said plight of the Southern country and its temples. She said "Where there resounded once the joyous sound of the *mṛdaṅgams* there is heard at present the howl of the jackal, that has made its abode. The river Kāverī that had been regulated by proper dams and flowed into regular channels has begun to flow in all directions. In the Agrahāras where the Yāgadhūma was largely visible and the sound of the chanting of the Vedas was everywhere audible, we have now the offensive smelling smoke issuing from the roasting of flesh by the Muslims and their harsh voice alone is heard. The beautiful coconut trees which were gracing the gardens surrounding the city of Madhurā; have been cut down and in their place we see plenty of Sulas with garlands made by stringing human heads together resembling in a remote manner the coconut trees. The waters of the river Tamraparṇī which used to be white with sandal paste and rubbed away from the breasts of the young and beautiful maidens, who were bathing in it, is now flowing red with the blood of brāhmins and cows slaughtered by the Muslims.

After having described the pitiable condition of Tamil country as above, the mysterious lady exhorts him to extirpate the invaders and restore the country to its ancient glory, presenting him at the same time with a divine sword and ordered him to proceed against the Sultan of Madhurā who was the enemy of the world. Kampaṇa proceeds against Sultan of Madhurā, and in a battle the Sultan was killed by him. Then he makes grants to several temples. At this point the Manuscript breaks off and the narrative is left incomplete.

IX Canto

Most probably verses at the end of the VIII and beginning of IX Cantos are broken off and the narrative is left incomplete. It begins with the description or the battle between Kampaṇa and Turaṣka king (Sultan) of Madhurā. It is fully devoted to describe the battle scene of Kampaṇa and Turaṣka king. The fighting scene is also dreadful and loathsome.

The Yavana king met Kampaṇa even as Vṛtra did the King of Gods. The two proud opponents fought in a manner befitting the respective might of their arms, by showering arrows on each other with their bows sent upto their ears. Afterwards Kampaṇa took the sword which was given by the Madhurā Goddess and cut the head of the Sūratrāṇa. The head of the Sūratrāṇa fell on the ground the head that never knew the art of cajoling servant like Samrāja (Supremacy) and the head not bowed down even to gods. Hero Kampaṇa was astonished to see that even after the head fallen the trunk on the horse back still held the reins checking the horses course with one hand while the other was uplifted to retun the blow of the adversary. In this manner he defeated and killed the Sultan of Madhurā. Thus, the here ends the ninth Canto.

MADHURĀVIJAYAṀ—A MAHĀKĀVYA

In Sanskrit literature, there are many types of poetry which have gained the appreciation of the learned ones. Of them, the Raghuvaṁśa. Kumārasambhava, Kirātārjunīya, Śiśupālavadha and the Naiṣadhīya-carita have been regarded as the Mahākāvyas. In addition, there are other number of good poems which are fit to be called Mahākāvyas. But they are not identified so. The reason could be the lack of popularity out of disregard or carelessness of people during that past period. Yet the truth never dies but lasts forever.

The Madhurāvijayaṁ of Gaṅgādevī has been one of the good poems identified and accepted as the Mahākāvyas. It consists of all fundamental characteristics of a Mahākāvya. Following are the characteristics of the Mahākāvya :

1. The Mahākāvya should run into the sargas. It should consist of the sargas or cantos not less than eight but not more than thirty. Each canto has a uniform metre, which may get changed at the end of the canto. The end of the canto should suggest the subject-matter of the next canto.
2. The Mahākāvya should begin with an auspicious benediction.
3. It should deal with the life of a single hero, or of many kings belonging to the same race. If the hero is only one he must be either celestial, or a Kṣatriya of noble family and possessed of the qualities of Dhīrodātta type.
4. Any one of the sentiments of Śṛṅgāra, Vīra, Śānta, and Karuṇa should be predominant in the Mahākāvya and the rest of the nine sentiments remain as subordinate.
5. At least, one of the four goals of life should be fulfilled.

6. Denouncement of wicked ones and the praise of noble ones should be there.
7. It should consist of the description of city, sea, mountain, seasons, sun-rise, moon-rise, garden, water sport, marriage, separation of lovers, birth of son, sending the messengers, war.
8. It should be embellished with rhetorical figures of speech, sentiments and good-style.[35]

Following is a brief observation of all the characteristics of a Mahākāvya, fitting in the Madhurāvijayaṁ:

1. The Madhurāvijayaṁ runs into the sections of sargas or cantos. It consists of nine cantos. The verses of the different cantos run in a uniform metre :

   Canto I–Anuṣṭub Metre

   Canto II–Upajāti, sometimes Upendravajrā and Indravajrā metres are used.

   Canto III–Vaṁśastha metre

   Canto IV–Anuṣṭub metre

   Canto V–Drutavilambita metre

   Canto VI–Puṣpitāgrā metre

   Canto VII–Viyoginī metre

   Canto VIII–Apacchandasika metre

   Canto IX–Upajāti, sometimes Upendravajrā and Indravajrā.

   And the subject matter of the following canto is suggested in the previous canto. For example, Devāyī's conceiving, her longings during pregnancy coming in the opening of the second canto, are suggested at the end of the first canto by the words : *Sākam tayā hṛdaya-sammatayā-narendraḥ, kālocitānyanubhavār kramaśas-sukhāni* .... (I-75).
2. The Madhurāvijayaṁ begins with an auspicious benediction–in the form of salutation to God Gaṇapati.

3. This Kāvya deals with the life history of king Kampaṇa belonging to warrior class. King Kampaṇa himself is the hero of this Kāvya and does possess the qualities of Dhīrodātta type : He is said to be kind enough to the subjects, well-versed in all sciences, brave, handsome interested in philosophical discourses, strict in administration, etc.
4. In the Madhurāvijayaṁ, Vīra Rasa is predominant and sentiments like Śṛṅgāra (II, V Cantos) Bhayānaka, Bībhatsa Rasa (V Canto) have been subordinately entertained in a most befitting way.
5. In the form of destroying the enemies and protecting his subject, king Kampaṇa achieves the first goal of life *i.e.* Dharma. Wherever, Kampaṇa becomes victorious at Kāñchi, Madhurā etc., he establishes stable and legal government for the welfare of the society.
6. In the opening section of the first Canto, the poetess denounces the persons who do not realize the importance of poetry, and praises the Sahṛdayas; so also in the following cantos like the eighth, denounces the wickedness of Muslims.
7. The description of the city of Vijayanagara follows from 43rd to 66th verses of the First canto:

   Description of Oceans & Rivers : I-50, 60; III-40, VIII-4

   Description of Seasons : V Sarga

   Description of Mountains : I-45

   Description of Sunrise & Moonrise : VII-1-50

   Description of Hunting : II-6, V-747

   Description of Garden : VI Canto

   Description of Watersport : VI Canto

   Description of Marriage : III Canto

   Description of Birth of Kampaṇa : II-14-42

   Description of War : IV & IX Cantos.

8. Gaṅgādevī employs different figures of speech to enrich the meaning to be highlighted. Such figures of speech are : Upamā, Utprekṣā, Rūpaka, Pratīpa, Apahnuti and Vyatireka, etc.

   Upamā (III-5, IV-78, IV-19)

   Utprekṣā (I-68, III-33, 47, V-27, VII-2)

   Pratīpa (III-12, V-52)

   Apahnuti (I-36)

   Atiśayokti (V-10)

   Rūpaka (III-40)

   Parisaṅkhyā (I-65)

   Parisaṅkhyā (I-65)

   Vyatireka (I-61)

   Bhrāntimān (I-55)

   Dṛṣṭānta (I-19-20)

   Hetumān (III-27)

   Mālopamā (I-27-29, 73; II-12)

   Yamaka (III-48)

Vīra, Bhībhatsa, Karuṇa, Śṛṅgāra etc., sentiments and Vaidarbhi style for the composition of the Madhurāvijayaṁ have been employed.

Thus, the Madhurāvijayaṁ in a befitting way is rich with all characteristics of a Mahākāvya, and hence, undoubtedly it may be regarded as a Mahākāvya. It may not be an exaggeration, if it is said that this Madhurāvijayaṁ gains the grandeur of the five Mahākāvyas in all respects.

REFERENCES

1. शब्दार्थयोस्समो गुम्फः पांचाली रीतिरुच्यते।
   शीलाभट्टारिकावाचि बाणोक्तिषु च सा रविः।।
   के वैकटनितम्बेन गिरा गुम्फेन रंजिताः।
   निन्दन्ति निजाकन्तानां न मौग्ध्यमधुरं वचः।।

सरस्वतीव कर्नाटी विजयाङ्का जयत्यसौ।
या वैदर्भ गिरो वासः कालिदासादनन्तरम्।।

2. सूक्तीनां स्मरकेलीनां कलानां च विलासभूः।
प्रभुर्दैवी कविर्लाटी गतापि हृदि तिष्टति।।
पार्थस्य मनसि स्थानं लेभे लघु सुभद्रया।
कवीनां च वचोवृत्ति चातुर्येण सुभद्रया।।
नीलोत्पलदलश्यामा विज्जावां ता मजानता।
वृथैव दण्डिना प्रोक्ता सर्वशुक्ला सरस्वती।।

3. *cf.* M. Krishanamachariar, *History of Classical Sanskrit Literature*, Motilal Banarasidas, Delhi, 1970, pp. 391-92.
4. Rajaśekhara's Kāvyamīmāṁsā. Introduction. Bihar Rastra Bhashya Parishad, Patna, pp. 20-21
5. P. Subramanyaswami, Madhurāvijayaṁ : Shri Ajanta Arts Printers, Kolluru, 1969, Introduction, p. 30.
6. K. Raghavacharyalu, Quarterly Journal of the Mythic Society. *"Some Indian Poetess, Index,"* Vol. XXII, 1935, pp. 41-48.
7. It is only a supposition. But there is, however, a note-worthy interesting point. At the end of Canto I, there is a homage to goddess Mīnākṣī immediatedly after the colophon. It may be said that this must have been copyist of the manuscript, he would have written them at the end of every canto. It may be a fact Gaṅgādevī had dropped the salutation in other cantos and in the verbation copy of the original that dropping was perpetuated.

   Moreover, Kampaṇa lived in Kanchipuram after acquiring the possesson of it from Sambuvarāya. The cantos 6th and 7th describe his happy life with his queen.
8. *Madhurāvijayaṁ*, canto 3, verse 18 and 19; also cantos 6 and 7.
9. M. Krishmachariar, *History of Classical Sanskrit Literature*, Motilal Banarasidass, Delhi, 1970, p. 215.
10. Rāmayyapantulu, *"The Southern School of Telugu Literature"* Quarterly Journal of the Andhra Historical Research Society; Vol. II, Part 3 & 4, 1928, pp. 169-177.
11. N. Lakshminarayana Rao, Quarterly Journal of the Mythic Society, *"Eminent Women of Karnatak"*, Vol. 45, 1954-55, p. 14.
12. M. Winternitz, *A History of Indian Literature*, Vol. III, Motilal Banarasidass, 1963, p. 104.
13. V. Raghavan, *"Sanskrit and Prakrit Poetesses"*, Quarterly Journal of the Mythic Society, Vol. 25, pp. 49-74.
14. Renupant Lucknow, Madhurāvijayaṁ—A Historical Perspective, All

India Oriental Conference, Thirty Second Session, Ahmedabad, 1984-85, p. 257.

15. R.S. Mugali, *"The Heritage of Karnataka in Relation to India"*. Satyasodhana Publishing House, Bangalore, 1946, p. 207.
16. P.N. Chopra, J.K. Ravindran and N. Subrahmanian, *History of South India in Medieval Period*, S. Chand & Company Ltd., New Delhi, 1979, p. 31.
17. K. Krishnamoorthy, *Essays in Sanskrit Criticism*, Karnatak University, Dharwad, 1964, p. 4.
18. M.B. Paraddi, "The Poetry of Gangadevi", The Journal of the Karnatak University : Humanities, Vol. XXI, 1977, p. 36.
19, B.A. Saletore, Social and Political Life in the Vijayanagar Empire, Vol. II, Madras, Paual, B.G., 1934, p. 163.
20. शचीव शक्रस्तरमेव शर्ङ्गिणस्सतीव शम्भोस्सुगिरेव वेधसः।
    अतिप्रियातासु बभूव कांचिन्महीभृतस्तस्य कृताभिषेकाः।। *MV*. III-18
21. अथैनमासादितयौवनोदयं नरेन्द्रकन्याभिरयोजयन्नृपः।।
    घनागमस्सम्भृतरत्नसम्पदं वरापगाभिर्निधिमम्भसामिव।। *Ibid.*, III-17
22. W. Whitney, *'Sanskrit Grammar'* Introduction Ieipzing, 1879 Second Edition, 1889, p. XIX.
23. M. Winterniz, *A History of Indian Literature*. Vol. I, University of Calcutta, 1972, Introduction, p. 26.
24. *Ibid.*, p. 29.
25. P. Subrahmanyashastri, *Madhurāvijayaṁ*, Sri Ajanta Arts Printers, Kolluru, Introduction, 1969, p. 31.
26. *MV*. I-16.
27. *MV*. I-15.
28. *MV*. I-14.
29. *MV*. I-13.
30. V. Raghavan, *"Sanskrit and Prakrit Poetesses"*, Quarterly Journal of the Mythic Society, Vol. 25, 1934-35, p. 65.
31. N. Lakshminarayana, *"Eminent Women of Karnataka"*, Quarterly Journal of Mythic Society, Vol. No. , 1954-55, p. 14.
32. Karnataka-Nayanotsava Purnachandra. Sakam Tayahraya Sammataya Narendra Kalochitanyanubhavan Kramasha Sukhani Virchiraya Vijayapuramadyavaseef. (Kannada Script) M.N. Srinivas Iyangar, Sanskrit Kavicharitre, Samput II, I.B.H. Prakashan, Bangalore, 1986, p. 854.
33. S. Sundararaj, *"Early Muslim Conquest of Tamil Country"* Quarterly Journal of the Mythic Society, Vol. 71, 1980, p. 75.

34. N. Anantarangachar, *'Sahitya Bharati'* University of Mysore, 1970, p. 56.

35. सर्गबन्धो महाकाव्यं तत्रैको नायकः सुरः।
सद्वंशः क्षत्रियो वाऽपि धीरोदात्तगुणान्वितः।। 613
एकवंशभवा भूपाः कुलजा बहवोपि वा।
शृङ्गारवीरशान्तानामेकाङ्गिरस इष्यते।। 614
अङ्गानि सर्वेऽपि रसाः सर्वे नाटकसन्धयः।
इतिहासोद्भवं वृत्तमन्यदा सज्जनाश्रयम्।।615
चत्वारस्तस्य वर्गाःस्युस्तेष्वेकं च फलं भवेत्।
आदौ नमस्क्रियाऽऽशीर्वा वस्तुनिर्देश एव वा।। 616
क्वचिन्निछा खलादीनां सतां च गुणवर्णनम्।
एकवृत्तमयैः पद्यैरवसानेऽन्यवृत्तकैः।। 617
नातिस्वल्पा नातिदीर्घा सर्गा अष्टाधिका इह।
नानावृत्तमयः क्वापि सर्गः कश्चन दृश्यते।। 618
सर्गान्ते भाविसर्गस्य कथायाः सूचनं भवेत्।
सन्ध्यासूर्येन्दुरजनीप्ररोषध्वान्त वासराः।। 619
प्रातर्मध्याह्नमृगया शैलवर्त्तुवनसागराः।
सम्भोगविप्रलम्भो च मुनिस्वर्गपुराध्वराः।। 620
रणप्रयाणोपयममन्त्रपुत्रोदयादयः।
वर्णनीया यथायोगं साङ्गोपाङ्गा अमी दश।। 621
कवेर्वृत्तस्य वा नाम्ना नायकस्येतरस्य वा।
नामास्य सर्गोपादेयकथया सर्गनाम तु।। 622

Vishvanatha, *Sāhityadarpaṇa.* p. 540.

Chapter-2

History in the Madhurāvijayaṁ

History is a systematic account of the events that influence a nation, and an institution. Its purpose is to unveil the truth of the past events through which a human being can learn many novel and useful things and proceed a step further with all confidence to make his life meaningful.

It is defined that history combines in itself not only an account of past events, but also many important instructions or advices on the four goals of life, such as Dharma, Artha, Kāma and Mokṣa.

धर्मार्थकाममोक्षाणामुपदेशसमन्वितम् ।
पूर्ववृत्तं कथायुक्तमितिहासं प्रचक्षते ।।[1]

Thus, it is evident that history contributes a lot to the upliftment of society or nation.

History of Indians is just a means through which the inculcation in posterity of the fourfold object of life is to be attempted. That, the Europeans blaming Indians as totally lacking historical sense, is unreasonable. There have been nārāśaṁsis[2], the seeds of historical writing even in the earliest literature. The real cause that prevented the growth of strictly historical literature in Sanskrit, is the peculiar attitude of Indians towards life as a whole.

We can collect rich historical elements of different periods from the Vedic literature. This epic poem, the Madhurāvijayaṁ has been a standing proof of the historical facts relating to the ancestors and descendants of the Saṅgama dynasty. The Epics, the Purāṇas, the inscriptions coins, monuments, secular literature and the accounts of foreign travellers also help us towards this end. But the history that we find here is generally mixed with myths and legends peculiar to India. The Madhurāvijayaṁ occupies an important place in the field of historical Sanskrit Mahākāvyas. The historical facts are found to be well supported by the grants and inscriptions of the reigns of different kings of the period.

The contents of the Madhurāvijayaṁ are of great importance for the first hand knowledge of Vijayanagar Empire. A short time after its foundation, it throws light on some facts not known before Kampaṇa, the prince of Vijayanagar. The delimitation of history in the Madhurāvijayaṁ begins with the description of the Empire of Bukkarāya, the younger brother of Harihara. Either Harihara or his empire is described; rather he is referred to as younger brother of Bukkarāya.[3]

The evidence of Bitragunte grant[4] of Saṅgama II dated 1350 A.D. records that Saṅgama I, the Father of Harihara I, had five sons. Harihara being the eldest, Kampaṇa and Bukka were second and third respectively. But this leaves the question why did not Kampaṇa succeed Harihara I, though rightful successor? and 'why' historians refer to Bukka as the successor? This question has been attempted in various ways by many historians. But proper solution is not found out to supply the reason for Bukka's sucsession to throne. It is said that Kampaṇa the second brother of Harihara I, was holding the Government of the province of Udayagirirāja, under the title and designation of the Lord of the Eastern and the Western oceans. This fact is well corroborated by the colophon at the end of the Mādhavīya Dhātuvṛtti.[5] According to B.S. Row, the said Kampaṇa must have been contented with his administration in Nellore and probably he was not fully qualified for the post.[6] However, it is expressed by Gopinath Rao in his introduction to the Madhurāvijayaṁ[7] confirms that Kampaṇa had died even before the death of Harihara in Śaka 1268-69 and it gave accession for Bukka I. If he had not died, it would have been difficult for Bukka I to mount the throne. In view of the controversy above, it is not possible to arrive at a conclusion concerning Bukka's succession. But, so far as the Madhurāvijayaṁ is concerned, there is no scope for controversy in the fact that Bukka was the real successor (*MV*. I-26).

In A.D. 1356, Bukka succeeded his brother Harihara I, to the throne of Vijayanagar. Already, he had been well acquainted with the problems of the new kingdom. In fact, he was an efficient ruler in the administration of different regions of the kingdom. After obtaining the crown, he set himself to the task of getting rid of the hostile elements and consolidating the new kingdom. He was a Kṣatriya. This is borne out by the propriety of various descriptions in this Kāvya.[8] He is the most renowned of all the kings of Vijayanagar. Some inscriptions clearly say that Bukka had enjoyed a great honour of having various titles like Mahāmaṇḍaleśa, Arirāya, Vibhāda, Rājādhirāja, Rāja Parameśvara, Suratrāṇa etc.[9] He has adorned the crown of fame which is described as, the lord of Eastern and Western oceans as may be seen from another inscription.[10] He is compared with Arjuna and described as one who drove out the enemies from many royal cities and ruled over an empire perfect in seven parts.[11]

King Bukka as stated in the Madhurāvijayaṁ had two sons by his queen, Devāyi *viz.*, Kampaṇa and Saṅgama.

अथ क्रमात् पार्थिवधर्मपत्नी सुतावुभौ कम्पनसंगमाख्यौ।
असूत चिन्तामणिपारिजातौ पयःपयोधेरिव वीचिरेखा।।

स राजसूनुः सह सोदराभ्यां दिने दिने वृद्धिमुपाससाद।
शशीव सानन्दमुदीक्ष्यमाणः प्रजाभिरालोकसमुत्सुकाभिः।।

MV. II-41-42

Gaṅgādevī in her Madhurāvijayaṁ has added a new information to the stock of southern history.[12] The two sons of Bukka I, having the same name, have produced great confusion and difficulty in the already confused state of genealogy of the first Vijayanagar dynasty. The name Kampaṇa is addressed to both the sons of Bukka I. However, from the inscriptions available from Madras presidency and Mysore state, it is understood that the elder was called Hiriya and younger was called Chikka. However, some of the epigraphists of Madras assert that Kumāra Kampaṇa, Chikka Kampaṇa. Vīrabukkarāya Kampaṇa and all those in which the prefix Hiriya etc., is used before the name Kampaṇa, are assigned to his paternal uncle, Kampaṇa (Intro., pp. 30-31). According to T.A. Gopinatha Rao, the second brother of Harihara I, is presumed to have died before Śaka 1268 or 1346 A.D. Now, the inscriptions that belong to a date later than this one, and having the name Hiriya Kampaṇa, should be ascribed to the elder son of Bukka I, and those which give the name of the prince as Chikka Kampaṇa should be assigned to the reign of the younger son Kampaṇa. Anyhow, the conclusion derived can be that Bukka I, had two sons having the same name (Intro., pp. 30-31).

Kampaṇa II, son of Bukka I[13] bore the titles of Mahāmaṇḍaleśvara subduer of hostile kings and lord of the four oceans.[14] His influence had extended from Mysore in the North to Rāmananda in the south.[15]

The Madhurāvijayaṁ states that Bukka I named his first son Kampaṇa, because after his birth, the enemies of Vijayanagar began to shake with fear. This description of Kampaṇa's greatness in fact is not an healthy praise. Yet it is corroborated. by epigraphical evidence also. An inscription from Kolar, praises Kampaṇa in the following words: A Sun of unbounded valour, a moon incarnate inserenity, a unique treasure of music, a tree of paradise to the learned, intent upon establishing Dharma, Lord of the Goddess of Sovereignty with a name renowned among kings, was Vīra

Kumāra Kampaṇa. (Epigraphic Carnatica, Vol. X, Kolar) Kumāra Kampaṇa's main achievements were two; one, the conquest of the Śambuvarāya territory and the second annihilation of the Sultanate of Madhurā. For the discussion of these two achievements, the Madhurāvijayaṁ and the epigraphical evidences engraved during the period of Kampaṇa's conquest and his rule in the Tamil country add significant contribution.

As stated by Gaṅgādevī, Bukka I advised his son Kumāra Kampaṇa to march against Śambuvarāya the chieftain of Padaividu in Tondaimandalam to defeat him in the battle and then to establish himself at Kāñcī. The Śambuvarāya is the leader of Vanninyas and he is preparing for war. If the Vanniya ruler is subdued, it would be easier to break the power of the Muslims at Madhurā. The Sultan of Madhurā is ruling like the Rakṣasas of Laṅkā. Just as Rāma destroyed the Rākṣasas including their leader Rāvaṇa, so too Kampaṇa is advised to destoy the Muslims (Madhurāvijayaṁ 41-43). The fourth canto of the Madhurāvijayaṁ deals with in detail, Kampaṇa's marching against the forces of the Śambuvarāya. The ending portion of this fourth canto states that Kumāra Kampaṇa arriving with his army at Virinchipuram attacked the forces of Śambuvarāya which were then completely defeated and the leader took refuge in the hill fortress called Rājagambhīramāla. But the fortress was besieged.

Being unable to stand the siege for a long time, Śambuvarāya came out of the fort with sword in hand. Then duel took place between them. At last, king Kampaṇa despatched Śambuvarāya as a guest to Indra's city. Having thus reed a Śambuvarāya in the field of battle, king Kampaṇa received the decree of his father that he should rule the territory thus conquered with the fame of his victory duly established in Kāñcī, he inaugurated a just and prosperous rule over Tundiramandalam destroying all confusion in castes and religious orders (Madhurāvijayaṁ IV-75-83).

At this juncture, it should not be forgotten that the history of the Tamil country refers to two great Śambuvarāya ruler-Venrumankonda Śambuvarāya (c.1321-1339 A.D.) and his son Rājanarayana Śambuvarāya (c.1339-1363A.D.).[16] Here, a doubt arises as to who was the Śambuvarāya that came into conflict with and defeated by Kampaṇa of Vijayanagar. It has been an admitted fact that Kampaṇa's conquests over different territories took place after A.D. 1340. Venrumankonda Śambuvarāya flourished before the reign of Kampaṇa. And the date of Rājanārāyaṇa Śambuvarāya goes well with that of Kampaṇa. A. Krishnaswami asserts–"the inscription from Madampakkam dated A.D. 1363 simply mentions that Gandaraguli Mārayya Nāyaka, the General of Kumāra Kampaṇa captured one Venrumankonda Śambuvarāya as prisoner and occupied Rājagambhīramalai. Does this name Venrumankonda Śambuvarāya in any way suggest that he was the son and successor of Rājanārāyaṇa? The fact seems to be that Rājanārāyaṇa himself is referred to in the record as "Venrumankondan" which was the title assumed by his father.[17] Therefore, it was Rājanārāyaṇa Śambuvarāya who was defeated by Kumāra Kampaṇa. But the above inscriptional evidence disproves the statement of Gaṅgādevī that the Śambuvarāya was killed in a duel with Kumāra Kampaṇa.

However, Gaṅgādevī gives no date of the conquest of Tondaimandalam ruled over by Rājanārāyaṇa Śambuvarāya, by Kumāra Kampaṇa. For this, one should rely on the inscriptional evidence. It is already known that Rājanārāyaṇa Śambuvarāya ruled over Tondaimandalam from A.D.1336 and lived upto 1363. His last regnal record from Ukkal (N.A.Dt.) bears the date of Śaka 1284. It refers to the 26th year of Rājanārāyaṇa's rule and yields correct date 30th March 1362. No inscription of Rājanārāyaṇa Śambuvarāya mentioning him as a ruler, after that date, is so far available. "Two other inscriptions of Kumāra Kampaṇa enable us to determine the date of the conquest with some accuracy. They are available from Serkadu in North Arcot district and both of them are dated 3rd January 1363.[18] They registered the free Colonization of the temple precincles by the people and the order of Kumāra Kampaṇa that the taxes collected from them should be utilised for worship in and repairs to the temple of Serkadu. This was done at the instance of Mahāpradhāni Somappa Udaiya for the continuity of Kampaṇa's rule. Its clear from these two records that Kampaṇa's rule was established in the Śambuvarāya's territory before 3rd January 1363. Hence, the nearest approximate date of the conquest may be fixed between October and December 1362.[19]

In course of his expeditions, Kampaṇa crossed the borders of the Karnātaka and reached the Kantakanana.[20] Kampaṇa's army commanded by eminent Generals moved on to the banks of river Kṣīrataraṅgiṇī and entered Virincipuram. Kampaṇa made Virincipuram to be the base of his military operations. As soon as the army of Kampaṇa was seen at Virinicipuram, Champarāja or Śambuvarāya opposed it and a fierce battle took place at Virincipuram. Campa's army suffered defeat at the hands of the powerful army of Kampaṇa and being driven by it, fled towards the capital.[21] Kampaṇa pushed Campa to his Capital. (अथ तस्य पुरीमेव नीत्वा). King Camparāja with some selected solidiers took to the strong fortress on the hill Rajasambutra which was surrounded by the enemy.[22] A fierce battle took place between the armies of Kampaṇa and Campa.[23] At last Campa came out to fight personally in a single combat. King Campa of Kāñcī was killed by Kampaṇa.[24] The Madhurāvijayaṁ is the only work stating that the Dravida king Camparāya was killed by Kampaṇa. After conquering the Dravida king, prince Kampaṇa proceeded to Kāñcī. Then he began to rule at Tundiramandala.

An inscription of Kampaṇa dated 1287 found in Tirupputkuli near Kāñcī records that Bukkannaudaiyara's son Kampaṇa Udaiyar became established on the throne after taking possession of the Rājagambhīrarājya.[25] When he was returning from Kancipuram he was described as a Samrat (Emperor).[26] He won the hearts of the people there.

It also indicates, the same that is a part of the scheme as mentioned in śloka 42 in sarga 3 of the Madhurāvijayaṁ.[27]

His subjects had considered him as another incarnation of Viṣṇu and his fame spread far and wide after establishing himself at Kāñchi.

The concluding canto *i.e.*, the ninth one of the Madhurāvijayaṁ describes at full length the battle between the forces of Kumāra Kampaṇa and the Sultan of Madhurā. "Where there resounded once the joyous sound of the Mṛdaṅgam (South Indian Musical Instrument). There is heard at present the howl of the Jackal, that has made it its abode, the river Kāverī that had been regulated by proper dams and flowed into regular channels has began to flow in all directions. In the Agraharas where the Yāgadhūma was largely visible and the sound of the chanting of the Vedas was everywhere available, we have now the offensive smelling smoke issuing from the roasting of flesh by the Muslims and their harsh voice alone is heard; the beautiful coconut trees which were gracing the gardens surrounding the city Madhurā, have been cut down and in their places we see plenty of Sulas, with garlands made by stringing human heads together resembling in a remote manner, the coconut trees. The waters of the river Tāmraparṇī which used to be white with sandle paste rubbed away from the breasts of the young and beautiful maidens, who were bathing in it, is now flowing red with the blood of brāhmins and cows slaughered by the Muslims.

After having described the pitiable conditions of the Tamil country as above, the mysterious lady was said to have presented Kumāra Kampaṇa with a divine sword and ordered him to proceed against the Sultan of Madhurā who was the enemy of the world. This description of the condition of the temples and the people, though poetic in character, cannot be regarded as opposed to facts of history. Ibn-Batuta and the Hindu chronicles paint equally horrible pictures of the rule of the Sultans of Madhurā and the difficulties which the people had to experience.[28] At the end, it is described "Seated on his agile horse, king Kampaṇa who was the glory of Karnātaka race, avoiding the sword blow aimed by Yavana, cut off in an instant the head of the latter. The head of the Suratrāṇa (Sultan) fell on the ground, the head that never knew the art of cajoling servant-like, the head that had borne the royal burden of the Turuṣka Samrājya and had not bowed down even to Gods.[29]

King Kampaṇa being a pious Hindu, must have had a holy bath at Rameshvaram after his victory over Madhurā and made some gifts to the temple. The earliest of these inscriptions is dated Virodhikrit saṁvatsara, 8th vaikāśi, which is equivalent to 4th June 1371.[30] Hence, the battle of Madhurā may be considered to have taken place in April or May 1371. The Madhurāvijayaṁ does not refer to the name of the Sultan of Madhurā, who was defeated by Kampaṇa. Yet the history of the Tamilnadu does throw a light on the identification of the Sultan of Madhurā who was defeated by Kampaṇa.

Despite the chronological list of Sultans of Madhurā, opinion differs from historian to historian. Yet the coins discovered in South India would be of much help to identify the Sultan of Madhurā conquered by Kampaṇa. The existence of coins cannot be denied as an imaginary one. Those coins mention three Sultans : (1) Adil Shah, (2) Fakhruddin Mubrak Shah and (3) Allauddin Sikhandar Shah. Of these three Sultans, who could be the person defeated by Kumāra Kampaṇa? As has already been maintained the date of the conquest of Madhurā by Kampaṇa to be the April or May 1371, it may be decided whether it was Fakhruddin Mubrak Shah for whom there are number of coins dated A.H. 761 to 770 *i.e.*, 1359 to 1370 A.D. If the numismatic evidence is to be believed, the Sultan defeated by Kampaṇa must be Fakhruddin Mubrak Shah. Because the coins of his successor are dated upto A.D. 1378, when Kumāra Kampaṇa was not alive. Thus, it was Fakhruddin Mubrak Shah who was defeated by Kampaṇa in A.D. 1371.[31]

In fine, it may be undoubtedly taken for granted that Fakhruddin Mubrak Shah was the Sultan defeated by Kumāra Kampaṇa and took the possession of Madhurā.

REFERENCES

1. Apte, V.S., *Sanskrit-English Dictionary*, 2nd edition, 1912, See Itihasa, p. 94.
2. Chandraprabha, *Historical Mahākāvyas in Sanskrit*. Published by Khazanchi Ram, Jain Meharchand Lachhmandas, 2736, Daryaganj, New Delhi, Introduction, 1976, p. 2. *RV*. X. 85. 6, *AVV*. 6. 4. *Tait. Sam.* VII. 5, 11, 2, *Kaṭhaka Sam*. V. 5.2. etc.
3. आसीत् समस्तसामन्तमस्तकन्यस्तशासनः।
   बुक्कराज इति ख्यातो राजा हरिहरानुजः।। *MV*. I-26
4. *Epigraphica Indica*, Vol. III, p. 23.
5. *E.I.*, Vol. III, p. 23.
6. B.S. Row, *Short History of Vijayanagar*, p. 93.
7. *Madhurāvijayaṁ*, Introduction, p. 32.
8. *MV*. I. 30, 68, 72.
9. *EC*, Vol. IV, Part II ch. TL No. 117 NG TL No. 61.
   EC, Vol. X, Kolar Dist. Mb. TL. No. 158.
10. *EC*, Vol. IV, Part II ch. TL No. 113.
11. *EC*, Vol. IV, Part II ch. TL No. 64.
    EC, Vol. IV, Part II ch. TL No. 46.
12. *MV*. II, 40, 41, 42.
13. *EC*, Vol. X, Kolar Dist. TL No. 222.
14. *EC*, Vol. X, Kolar Dist. TL No. 203.
15. *EI*, Vol. IV, Insc. No. 33.
16. A. Krishnaswami, *The Tamil Country under Vijayanagar*. The Annamalai University, 1964, p. 10.
17. *Ibid.*, p. 15.
18. *Ibid.*, pp. 17-18.
19. *Ibid.*, pp. 17-18.

20. *Madhurāvijayaṁ* IV, 47.
21. *Madhurāvijayaṁ* IV, 60-66.
22. *Ibid.*, IV, 67.
23. *Ibid.*, IV, 68-76.
24. *Ibid.*, IV, 82.
25. *Annual Report in Epigraphy*, 1896, No. 18.
26. *Madhurāvijayaṁ* V, 8, 9.
27. *Ibid.*, III, 41.
28 *Ibid.*, VIII, 2, 7, 13, 16, 29.
29. *Ibid.*, IX, 37, 38.
30. A. Krishnaswamy, *Tamil Country under Vijayanagar*, Annamalai University, 1964, p. 34.
31. For details, see A. Krishnaswami, *The Tamil Country under Vijayanagar*, pp. 34-40.

    In spite of the conclusion above, some scholars like S. Tiruvenkatachar, Venkataramanayya hold the similar view that it was Qurbat Hasan Kangu, the Sultan of Madhurā flourished during 1353-1371, and defeated, by Kampaṇa by the following arguments.

    (1) According to inscriptional evidences, Princes Savana Udaiyar and Kampaṇa Udaiyar invaded Madhurā and tried to Qurbas Hasan Kangu from power about A.D. 1352-53 though it cannot be asserted that the Sultan suffered defeat.

    (2) Bukkan, an enemy who was on the frontiers of Mabar with a large army and powerful elephants, invaded Mabar, defeated Qurbat Hasan and killed him. Then he took possession of the city of Madhurā.

    The first argument mentioned above says that it was a joint invasion of Kampaṇa and Savana Udaiyar during A.D. 1352-53. But, it is crystal clear from the Madhurāvijayaṁ that Kampaṇa alone invaded Madhurā and Savana Udaiyar did not take part in the compaign against Madhurā undertaken by Kampaṇa.

    The second argument clearly says that Qurbat Hasan was defeated by Bukkan and not by Kampaṇa. It is said, Bukka had been sent against Madhurā during the reign of Harihara I. Anyway, both the arguments above are insufficient to maintain the view that it was Qurbat Hasan who was defeated by Kampaṇa.

Chapter-3

The Art of Narration

The entire corpus of a Mahākāvya invariably consists of descriptions and narrations. Since technically the Mahākāvya is of the "Prabandha" type, narration has to occupy an important position in it, for, otherwise, the thread of the story cannot be maintained. But at the same time, the poetic faculty of the author of a Mahākāvya cannot find its fulfilment merely by narrating a series of events or incidents. He has invariably to create opportunities for introducing lengthy descriptions of objects which are grand, majestic and beautiful. It is at times, very difficult to draw a line of demarcation between the narrations and the descriptions.

So far as the present Mahākāvya is concerned, we can distinguish narrations from descriptions on the basis of the attitude of the poetess. Those portions of this Mahākāvya which narrate the various incidents of the story and also those which tend to carry the Kathāvastu of a Mahākāvya further and serve as a connecting link between what precedes it and what follows it, should be counted as narrations. There is no doubt that narration holds a subordinate position in Mahākāvya, the major portion being occupied by descriptions.

Gaṅgādevī's Madhurāvijayaṁ is a Mahākāvya, in which descriptions occupy a major portion as compared to narrations. The narrations are very brief and are presented in a summarised form.

The method of narrative skill in this work has some resemblance that in Raghuvaṁśa of Kālidāsa, Kirātārajunīyaṁ of Bhāravi, Śiśupālavadha of Māgha, Rāmāyaṇa of Vālmīki. For instance, in the first canto of the Raghuvaṁśa, Kālidāsa praises Lord Śiva and Pārvatī in the following words: "I bow down to Pārvatī and the Supreme Lord, the world's parents, who like word and meaning are united that I may attain right knowledge of word and sense."[1] Similarly, the poetess Gaṅgādevī also praises God in the first canto of Madhurāvijayaṁ. She says, "For the sake of wisdom, I prayerfully approach god Śiva and his pouse who embody the light of universal consciousness and who bear the, form of the creators's model for making man and woman."[2] In Raghuvaṁśa : Dīlipa was loving his wife Sudakṣiṇā. Many were the women that claimed him as their lord, but in this wise lady and in Lakṣmī he found a true wife.[3] Similarly, in Madhurāvijayaṁ, though the king Bukka had other wives, Devāyī alone became the object of his love and was regarded even as Rohiṇī to the Moon among celestial luminaries.[4] Dilīpa performed the Puṁsavana saṁskāra to. Sudakṣiṇā in a manner befitting his love for his queen and the generosity of his mind, as also befitting the wealth of the ends of the quarters which he had earned by (the prowess of) his arms and the joy he felt.[5] So, it was done to Devāyī also in the Madhurāvijayaṁ The king Bukka who was as prosperous as Indra and who was ever bent on ameliorating the hardships of his subjects, celebrated the ceremony of Puṁsavana as ordered by his preceptor on the appointed time on a scale befitting his royal rank.[6]

In Raghuvaṁśa, Kālidāsa has explained very beautifully Sudakṣiṇā's Garbhalakṣaṇa *i.e.*, pregnancy, due to which her body has changed a lot. She was wearing a few (*i.e.*, limited number of) ornaments on account of the attenuation of her frame with contenance pale as the Lodhra flower, she looked like the night bordering on moon, in which the stars require a search, owing to the moon having pale light.[7]

Similarly, in Madhurāvijayaṁ, poetess Gaṅgādevī explained the Garbhalakṣaṇa of Devāyī like this: The queen put aside her jewels. Her face was some what pale like the sara reed and her form unusually slender. She shone like a river in autumn with lotuses and with the globe of the moon reflected on its watery surface.[8]

In Raghuvaṁśa Kālidāsa has explained the Garbhābhivṛddhi of Sudakṣiṇā very beautifully. He says: As days rolled on, her full and, plumpy breasts, with dark nipples, put to shame, as it were, the loveliness of two harming lotus-buds surmounted by black bees.[9]

Similarly in Madhurāvijayaṁ, Gaṅgādevī described the changes of Devāyī's body like this : Her breasts, with black nipples surpassed in their attractiveness the Cakravāka couple with a bit of blue Utpala flower in their beaks.[10]

Dilīpa was blessed with a son who was named Raghu. "Rituals connected with the birth of the son were performed by Dilīpa as ordained by the royal preceptor. This great son Raghu shone more like a jewel from the mine when duly polished.[11]

Similarly, in Madhurāvijayaṁ, Bukkarāja also performed for Kamparāja on an auspicious day the Jāta-karma rites of the child, as directed by the royal priest and the child grew in splendour like the god of fire that witnessed those rites.[12]

As there is Daśaratha in Raghuvaṁśa, so is the king Bukka in the Madhurāvijyaṁ. In Raghuvaṁśa the Lord of kings on account of the four princes who were portions of Viṣṇu, appreared like the celestial elephant Airāvata with his four tusks that had blunted the edge of demon's swords, like Viṣṇu himself with his four arms as long as a yoke and like politics accompained by four political expedients, the use or adoption of which is inferred from the success attained.[13]

Similarly, in Madhurāvijayam Gaṅgādevī also explained the personality of Bukkarāja like this: The king, with his three children, shone like Śiva with his three eyes, the moon, the sun, and the fire, or like statesmanship, with its three unfailing aspects, power, daring the counsel, or like life with its three ends, virtue, wealth and enjoyment.[14]

In Raghuvaṁśa Rāma loosed arrow piercing Rāvaṇā's breast, entered the earth as if to bear the glad tidings to the serpent world.[15]

Similarly, in the Madhurāvijayaṁ, the poetess describes the sunsetting as below. The sun as if anxious to inform the serpent king who bore this earth (Śeṣa) that his burden would boon be lightened, sank in haste into the nether regions.[16]

In Raghuvaṁśa, as the naked swords of nailed warriors fighting desperately, fell upon the huge tusks of elephants, (sparks of) fire rose which the frenzied elephants quenched with water sprayed from their trunks.[17]

Similarly, in the descriptions of the orderly march of the Kamparāja's forces, she states that particles of the dust fanned out by big war elephants flapping their ears were kept back by the rain of spray from the trunks of elephants.[18]

In the Raghuvaṁśa, when Kuśa left Ayodhyā and went to Kuśavatī from where he began to administer the presiding deity of Ayodhyā appeared before Kuśa at night and implored him to save her. This may be read in detail as below:

"Once, when it was still midnight, people were asleep and lamps were burning mildly, Kuśa awoke and saw in his sleeping chamber a woman, never seen before, dressed like one whose husband has gone on travel.

"Standing before him, of the refulgence of Indra, who was the conqueror of his foes, whose royal wealth was common to the good people and who had friends and relations, she folded her hands having first hailed him victory.

"Then the astonished son of Daśarathī (*i.e.*, Kuśa) leaving the bed by the forepart of his body, spoke to her, who had, like a reflection into a mirror, entered the palace, though the bar of its gate was long since undrawn.

"Finding access in a sheltered home, your power of yoga undiscerned, your wearing the form of one woebegone, like a lotus-vine, in winter's chill outrage, who art thou, O fair.

"Woman, whose wife art thou and what is the reason of your coming to me so promptly, tell me for Raghu's mind is averse to stranger's wife.

"That faultless woman spoke: "Know me, O Lord, to be Lordless, presiding deity of the city, whose citizens where raised by your father prone to repair to heaven.

"That I have been brought to a pitiful plight, out of a splendour, lying with that of Alakā with a prosperity, engendered by good rule, that enables people to indulge in festivities, while thou of the family of the sun descended race rulest the earth, so happy and blissful under thy lead.

"With hundreds of its turrets shattered, and with ramparts demolished, my place bemocks the day's end, whose sun is sunk in setting while fierce winds have scattered the clouds.

"That royal highway, the haunt of Abhisārikas, gleaning with tinkling anklets digit with gleaning meteors in their cavernous mouths, is now the haunt of female jackals.

"The waters in swimming pools which imitated the solemn music of drums when beaten by the finger of damsels (at the time of water-sports) are now crying, being beaten by the horns of wild bisons.

"The sporting peacocks, living on the trees because of the breach of their perching rods, and bereft of their dance in consequence of the absence of the music of drums, are reduced to the wild peacocks, as they had only the remnants of their plumage as it was singed and ruined by flaming meteors.

"On the stairways wide, where gorgeous damsels planted their lovely feet, which with paint they smeared, there, now the tigers plant their feet, and leave their pub-marks, ugly, soaked in the blood, in the carnage of the deer they killed (in raging fury).

"Elephants in the pantings as entered into lotus-beds and as being proffered with snicks of lotus-stalks by their mates (now) bear the blows of the enraged lions having their (elephants') temples smashed by the blows of their lions' goad-like nails.

"The sloughs of snakes become the covering upper garment of the breasts of the statues of women on the columns, which have dusky appearance and the lines of colour on which have been disfigured.

"By the lapse of time, the stately mansions with grass overlaid, their whitewash turned grey, do not reflect the rays of the moon, though serene like ropes of pearls.

"My garden creeper, whose flowers were plucked by damsels, bending their boughs with compassion, are now tortured by monkeys of the forest and by wild pulindas.

"The lattices displaying no light of lamps at night and void of the lustre of the faces of the beautiful ladies during day, are now covered with the cob-webs of spiders with the lines of smokes completely destroyed.

"I am afflicted on seeing the waters of Sarayu not coming into contact with perfumed powders, with sandy beds void of the rites of Bali offerings and having on their sides buts made of canes (now) deserted.

"Therefore, deign you to leave your present habitation and come to me, the capital of your royal family, as did your father before you, having shuffled off his mortal coil, which on purpose he assumed, to attain Viṣṇu's form.

"Saying 'So be it', the foremost of the Raghus accepted her submission happily, and the city, too, with her face bright and serene, in her human form, disappeared."[19]

The Madhurāvijayaṁ also contains a similar narration where the presiding deity of Madhurā explains the atrocities of the Muslims and implores Kampaṇa to save from them. This narration follows as below:

"In Srirangam, the lord of serpents is seen warding off the tumbling debris of brick with his bood lest their fall disturb the sleep of yoga in which Hari is wrapped up there.

"When I look at the state of the temples of other gods also my distress knows no bounds. The foldings of their door are eaten up by wood worms. The arches over their inner sanctuaries are rent with wild growths of vegetation.

"Those temples which were once resonant with the sounds of Mṛdaṅga drums are now echoing the fearful howls of fackals.

"The river Kāverī, uncurbed by proper bunds or dams, has become deflected very much from her time-honoured course, and flows in all sorts of wrong directions as if imitating the Turuṣkas in their actions.

"The brāhmin-streets, where once the sacrificial smoke was even seen rising, and the chanting of the Vedas always greeted the ears, now exude the musty odour of meat, and resound with the lion-roars of drunken Turuṣkas.

"I very much lament for what has happened to the groves in Madhurā. The coconut trees have all been cut and in their place are to be seen rows of iron spikes with human skulls dangling at the points.

"In the highways which were once charming with the sounds of anklets of beautiful women, are now heard ear-piercing noises of brāhmins being dragged, bound in iron-fetters.

"Webs worn by spiders have since taken the place of silk veils with which the dolls adorning the outer-towers of the city were once covered. Royal court-yards which were once cool with the spraying of ice-cold sandal, now distress me, wet as they are with the tears of brahmins taken as prisoners.

"Screechings of owls in worn-out pleasure groves do not afflict me so much as the voice of parrots taught to speak Persian in the houses of Yavanas (Turuṣkas).

"The waters of Tāmraparṇi which were once white with sandal paste rubbed away from the breasts of charming girls are now flowing red with the blood of cows slaughtered by the miscreants.

"Earth is no longer the producer of wealth. Nor does Indra give timely rains. The God of death takes his undue toll of what are left, lives of the undestroyed, by the Yavanas.

"I am very much distressed by looking at the tearful faces of Dravidas, their lips parched by hot sighs, and their hair worn in utter disorder.

"The Kali age deserves now deepest congratulations for being at the zenith of its power; for, gone is sacred learning; hidden is refinement; hushed is the voice of Dharma; destroyed is discipline, and discounted is nobility of birth.

Having thus narrated the sickening career of the Yavanas, she (the strange woman that appeared before Kampaṇa) by her wonderful power of magic caused a terrible looking sword to appear.

"In its shining silver sheath and handle, it looked like a serpent that had recently sloughed. In its darkish brilliance it resembled the Agaru paste that one might imagine on the person of Bhadrakāli whose advent marks the end of this universe. With the images of burning lamps reflected in its surface, it looked like a fresh cloud bright with lightening within it. This sword, efficacious in drawing tears of sorrow from the eyes of enemies' spouses, she placed before the king, as if it were the personification of the prosperity—Goddess of Colas and Pāṇḍyas and began to further address him thus:

"O King, in olden times, this sword was made by Viśvāmitra with the melted splinters of all divine missiles, and he gave it as a present to God Śiva for the destruction of asuras.

"And that God gave it as a boon to the Pāṇḍya king,

pleased with his severe austerities, and his successors had it for a long time and were the unchallenged rulers of their earth.

"Sage Agastya, seeing that the Pāṇḍya race has lost its old virility by the wearing influence of time, has sent this scimitar to you, O powerful king.

"You are by nature daring and wedded to risky enterprises. The possession of this weapon will make you formidable in battle. Forest fire is terrible enough, and if high winds also assist it, who can gauge its all-consuming ferocity?

"By the wonderful virtue of being armed with this weapon you will never flag in the field of battle; nor would any harm result from enemy missiles such as sword, disc or bow.

"As you wave this lightening-like sword in battle, not even the god of death can dare oppose you, let alone, others.

"Do you now proceed to southern Madhurā and destroy Śrī Kṛṣṇa the cruel king of Yavanas who is the enemy of the world, even as killed the demonic Kaṁsa who once ruled there (northern Madhurā).

"Not for the first time will you now be wearing this bracelet on your hand, which has been even on prior occasions, the emblem of your vow of protecting the three worlds, bracelet which none but you can wear.

"Do you scatter the heads of Turuṣkas, heads with those swinging to tufts those bloodshot eyes, those ferocious beards and furious-browed foreheads.

"May the Sun of your prowess in battle wipe off the smile of moon-light of the face of the drunken Yavana ladies.

"Dharma is in great distress by being now subjected to the scorching influence of the evil-natured Yavanas, and earth in consequence looks parched, as it were; and so may you, by the rain of enemies blood, allay the latter's sufferings.

"May this sword of yours feast the evil spirits such as

Katas, Putanas and Yatudhanas with the blood flowing down from the headless trunks of your evil adversaries.

"May you erect many a pillar of truimph in the middle of Rāmasetu by dealing destruction to the Turuṣka lord who is wedded to nothing but evil doings and who therefore is to be regarded as the thorny shrub of the three worlds.

"The Kāverī like a tamed female elephant will regain her of course in the proper place only if and when you become supreme Governor, O Your Majesty."[20]

Moreover, the description of the battle occuring twice in the Madhurāvijayaṁ is in consonance with the descriptions of battle between Raghu and Indra, Aja and his enemy kings, as also between Rāma and Rāvaṇa. The description of Kampaṇa's battle with the Śambuvarāya king, forms the fourth canto. It runs into the following heads :

1. Preparations for the march against the Śambuvarāya territory.
2. Prince Kampaṇa starts on the campaign: He is accompanied by the Cola, Kerala and Pāṇḍya kings.
3. The orderly march of the Karnata forces.
4. Prince Kampaṇa at first struck camp at Mulbāgal and then arrived in Virinchipuram for the fight.
5. The siege of Padaividu the stronghold of the Śambuvarāyas. The defeat of the Tamil forces.
6. The battle on Rājagambiranmalai The defeat and destruction of the Śambuvarāya by Kampaṇa.

These points have been described in detail as below:

"When the divine sun, the sustainer of lotuses, and the unequalled lamp of universe, rose the next day, the prince woke from his sleep, and after duly performing the morning rites of worship, ordered his generals to get the army ready for marching.

"Then, like the noise of the ocean, churned with the mountain of Mandara, the sound of war-drums beaten, arose at the beginning of the march.

"The sound grew louder and ruder, and filled the skies if it emanated from Caṇḍīśa's ḍamaru (drum) beaten at the time of the Great Deluge.

"It raised echoes from the caverns in the mountains as if to scare the fear-ridden enemies who might otherwise take shelter in them.

"As the uproar entered the bowels of earth, Śeṣa closed his eyes (which were also his ears), and he became both blind and deaf by a single act.

"The army at once got ready with each of its units, *viz.*, elephants, horses and foot soldiers. suitably covered and dressesd; elephants with carpets on their backs, horses fully aparisoned and men protected in their mailed coats.

"There mustered hundreds of formidable war-elephants with ichor streaming forth from their extensive temples.

"Horses with foaming mouths, and swift as wind, were seen founding like waves in the army-ocean.

"There gathered in no time, hosts of footmen from different countries, armed with swords, daggers, lances and bows.

"Wearing suitable ornaments, kings renowned for the might of their arm, waited near the outer gate awaiting the arrival of their overlord (Kampaṇa).

"The space of the sky was completely filled with uplifted umbrellas resembling white lotuses in the river of the army, and also looking like the play mirrors of the Goddess of Victory.

"Should the stirring period of the march be compare to the advent of the autumnal season, the fly-whisks waving by the side of kings appeared like swans hovering about.

"The rays of the sun never left their natural redness, as the colour of the sparking gems set in royal crowns, beautiful as a cluster of flowers, was ceaselessly mingling with them.

"As the passage of the sky was completely blocked by the flags flying aloft, Aruṇa experienced much difficulty in conducting the chariot of the sun across.

"Fed by the neighing of the horses, intensified by the loud trumpeting of the elephants and extended by the sound of the instruments of war-music (war-drums) the din that arose was something inconceivable.

"The king who had himself knowledge of the appropriate hour, however, awaited with his retinue, the formal fixing of the auspicious moment by his loyal priests.

"His throbbing right hand foretold the auspicious event of the forthcoming embrace by the Goddess of Valour, before everybody else.

"Brahmins chanting the Atharva Veda, augmented the chances of his victory with their (hearty) blessings, just as the sacrificial fire is made a glow by oblations sanctified by hyms his bodily form.

"The wind, blowing from the end of his waving tail which attended on him, was like a disciple taking secret lessons in speed.

"By raising his head up, and letting it down again, frequently, to keep his swiftness in bounds, he appeared to be offering salutations to the Goddess of Victory standing in front of him.

"With the heaps of dust raised by his hoofs, the regions of the sky were rendered like floor; and served to give the lie direct to the claims of the sun's horses that they trod on airy tract.

"The king mounted the horse, the personification of strength, and (in his elation) felt as if the entire kingdom of the earth had already passed into his hands.

"With numberless troops pouring in from all directions, the king, with his view unconcealed, crossed the outer gate.

"With crowns on their bent heads, with their hands folded (in reverence), the monarchs of earth saluted him, as he emerged, seated on the back of his horse.

"With shouts of joy on seeing him, the Cola, Kerala and

Pāṇḍya monarchs assumed the role of staff-bearers, and chose to walk in front of him.

"Like a row of clouds raining drops of water on a mountain, the respectable matrons of the town, showered the customary parched grain on him.

"As he marched in state, king Kampaṇa caused a quiver in the hearts of his rivals, and tuned to the direction of the quarter which had the Malaya mountains for its boundary.

"Leading such a huge army, the great hero looked like the eastern wind dragging behind it a string of heavy clouds.

"The load of the earth having become lightened by heaps of dust rising up, Ādiśeṣa managed to bear the weight of the royal army.

"The dust that rose up acted simultaneously as an eclipse of both the sun of prowess and the moon of fame of the enemy (and thus effected a double eclipse at the same time).

"The aggregate of dust caused the illusion of a huge dung heap capable of manuring the creepers of (Kampaṇa's) fame that had begun to sprout out in all the quarters.

"Under the pretext of being hidden away by the dust, the sun (in fact) fled to some unknown quarter, afraid that he might be pierced through by warriors transformed into gods in the approaching conflict (Warriors who go to vīra-svarga after a heroic end may pierce the sun in their journey to that destination).

"As if apprehending early extinction, grains of dust entered the pores of glands of lordly elephants through which ichor was coming out.

"The collection of dust plunged into the great oceans having been subjected, as it were, to unbearable heat when trying to absorb the rays of the sun.

"Water particles sprayed from the trunks of female elephants gave the shape of a fine hail to the cloud of dust raised by the marching army.

"Particles of dust fanned out by big war-elephants

flapping their ears were kept back by the rain of spray from the trunks of elephants.

"The army which looked like the grand confluence of all the seven oceans at the time of Mahāpralaya (the Great Deluge) began its orderly march with a great uproar.

"Caught up in the temples of great elephants overflowing with ichor, dust no longer rose, though the ground was continuously being broken by the toe-like hoofs of horses.

"The cool breeze, cool by reason of its contact with fine drops of water from the waves of the Tuṅgabhadrā, proved quite welcome for the onward march of the army.

"King Kampaṇa reached Muluvayipattanam after crossing the Karnata country within five or six days (*i.e.*, after a march of five or six days).

"In that city he was biding his time; and when the appropriate hour arrived he started to launch his attack against the Śambuvarāya ruler.

"The dust raised by his army made both the Palar and the fame of the Śambuvarāya monarch look dirty.

"King Kampaṇa struck camp with his army near Virinchinagara (Virinchipuram) where the branches of the trees were being shaken by the wind proceeding from the (waves) ripples of the Palar.

"Having come in all readiness, king Kampaṇa started to lay siege to the town of the Lord of the Tamils, like the dewy season blocking up the course of the sun with intermittent snow.

"The arrayed forces of both the Karnata and the Tamil kings attacked each other, like two oceans brought against each other by stormy winds at the time of the Great Deluge.

"The fight began to rage, foot-soldiers falling on foot soldiers elephant-herds attacking elephant-herds, troops of horses colliding with troops of horses.

"Unable to bear the lion-like roars emanting ting from

warriors on both sides, the elephants of the quarters, with their trumpeting completely silenced, almost lost their consciousness.

"Sparks generated in large numbers by the clash of the weapons of the warriors on either side bore a close likeness to a collection of glow-worms in the darkness of the dust.

"Even like the fancied side-glances of the amourous Goddess of fight, the sharp-pointed arrows let fly against one another by bow-men fell to the ground.

"The blood-stained sword-blades waving in the hands of heroic warriors appeared like the lolling tongue of Yama eager to make a meal of them.

"In the countless rivers of blood which began to flow on all sides, the faces of soldiers cut off by the bhalla arrow looked like lotuses.

"The arms of kings severed by swords resembled the trunks of elephants but were mistaken for snakes by the eagles that snatched them away.

"The blood flowing from human trunks was very much liked by the Rākṣasis who deftly seated themselves on the trunks of elephants as if on tops of places.

"Brave fighters sent to (everlasting) sleep by enemy arrows on the protrusion of their elephants, soon woke up on the pot-like breasts of divine damsels.

"Then the army of the Tamil king routed by the mighty forces of Kampaṇa took to flight.

"Some men fleeing in great disorder let fall their weapons in great terror and swore they would never fight again.

"Others, feigning death, dropped down; but fearing the presence of jackals, they at once rose up and started running pell-mell, affording no small mirth to the Karnāta forces.

"Yet others, mistaking a mirage for water (river) made futile attempts to cross it with a boat improvised out of the shields which they had forgotton to abandon (in their flight).

"There were still others who in their flight mistook their

own shadows for the pursuing enemy in the extremity of their fright and began to prostrate before them, biting their fingers.

"King Kampaṇa, then converted the Tamil king's town into an encampment for his own forces, and from there began to lay stage to the hill fortress named Rājagambhīra (Rājagambīrammalai) in which the enemy had sought asylum.

"The sound of his war-drums raised echoes from every cave of the hill and it looked as if the hill itself had begun to yell out in fright.

"With flags flying in the direction of high winds, the hill (fort) gave the impression that it was greeting king (Kampaṇa) and welcoming him with its arms (the flags) to come to its top.

"Again, fierce fighting commenced between the two sides, and the weapons falling down and shooting up, lit up both earth and sky by their resplendance.

"Heads severed by arrows resembled palmyra-fruits as they fell down from the ramparts and caused an illusion of balls belonging to the Deity of War (for playing with).

"Like messengers (tax-collectors) sent by the stronghold itself claiming the tolls for the entry (of the Karnāta troops) the stones let down from catapults fell just in front of the king.

"The hill, with the houses lit up by the fire from the missiles of bow-men, looked like holding lamps in readiness for the happy ceremony of harati to mark the auspicious victory of the king.

"The ascent of the hill was accomplished by heroic men by means of rows of lances planted as ladders and climbing up to the tops of sāla trees.

"With all means (and chances) of (escape) coming out completely blocked, the stronghold was subjected to such great distress that the, embryos of women, big with children, slipped out at the very sight of the fierce troops jumping in, and people immersed in the river of blood of the slain prayed for their lives.

"The Śambuvarāya monarch, with drawn sword, came out of his palace in great anger, even as a snake with its lolling tongue might come out of a mole-hill.

"Though many a soldier of valour eagerly came forward to fight saying, "let me do it", king Kampaṇa preferred to face Śambuvarāya himself.

"With the forepart of their bodies bent and eyes fixed, the two kings, sword in hand, stood still for a moment like a picture on a piece of painting.

"The gods were thankful for the total absence of winking in their eyes, as they were looking on with fixed gaze, the flight (of the two heroes), their bodies divided at the waist.

"Kampaṇa's sword, reflecting as it did, the image of the Śambuvarāya monarch, looked like a pregnant daughter about to give birth to a husband for the celestial nymphs.

Then escaping deftly a sword thrust, king Kampaṇa despatched the Śambuvarāya (monarch) as a guest to Indra's city.

"Having thus reduced (killed) the Śambuvarāya in the field of battle, king Kampaṇa received the decree of his father that he should rule (the territory thus conquered). With the fame of his victory duly established in Kāñcī, he inaugurated a just and prosperous rule over Tundiramandalam destroying all confusion in castes and religious orders."[21]

So also, Kampaṇa's second and final battle with the Turuṣka king, forms the ninth canto of the Madhurāvijayaṁ. It follows as below:

"Bow-men severed the hands of elephant riders with Ardhachandra arrows; and they fell down in the pool of blood in the battlefield like serpents in the sacrificial fire of Parīkṣit's son.

"Pearls from the broken heads of elephants in rut attacked by heroic warriors, fell down blood-tinged like sparks produced in sudden collision.

"No sooner did a horseman begin to return after having cut with his sword the frontal globe of an elephant than that elephant was seen seizing his horse between his legs and squeezing him.

"The blood flowing from the wounded frontal globes of elephants was seen, being drunk through their trunks by some night-prowling demons in great glee, spitting the pearls that also came with the blood stream.

"Birds of prey with a view to taste the inner flesh entered into the body of a dead elephant making it quiver; jackals that mistook it for sign of life fled away, though they very much loved to feast on the body.

"Just as the heads cut by wheels were about to fall down, they were snatched away quite afresh with life by Rākṣasa women who desired to wear them as wreath on their ears.

"A certain elephant having seized by the foot, and thrown up a warrior with his trunk, wanted to catch him again, as he fell, with his pair of tusks.

"A certain brave warrior thrown up by his adversary elephant alighted on his back with his sword with which he despatched the enemy rider, and installed himself in his place.

"A certain warrior, after having been killed by the rain of arrows of his angry adversary, became a god and from his place in swarga rained flowers upon the latter praising his valour with genuine delight.

"A certain warrior was struck with a (double-edged) lance by his opposing foe, and by embracing the latter with the same lance sticking in his body, wounded him. This act evoked great admiration. Who is there that is not moved by real exhibition of daring qualities?

"Two warriors, meeting in single combat, cut each other's

head with their swords after a long fight; leaving their bodies there, they went up together at once to celestial regions as close friends.

"Some royal warriors, like lions, wandered in the field of battle, and tore the heads of their adversaries with their sharp nails as if the latter were opposing elephants.

"With one blow of his sword he (king) split two both the elephants and their riders with their coat of mail. Their bodies, lying mingled, gave but a slender clue for distinguishing the ranks of elephants from those of foot soldiers.

"The king, by smiting the elephants on their globes, produced many a river of blood scattering the pearls on their head like sands.

One thought, by looking at them, that there was not only one Tāmraparṇi river but several hundreds of Tāmraparṇis.

"The heads of other elephants he pierced with his javelins and pearls came out from them. This reminded one of Subrahmaṇya boring a hole in the Krauñca mountain through which hosts of swans came out.

"The agile king cut and wounded the bodies of those that opposed him, even as a hyena destroys, with his sharp nails, deer caught in front of him.

"The brave king pounded the turbaned heads of his enemies with his mace in such a way that the eyes which came out of the sockets sank again in their old places.

"When the king, thus began to work destruction in the enemy ranks with his several weapons, the opposing army fled before him and disappeared like rains in the huge fires that are started at the end of universe (Pralaya).

"Not even Paraśurāma, Rāma, Bhīma or Arjuna provided such entertainment as the king did to that sage (Nārada) who always loved the sight of good battle.

"Then seeing all his Turuṣka forces routed in battle, the

Yavana king, stringing his fearful bow, met the king Kampaṇa in single combat even as Vṛtra did the kind to the gods.

"The warriors regarded him as the embodiment of both anger and intoxication, his eyes red with the drink of Vīrapana, and knitted brows on his forehead fearful to look at.

"His jewelled tuft in a line of unbroken brilliance as he rode on his fast horse looked like the wreath of his smoking anger which was about to blaze.

"The sound produced by his forceful stringing of the bow seemed as if it were emanating from the anklets of the Goddess of Victory, who, after having deserted him so long, was now returning to him in haste.

"The brave king Kampaṇa delighted in his having an opponent like the Suratrāṇa (Sultan) who had by his valour reduced the Colas and Pāṇḍyas and despoiled the wealth of Vira Ballala (the Third).

"The two proud opponents fought in a manner befitting the respective might of their arms, by showering arrows on each other with their bows bent up to their ears.

"The king of the Yavanas warded off the arrows let fly by king Kampaṇa, which were like the side glances of the Goddess of Heroism. And the king, similarly, checked the Parasika's (Persian's) arrows which resembled the eye-darts of Yama's sister.

"King Kampaṇa let fly against the Yavana king his arrows that had, like serpents, drunk the life-breaths of Keralas, like fire had consumed the lords of the Vanya kingdom, and like the sun had destroyed the dark Āndhras.

"The scratches caused by the Yavana king's arrow on the person of king Kampaṇa shone like the nail marks of the Goddess of Victory who was passionate to enjoy her privacy.

"The crow banner of the Yavana king which looked like

the typification of the crown of Kali age was destroyed by king Kampaṇa, and with that the former's hope of victory also.

"The king, with his arrow, cut the bow-string of the Turuṣka king who was, in his fury, raining arrows at the former. It was as if the knife was laid on the auspicious chord round the neck of the Rājyalakṣmī (kingly prosperity) of the Turuṣkas.

"The Turuṣka hero blazing with anger, then threw away his bow, and hastily drew out his terrible sword that was hanging on the side of his horse's saddle.

"Determined to make an end of the Yavana king, king Kampaṇa also armed himself with that sword which Agastya had sent him, and which looked as terrible as Yama himself.

"That sword, grew-coloured like poisoned fumes as it was being waved by the hand of king Kampaṇa, looked like a serpent about to drink the life-breath from the Yavana's body.

"Seated on his agile horse, king Kampaṇa, who was the glory of the Karnāṭa race, avoiding the sword blow aimed by the Yavana, cut off in an instant the head of the latter.

"The head of the Suratrāṇa (Sultan) fell on the ground, the head that never knew the art of cajoling servant-like, the head that had borne the royal burden of the Turuṣka Sāmrājya (Supremacy) and had not bowed down even to gods.

"The hero, Kampaṇa, was astonished to see that, even after the head had fallen, the trunk on the horse-back still held the reins, checking the horse's course with one hand, while the other was uplifted to return the blow of the adversary.

"On the head of king Kampaṇa, held high in pride, fell heaps of flowers rained from the celestial regions, and those heaps had the appearance of auspicious yellow-rice (akṣata) let fall by the Goddess of Kingly Prosperity, on Her self-chosen Lord.

"Like the beauty of the forest saved from forest-fire, like the view of the sky after the vanishing of an eclipse, or the calm appearance of the river Yamunā after the eradication of the serpent Kaliya, the region of the South shone after the overthrow of the Parasikas.

"King Kamparāya guaranteed the safety of the remaining men in his enemy ranks and was crowned with happiness and glory."[22]

Similarly, the third canto of the Raghuvaṁśa describes the battle between Raghu and Indra as below:

"The son of Dīlipa (*i.e.*, Raghu) honoured by the good wiped his eyes with the holy water dripping from Nandinī and thus was blessed with a vision of things veiled from sense.

"And in the east, he–this son of the lord of men beheld the God who clips the wings of mountains, carrying away his horse tethered by reins to his chariot, whose restiveness was ever and anon being curbed by his charioteer.

"Recognising him to be God Indra, by his hundred unwinking eyes, and his bay horses, Raghu now addressed him in a deep voice that pierced the sky, as if to win him from his purpose.

"O Lord of Gods, the wise ever describe you as the chief of those that share all sacred oblations; how is it then that you are bent upon obstructing the sacrifice of my father who is constantly engaged in sacrificial vows?

"Being the lord of the three worlds and possessed of divine vision, you should restrain those that hate sacrificial acts; but if you yourself prove an obstacle in the acts of the righteous, there indeed, farewell to all sacred rites!

"Be pleased, therefore, O Indra, to set free this horse who is the principal element of the great sacrifice; for great ones who point the way (taught by) the Vedas never stop to unrighteous ways.

"The Lord of the gods, hearing those bold words uttered by Raghu, wonderingly turned back his chariot and began to make the following reply.

"What you say, O son of a Kṣatriya, is true; but then those who regard their fame as their prized possession, must need guard it from their enemies; and your father seeks, by his sacrifice, to rob me of all my world-wide renown.

"As Puruṣottama conveys none but Viṣṇu, or 'Maheśvara' denotes the three-eyed God alone, even so the sages understand me by the title 'Satakratu'; these our titles do not belong to any other person.

"And therefore, following in the wake of Kapila, I carried away this your father's horse; do not make any further efforts in this regard; seek not to tread the path which the sons of Sagara trod.

"At this, the horse's protector laughed and fearlessly addressed Indra once again: 'Take your weapon if that is your resolve; for you cannot consider yourself to have achieved your object, so long as Raghu remains unconquered.'

"So he said to Indra, and as with his face raised up, he was about to place the arrow on his bow, he seemed to resemble the great God Śiva by his eminent form looking very handsome in the Ālīḍha posture (he assumed).

"Struck in the breast by Raghu's arrow breathing defiance, the mountain-cleaver was filled with indignation and put an unfailing dart upon his bow which for a moment becomes the emblem of a host of fresh clouds.

"That arrow, accustomed to taste the blood of grim demons, plunged into the broad space between the two arms of Dīlipa's son, and seemed to drink human blood, untasted before, out of curiosity as it were.

"The prince too, brave as Kumāra, planted an arrow,

bearing his own name, on the arm of Indra, the fingers of which were hardened by the constant goading of the celestial elephant, and which marked by leaf-like figures in paint on Sachi's (person).

"And with another, fledged with peacock's plume he rent the great lightning flag of Indra; whereupon Indra was greatly enraged to him, as though he had forcibly torn the heavenly Lakṣmī's hair.

"And now ensued a fierce fight between them who strove for the mastery, their arrows hurtling upwards and downwards, like so many fierce-looking winged serpents, while the siddhas and the soldiers stood by.

"Nor could Indra, even with a ceaseless shower of missiles, repress him who possessed such irresistible fire, just as a cloud is unable to extinguish the lightning-fire released from itself.

"Then with a cresent-headed arrow, Raghu snapped asunder the bow-string of Indra, which was roaring aloud, like the ocean when churned, at his wrist smeared with yellow sandal.

"Highly incensed, he flung aside his bow, and desiring to slay his gallant foe, took up the missile used by him in clipping the wings of mountains, bright shining with a halo of light.

"Struck in the chest by that he fell to the ground along with the tears of his soldiers; but shaking off his agony in a moment he rose up with their joyous shouts.

"However, Indra was pleased with his great heroism, who for long stood in a state of hostility, a state made terrible by the use of weapons; for indeed virtues and access everywhere.

"No other person save yourself has withstood my weapon which by its might did not suffer resistence even from mountains; know me to be pleased with you; say what you desire, save this horse," thus Indra clearly spoke to him.

"Then putting back the arrow which was not wholly drawn out of the quiver; and which by its folden feathers made his fingers radiant, the sweet-voiced prince made answer to the king of the gods.

"O Lord, if you think that the horse cannot be restored then let my father, who is hallowed by constant vows, be blessed with the entire fruit of the sacrifice, as if the rite were concluded in the proper manner.

"And O Lord of the worlds, so arrange that the king sitting in his assembly, irresistible by reason of his being a portion of the three-eyed god, hears this news from your own envoy.

"With the words 'so be it' Indra who had Mātalī for his charioteer, promised to grant Raghu his desire and went away as he came; and the son of Sudakṣiṇā (Raghu) too, not quite well-pleased in his heart, returned to the king's assembly hall.

"The king of men, already enlightened by a messenger of Indra greeted him and gently stroked his limbs, marked by the scars of the thunderbolt, with his hand numbed by joy.

"Thus did the lord of the Earth, whose commands deserved to be respected, perform ninety-nine sacrifices, as though they were the flight of steps whereby at the close of his life he would ascend to heaven.[23]

So also the battle of Aja with the enemy kings occurs in the seventh canto. The context is that–after Aja's marriage with Indumati, the enemy kings who had been already deprived of their possessions by Raghu, could not bear to see his son (Aja) winning the gem of a woman *i.e.*, Indumati. These enemy kings obstructed himon the way, while he was taking with him the Bhoja princess, Indumati. And there a fight between them takes place. It follows as below:

"Having directed a trustworthy counsellor with a large number of warriors to guard her, the prince dashed on the ranks of those enemy kings, like Śoṇa with his rising billows, smiting the Ganges.

"Foot to foot, car to car, horse to horse, and elephant to elephant–thus fought warriors that battle in which the antagonists were equally matched.

"And as the clarions brayed, the archers did not announce their names; for their voices were scarcely audible; but by the letters, inscribed on their shafts, they made known to each other their lofty titles.

"The dust of battle, stirred by the horses, thickened by the wheels of multitude of chariots, and spread by the flapping ears of elephants, veiled the Sun in the manner of an awning.

"The fish-shaped pennons, whose mouths were rent by the wind, devoured the growing dust raised by the hosts, so that they looked like real fishes drinking fresh muddy water.

"In that thick dust, the noise of wheels proclaimed the chariot, tinkling of danglings bells betrayed the elephants; while friend and foe were only known from shouted names of chiefs.

"The blood that streamed from horses, elephants, and warriors shone as the morning Sun in the darkness of dust that grew intense in the strife, and hemmed in the field of men's vision.

"The dust, whose root the blood had cut, and which was blown about over it (the blood), looked like smoke that had streamed up before the fire had been reduced to glowing cinders.

"Car-borne heroes, waking from their swoon that was caused by blows, rebuked their drivers, and turning their horses, angrily smote those (very warriors) who gave them wounds, recognizing them by their pennons previously marked.

"Now skilful archer's shafts, though split in mid-fight

by enemy's darts, yet reached their aims, with their barbed fore-halves, through the continuity of their speed.

"In the elephant-fight, the heads of drivers, smit off by razor-keen quoits, dropped down after a while, having been caught up by the hair in the pointed extremities of hawks' talons.

"A horseman, who was the first to strike, did not again strike his foe so long as he was unable to return the blow, but waited until the latter woke from his swoon, his body reclined on his horse's neck.

"And as the naked swords of mailed warriors, fightind desperately, fell upon the huge tusks of elephants, (sparks of) fire rose which the frenzied elephants quenched with water sprayed from their trunks.

"Like Death's drinking-booth showed that field of battle abounding in the shaft-severed skulls for fruit, the fallen helmets for breakers, and blood for streams of wine.

"A female jackal snatched from birds a broken arm, which was pecked at the extremity by them; but she flung it away, although fond of flesh, as the roof of her jaw was hurt by the end of the armlet (worn on the arm).

"A certain hero, when his foeman's sword had severed his head, that very instant found himself the master of a celestial car, with a heavenly nymph clinging to his left side, and saw his (lifeless) trunk dancing on the battle-plain.

"Two other warriors, finding that each had slaughtered the other's driver, themselves became both drivers and car-borne heroes; when their horses were dead, they fought long with their maces; and when these were broken they closed in a hand-to-hand scuffle which ended in their death.

"The other heroes, who, having struck each other, breathed their last at the same moment, yet renewed their fight, even in their immortal state, being suitors to the same heavenly nymph.

"The two rival hosts swayed between victory and defeat over one another like ocean's waves that alternately swell when driven by contrary winds.

"The mighty Aja rushed at the opposing host, although they had worsted his army; wind may repel smoke, but fire will assuredly reach straw.

"That high-spirited peerless hero, car-borne and mail clad, with his bow and quiver, repelled the kingly host, like the great boar the waves of the ocean that overflowed the shores at the end of an acron.

"He was seen on the battle-field deftly moving his right hand at the mouth of his quiver; while the string of the bow stretched but once upto this warrior's ear, seemed to produce the arrows that killed his enemies.

"He strewed the battle-field with the heads of his enemies, severed from the neck by his Bhalla arrows—the heads which had their lips more red as they were bitten in anger, which bore frowns whose upward lines were clearly seen, and which still had the sound of defiance within them.

"With every kind of force, among which elephant were the chief, with every kind of weapon that could penetrate armours and with all their might, all those kings fell on him.

"As volleys of missiles veiled his chariot, the top of his pennon alone betrayed his presence, as the dimly shining Sun shows the mist-veiled morning.

"Then the prince, this son a universal sovereign, fair as the God of Love, and ever vigilant, now launched at the kings that sleep compelling missile, which, presided over by Gandharvas, as given to him by Priyamvadā.

"Struck to sleep, the kings's armed host stood powerless to draw the bow with their hands, the helmets swerving to one shoulder, while they leaned against the staves of their flags.

"Then the prince placed on his lower lip, whose seets

his Bride had tasted, a conch-shell, and blew it, so that he seemed thus to drink emgodied glory, won by his own hands.

"His warriors, recognising the sound of the conch-shell, returned and saw him in the midst of his foes over powered by sleep, like the image of the Moon bright-quivering in the midst of sleeping lotuses.

"Then, with the blood-stained points of his darts he wrote letters on their banners; 'Raghu's son now has taken from you your glory, but has spared your lives out of mercy.

"Then with one arm resting upon the end of his bow, his hair loosened by the removal of his helmet, and his brow moist with the drops of sweat, brought on by fatigue, he advanced to his timid bride and spoke:

"Look, Vaidarbhi-I give you leave–look at these our foes; even infant hands may seize their weapons; it is with such feats of war that they seek to win you from my hands!

"Then her face, recovering from the alarm, caused by the foes, shone like a mirror which has gained its transparency when damp breath is wiped away.

"Rejoicing, yet by shame overpowered, she praised him not herself, but, by the lips of her handmaids as a natural landscape, when sprinkled over by drops of rain, thanks to the rows of cloud, by peacock's cries.

"Then he set his left foot upon the heads of the kins, and faultless, bore off his flawless bride, who with the ends of her hair made rough by the dust raised by chariot and horse, shone like incarnate victory of the battle.[24]

In like manner, the twelfth canto of the Raghuvaṁśa describes a fierce fight between Rāma and Rāvaṇa.

"The fight between Rāma and Rāvaṇa in which after a long time their valour found scope by this their mutual encounter, seemed not in vain.

"Rāvaṇa, alone, and not like what he was before, yet by his many arms, and heads and thighs appeared encircled by-his mother's kin.

"Rāma highly esteemed his foe, who had conquered the world's Guardians, who had worshipped God Śiva by (offering up) his heads, and who had poised aloft the Kailāsa mountain.

"Fiercely wroth, Rāvaṇa drove deep his arrow in his right arm which throbbing foretold old his union with Sītā.

"Then an arrow, loosed by Rāma, piercing Rāvaṇa's breast, entered the earth as if to bear the glad tidings to the serpentworld.

"As each matched his foes with missile for missile their zeal to triumph over their rival brew like that of two disputants who match argument with argument.

"Owing to an alternate display of valour the fortune of war wavered between them, like an altar-shaped wall set between two raging elephants.

"The volleys of shafts, that each other poured, did not endure the flowers rained down by the Gods and Demons over them when pleased with their asults and repulses.

"Then the Demon dashed at his foe with his Sataghni mace studded with iron spikes, as if it were the club, Kutasalmali.

"With crescent-tipped arrows, Rāma cut that (made) in twain before it reached his chariot, as easily as a plaintain-tree, and also shattered the hope of the enemies of the Gods.

"Then the matchless archer, laid across his bow that unerring Brahmā missile, directing the same against him—a physic to extract the iron of grief from his beloved's heart.

"Split a hundred fold in the air, with flaming points, it looked like the body of the serpent Śeṣa, with its awful circle of hoods.

"With that (shaft) winged with spells, he brought down, in half a moment, the row of Rāvaṇa's heads, which did not even feel the pain of the wound.

"The line of severed necks of the demon's body that was

about to fall shone like the images of the morning Sun in water, broken by wavelets.

"The minds of the Gods could yet not fully believe it, even when they saw his heads fall, for fear that those heads might join with the trunk once more.

"Then fell on Rāma's head, which soon should wear the jewelled crown, a rain of fragrant flowers, poured by the Gods, which was followed by swarms of bees that with their wings, heavy with ichor, forsook the broad temples of the elephants of the guardians of the world."[25]

Thus, ends the beautiful narration of the battles in the Raghuvaṁśa. A few of the similarities found in the Madhurā-vijayaṁ and the Raghuvaṁśa, may be observed as below :

1. Being impelled by his father, Dilipa, prince Raghu in the third canto called out Indra for fight, and become victorious; so too at the behest of his father, Bukka, prince Kampaṇa in the fourth canto of the Madhurā-vijayaṁ, marched against the Śambuvarāya king and was victorious.
2. Raghu's heroic deeds and his bold steps in the battle with Indra bear some resemblance with that of Kampaṇa.
3. Though all enemy-kings got together and attacked Aja fiercely, yet Aja like Agni fought with them alone which in fact caused a sort of astonishment in his rival kins. Similarly as Kampaṇa was marching with his powerful forces, he caused a quiver in the hearts of his rivals.
4. Seeing all his forces destroyed, the demon-king Rāvaṇa met Rāma in single combat. Similarly, seeing all his Turuṣka forces routed in the battle, the Yavana king, stringing his bow met the king Kampaṇa in single combat.
5. Just as Rāma experiences the throbbing in his right arm which foretold his union with Śita (XII-90), so too, when Kampaṇa started on compaign to Kāñcī, his

throbbing right hand foretold the auspicious event of the forthcoming embrace by the Goddess of Valour (IV-18).

6. The rain of arrows in battle between Rāma and Rāvaṇa, and Kampaṇa and Sultan bears much resemblance.
7. Description of Rāvaṇa (XII-99) and of the Sultan (IX-37) after their heads being cut off, holds much consonance with each other.
8. When Rāma in the Raghuvaṁśa (XII-102) and Kampaṇa in the Madhurāvijayaṁ (IX-38) became victorious, a rain of fragrant flowers poured from the celestial regions.

Thus, in many contexts, the Madhurāvijayaṁ holds much resemblance with the Raghuvaṁśa so far as poetess's art of the narration of battle is concerned.

Though the description of the battle scence appears to come under descriptive aspect, it is included in the narration part. As such, here, the battle scene is given in full to realize the poetess's narrative skill. In this narration, descriptive points are included as a part and parcel of the former. Hence, it leaves no confusion.

Further, it may be seen that the method of narrative skill of Gaṅgādevī is similar to that of Vālmīki in his Rāmāyaṇa. The story of Rāmāyaṇa begins with the king Daśaratha, as the story of the Madhurāvijayam with Bukka. Both the kings, Daśaratha and Bukka followed the custom of having more than one wife. Kauśalyā was the chief queen of Daśaratha and Devayī of Bukka. Daśaratha had made Ayodhyā as his capital city; so also Bukka's capital place was Vijayanagara. Rāma was the eldest son of Daśaratha, so too, Kampaṇa was of Bukka. As Rāma had three brothers—Lakṣmaṇa, Bharata and Śatrughna, Kampaṇa had two brothers, Kampaṇa and Saṅgama. The mandate of the father was responsible in both the cases for their respective achievements. The killing of Khara in Daṇḍaka forest by Rāma is similar to the killing of

Śambuvarāya king in Kāñci. Sage Agastya gifted some divine weapons to Rāma to facilitate his act of killing Rāvaṇa; so also a sage with the same name sent through, the goddess of Madhurā divine weapons to Kampaṇa for his killing, the Sultan of Madhurā (IX-29). Rāvaṇa's capital was Ceylon while Sultan's capital was Madhurā in the Southern part of India. Rāvaṇa was very trouble-some to the world; even as Sultan was a curse to the upliftment of the society. As Rāma destroyed Rāvaṇa, Kampaṇa killed the Sultan of Madhurā. Carrying away Sītā by force and unlawfully was only the proximate cause in killing Rāvaṇa. But, for Rāma, the ultimate goal was the establishment of Dharma, saving the world from hindrances and the upliftment of the society. Kampaṇa too, had the same ultimate goal in killing the Sultan of Madhurā. As Dīlipa performed the rituals for Raghu, so Bukka did for Kampaṇa.

Thus, there are many a point of resemblance. Gaṅgādevī owes much of her inspiration for her works to the great epic, the Rāmāyaṇa of Vālmīki, as she mostly follows Vālmīki in the art of narration of the Madhurāvijayaṁ. It may therefore, be said the theme of the Madhurāvijayaṁ has been on the analogy of the themes in the Rāmāyaṇa of Vālmīki when narrative aspect of the Kāvya is taken into consideration.

REFERENCES

1. वागर्थाविव सम्पृक्तौ वागर्थप्रतिपत्तये।
   जगतः पितरौ वन्दे पार्वतीपरमेश्वरो।। *Raghuvaṁśa* I-1
2. स्रष्टुः स्त्री पुंसनिर्माणमातृकारूपधारिणौ।
   प्रपथे प्रतिबोधाय चित्प्रकाशात्मकौ शिवौ।। *Madhurāvijayaṁ* I-2
3. कलत्रवन्तमात्मानमहरोधे महत्यपि।
   तया मेने मनस्विन्या लक्ष्मया च वसुधाधिपः।। *RV*. I-32
4. सत्स्वप्यन्येषु दारेषु तामेव मनुजाधिपः।
   बह्वमस्त निशानाथो नक्षत्रेष्विव रोहिणीम्।। *MV*. I-74
5. प्रियानुरागस्य मनः समुन्नते भुजार्जितानां च दिगन्तसम्पदाम्।
   यथाक्रमं पुंसवनादिकाः क्रिया धृतेश्च धीरः सदृशीव्यधत्त सः।। *RV*. III-10

6. ततः परं तापहरः प्रजानां पुरोहितोक्त्या पुरुहूतकल्पः।
व्यधत्त काले विभवानुरूपं पुसां वरः पुंसवनक्रिया सः।। *MV*. II-13

7. शरीरसादादसमग्रभूषणा मुखेन सालक्ष्यत लोघ्रपाण्डुना।
तनुप्रकाशने विचेयतारका प्रभातकल्पा शशिनेव शर्वरी।। *RV*. III-2

8. मुखेन तन्वी शरपाण्डरेण विमुक्तरत्नाभरणा विरेजे।
विलूनराजीववना दिनान्ते छायाशशाङ्केन शरन्नदीव।। *MV*. II-2

9. दिनेषु गच्छत्सु नितान्तपीवरं तदीयमानीलमुखं स्तद्वयम्।
तिरश्चकार भ्रमराभिलीनयोः सुजातयोः पङ्कजकोशयोः श्रियम्।। *RV*. III

10. श्यामायमानच्छविना मुखे न स्तनद्वयं तामरसेक्षणायाः।
संदष्टनीलोत्पलयोरभिख्यां रथाङ्गनाम्नोरधरी चकार।। *MV*. II-11

11. स जातकर्मण्यखिले तपस्विना तपोवनादेत्य पुरोधसा कृते।
दिलीपसूनुर्मणिराकरोद्भवः प्रयुक्त संस्कर इवाधिकं बभौ।। *RV*. III-18

12. ततः प्रतीतेऽह्नि पुरोहितेन नरेन्द्रसूनुः कृतजातकर्मा।
समिद्धतेजाः समतामयासीन्मन्त्रप्रणीतेन मुखानलेन।। *MV*. II-33

13. सुरगज इव दन्तैर्भग्नदैत्याभिधारैर्नय इव पणबन्धव्यक्तयोगैरूपायैः।
हरिरिव युगदीर्घे र्दोर्भिरंशैस्तदीयैः पतिरवनिपतीनां तैश्चकाशे चतुर्भिः।। *RV*. X

14. पशुपतिरिव नेत्रैः सोमसूर्याग्निरूपैः नय इव निरपायै प्राभवोत्साहमन्त्रैः।
भव इव पुरुषाथैः धर्मकामार्थ संज्ञेस्त्रिभिरपि नरपालस्तैस्तनूजैरभासीत्।। *MV*. II. 38

15. रावणस्यापि रामास्तो भित्वा हृदयमाशुगः।
विवेश भुवमाख्यातुमुरगेभ्य इव प्रियम्।। *RV*. XII-9

16. अथोरगाणामधिपाय भाविनं भुवो भरस्यापगमं दिनेश्वरः।
निवेदयिष्यन्निव गाढरंहसा रथेन पातालगुहामगाहत।। *MV*. III-46

17. तनुत्यजां वर्मभृतां विकोशैर्बृहत्सु दन्तेष्वसिभिः पतद्भिः।
उद्यन्तमग्निं शमयाम्बभूवुर्गजा विविग्नाः करशीकरेण।। *RV*. VII-48

18. ततस्सेनागजेन्द्राणां कर्णतालानिलोद्धता।
अवार्यत रजोराजिः करशीकरदुर्दिनैः।। *MV*. IV-43

19. *Raghuvaṁśa* XVI. 4-23
20. *Madhurāvijayaṁ.*
21. *Ibid.*, IV. I-83.
22. *Ibid.*, IX. I-40.
23. *Raghuvaṁśa*, III. 42-70.
24. *Ibid.*, VII. 36-70.
25. *Ibid.*, XII. 87-10.

Chapter-4

Description in the Madhurāvijayaṁ

Narration of legendary things or historical facts has been vital portion of a Mahākāvya of Prabandha type. Nonetheless it should not be forgotten that a mere narration of incidents, by itself does not fulfil the requirement of a Mahākāvya. As such Mahākāvya essentially brings in description of city, ocean, mountains, seasons, moon-rise, sun-rise etc., in a grand and charming style. With a view to bringing in these descriptions, poets have to seek for opportunities on various occasions, in course of the narration of the main story. Thus both narration and, description are primary requisites of a Mahākāvya. A perusal of the well-known Mahākāvyas makes it evident that the method in which descriptions are treated is found to be not in similar tastes. When we go through the pages of the Mahākāvyas like the Śiśupālavadha of Māgha; the Kirātārjunīya of Bhāravi, the Naiṣadhīyacarita of Śrīharṣa, etc. We come to notice that in these Mahākāvyās the narration of incidents occupies a very subordinate position, the major portion being reserved for descriptions. The authors of these Mahākāvyas have given so much importance to descriptions that the main story is almost overshadowed by descriptions and seems to be lost in the thick forest of descriptions. These poets have generally been fond of descriptions because the descriptions provide them wider scope to exhibit their unusual poetic skill and erudition. It is only in order to have an opportunity to give elaborate descriptions that they bring in some incidents. Moreover, these poets have seldom tried to seek novel stories for their poems. They generally select the theme for their Mahākāvyas from the legendary stock of the purāṇas, the Rāmāyaṇa, the Mahābhārata or the Bṛhatkathā, and give them a new currency in their poems, thus, as far as the theme is concerned, they exercise very little or no originality. Without bringing about any major modifications in the main theme, they concentrate their poetic faculty solely on descriptions. That is why Mahākāvya consists of descriptions in some places which appear somewhat independent of narration.

The Mahākāvyas in which the descriptions have been interwoven with the narration in such a way that their introduction may not cause any hindrance in the development of the theme, are very less in number. It is only Kālidāsa who, in his Raghuvaṁśa and the Kumārasambhava, has interwoven the descriptions with the theme in such a way that they appear as if they are evolved out of the theme itself. In these two Mahākāvyas the narration is hardly affected by introducing the descriptions. Rather, the description provides much lively beauty to the narration. Even when the descriptions are only remotely connected with the narration of the main incidents, their introduction can be justified on the ground that they refer to the characters of the poem, or prepare a suitable background for further narration, or present the Vibhāvas for the delineation of Rasas. Such descriptions may keep the reader poetically attuned to the incidents and make him appreciate the theme better. But, the description should be such as that the main theme is never lost sight of. Gaṅgādevī though an ardent follower of Kālidāsa is found to be not strictly faithful to the latter in this respect. This is obvious from her Madhurāvijayaṁ where she has devoted a major portion for descriptions, like Māgha and Śrīharṣa. Gaṅgādevī has focussed so much attention on the descriptions that the narration of the main theme appear to be almost veiled in her Mahākāvya. Hence, it is not convenient for any reader to follow the thread of the main incidents narrated. No doubt she has full aquaintance with the narration of the story of Kampaṇa. Yet, it is found that she has given much scope for description in the Mahākāvya so that more number of verses have been devoted to the descriptions than to the narration. This analysis clearly indicates Gaṅgādevī's fondness for description.

The following descriptions have been highlighted in this work *viz.*, description of the seasons, of swimming and bathing, of the setting of the sun and the rising of the moon, of battles of the king, of the capital of morning sickness, of birth, of childhood, of youth, of invasions, etc. For the convenience of study and appreciation, the descriptions occurring in the Madhurāvijayaṁ may be divided into three categories, namely :

1. Description of the Nature,
2. Description of the personal beauty, particularly of male beauty.
3. Description of miscellaneous items *e.g.*, city, battle scene, etc.,

Description of the Nature

Nature finds a prominent place in Sanskrit literature even from the earliest times. It bears a strong emotional appeal and thereby keeps the human mind ever delighted. Even an ordinary person gets inspiration from the enchanting beauty of the nature. Then what to say about the poets who are the keen observers of nature? The poets possess a special sensitivity towards the objects of the nature. Vālmīki the Ādikavi is well-known for his description of the nature which abounds the whole of the Rāmāyaṇa. Kālidāsa being an ardent lover of Nature is also well-known for his description of the nature. Two lyric poems of Kālidāsa, namely, the Meghadūta and Ṛtusaṁhāra, are nothing but the glorification of the role played by nature in human life. The Mahākāvyas as well as the dramas of Kālidāsa are rich with descriptions of the nature providing a background for the delineation of sentiments like *śṛṅgāra, karuṇa,* etc. Gaṅgādevī the author of the Madhurāvijayaṁ has sung the glory of Nature with great enthusaism undoubtedly. As far as the descriptions of Nature are concerned, she is one of the Sanskrit poets who follow faithfully the tradition of describing Nature started by Vālmīki and highlighted by Kālidāsa. In the Madhurāvijayaṁ also we find many elaborate descriptions of seasons evening scenes and morning scenes, etc., which are as follows:

Seasons

The various seasons have been beautifully portrayed in the Madhurāvijayaṁ. Numerous exciting pictures of seasons are found in this Mahākāvya. Being fond of nature, poetess Gaṅgādevī has displayed her skill in giving all details pertaining to the seasons. She closely follows Kālidāsa in presenting the charming picture of different seasons and influence of the seasons on all human beings.

Spring Season

Spring is the most favourite season of the poets. Particularly Sanskrit poets have a great fascination for describing the multi-faced nature of this season. This season claims the position of Ṛturāja (the king of seasons). It creates a pleasing atmosphere for love. During this season, the blossoming flowers, swinging creepers, humming bees, chirping birds, cooing-cuckoos, the fragrant smell of the wind, the beautiful lakes having the blooming lotuses the crackling of geese and the infatuating pleasure parks (Udyanas) all these bring about a pleasing and enchanting atmosphere all over.

In the Fifth Canto of the Madhurāvijayaṁ, Gaṅgādevī gives a captivating description of the spring season. A full account of the spring season is given in fifteen verses *i.e.*, 62 to 76. Though the description of the spring season, in the Madhurāvijayaṁ is in brief, it sings beautifully of the over all glory of the season. When the spring season sets in, beauty in abundance of flowers everywhere, is seen. Referring to the advent of the spring season Gaṅgādevī fancies that the spring season has come, with trees full of flowers as if for an offering with sprouting foliage like hands folded in veneration, with the cooings of cuckoos, as if uttering humble words of obeisance, the season seems to be paying homage to the king. First of all, the spring season becomes most pleasing because of healthy climate.[1] Gentle and fragrant breezes start blowing from the south carrying mango leaf-dust. Gaṅgādevī describes such breezes as appearing like sorcerers sprinkling ashes to turn the of anger-ridden damsels that turned the lovers. Gaṅgādevī referring to the charm of Kiṁśuka trees in this season fancies that these trees with buds of dazzling reds shone like lions with blood-stained nails that had torn the deer of lovely travellers during the vernal (*vasanta*) season.[2] Further she speaks of Campaka trees and describes them as rows of (campaka) clusters with collyrium-like bees settling on them looked like lamps lighted by the spring in commemoration of Cupid's festival.[3] Referring to the young sprouts of Aśoka tree, she says these sprouts of Aśokas with bees humming around in thick rows, indicated a sort of appropriateness, to the manure which the tree had by the touch of the tender feet of Kuntala ladies resounding with ornaments.[4] Referring to Kurubaka in spring, the poetess glorifies, the Kurubaka that looked like hair standing on end in the act of mutual embrace of lovers, raised love passion even in the heart of insentient beings.[5] The sweet pañcama notes (पंचमराग) of cockoos delighted the world immensely (and) lonely travellers that heard, it felt as if they heard sounds of cupid's bow shooting arrows at them.[6] Gaṅgādevī describes the flowering season of spring as follows:

Wild creepers that were the beloved of the black bees attracted the latter, very much as clusters of buds looking like breasts sprouted in them in the flowering season of spring.[7] She states, how the spring season influenced human beings. In the spring festival, ladies wanted to paint images of cupid on picture-boards but they ended in painting the images of king Kampaṇa who was always in their heart. Certain ladies smeared the cupid-like person of the king with sandal paste and their hands evidenced love passion by sweat drops and horripilation that marked them in the act. The tinkling of bracelets of those lovely ladies, the dropping of garlands and the flying of curls of them that marked, the practice in swinging play, looked like a rehearsal on the part of those lovely ladies of love sports with their lovers. Some queens felt ashamed before their female companions, and in singing songs in praise of Kāma they often introduced the name of the king in their foregetfulness. Those young lovely ladies desired to splash on the king, paste of saffron, but they were not aware that the substance had already leaked out of their sweat-bathed hands.[8]

Rainy Season

Usually the monsoon rains begin in the month of June in India. The advent of rain is a dramatic occurrence. This is the season for pollination in flowers. The monsoon comes as a rival to the earlier season. The commonest flowers are the Ketaka, Kadamba and Yūthikā, *i.e.*, jasmine. The sweet smell of the earth, the dancing of the peacocks, the अभिसारिका stealing off at night to visit her lover, the traveller's plight during these nights and the sadness of ladies left behind are the effects of the rainy season.

The rainy season follows the hot summer. It makes the earth wet with its showers and expels completely the scorching heat of the sun. The thick and water laiden clouds cover the orb of the Sun. The moon as well as the stars in the nights become invisible as they find their place in the womb of the clouds and lose their lustre. Cloud establish their realm in the sky. The whole earth becomes gladdened at the advent of the Rainy Season.

Gaṅgādevī is attracted by the Rainy Season, like other great Sanskrit poets like Vālmīki, Kālidāsa etc., who have described, the rainy season in their works in detail. The Rāmāyaṇa gives a full account of this season in the 28th Canto of the Kiṣkindhākāṇḍa. Kālidāsa has given a graphic account of the Rainy Season in Ṛtusaṁhāra (in Canto II) and other works. In the same way, Gaṅgādevī has also given a detailed description of this season in not less than fourteen verses occurring in the fifth Canto. The colourful aspects of the rainy season such as the water-laden clouds, rumbling thunders, swift lightnings, heavy rainfall, overflowing rivers, treams, etc., are vividly described with exhaustive material. Throughout the description of the rainy season Gaṅgadevī has shown her power of keen observation and her capacity for describing events in detail.

The very beginning of the description of the Rainy Season follows thus:

The Cātaka birds, intent upon drinking the rain-drops directly from the clouds, make sweet sound. Their sweet sound is, as poetess understands praise of clouds. And this sweet sound of the Cātakas appeared like rendering welcome to the king. And the nicula flowers, that usually bloom in rainy season have fallen on the ground here and there being blown by wind. Such nicula flowers appeared as fanning the king. She imagines that the clouds, which had covered the sky looked like the sporting pavilions of women called lightnings and the thunder that was heard resembled the sounds of *mṛdaṅga* drums.[9] Further, she describes that the bees like black clouds looked like dark coloured petticoat flashes of lightning that appeared now and then glittered like borders of gold-lace, and rain drops like pearl countings.[10] In a like manner, she gives a beautiful picture of the rainbow. The rain-bow with its colours green, red, and white, shone like the girdle, set with emerald, coral and pearl of the beauty of the Goddess of sky.[11] When clouds appeared here and there, peacocks started dancing in mountainous plateaus, singing sweet notes of *ṣaḍja* at the appearance of clouds that were their favourities.[12] She also refers to the effects of the rainfall. It is described, the travellers with desperate courage heard the thundering of clouds in the sky which sounded like clestial kettle-drums which cupid beat with the sticks of lightning. For some days, the forest presented this appearance: plantains putforth new shoots. The Arjuna, Kadamba and the Keṭaka trees blossomed. The Cātaka birds and peacocks were in great glee. Through the winds, as if with hands, clouds sprinkled Keṭaka dusts resembling holy ashes. The murmring of thunder was like the uttering of the hum. And all this was effective in exercising the evil-spirit of love, anger which sometimes possessed the ladies of the harem.[13] Frozen rain drops fell from the clouds that whirled round with the blowing of the eastern wind. Looking at them one wondered if they were not pearls which were taken along with the sea-water during the latter's formation.[14] Red insects looking like blood drops began to swarm the earth. They looked like sparks of lightning fire that had dropped down on earth when clouds clashed clouds violently.[15] The advent of the rainy season enacted the role of 'romance' confident to the king in the night time as it made even the newly married shy girls embrace him at every sound of thunder murmurings.[16]

Also it is described, the mind of the king was very much attracted by pleasure-hillocks. Eyes in the tails of dancing peacocks rendered them very picturesque, and camphor deposits in them exuded the most agreeable odour. The numberless Kadamba trees there, were in full blossom. King Kampaṇa was attracted by his beautiful ladies whose curling locks were decorated with the evening-blossoming Mālatī flowers. The king's love, passion was very much excited by gem-set pavilions, by fragrant breezes wafting the smell of Kūṭaja and Keṭaka flowers and by the musical notes of intoxicated peacocks.[17]

Autumn Season

Following the description of the rainy season, Gaṅgādevī portrays the picture of Autumn (*śarad*) in fifth Canto of the Madhurāvijayaṁ. The Autumn season is the time of harvest of sugarcane, barley and rice, the grass is still lush and the streams shrink back to their old channels, thus showing the evidence of recent flood. Autumn also heralds the arrival of flights of migratory birds.

Gaṅgādevī again displays here her proficiency in the description of the Autumn. She has touched upon almost all the aspects of this season such as the clear sky, crystal clear water of the lakes, gently flowing rivers and streams, sonorously blowing wind, blossoming of the flowers etc.

In the very beginning of the description of the Autumn, the poetess personifies this season as a beautiful lady with lotus like eyes desired as if it were to see her face every now and then in the mirror of the Sun whom she, therefore, frequently drew out from his wrapper of white clouds.[18] Further she describes beautifully such natural phenomena as the Sun and the Moon becoming brighter. The poetess says the clouds in Autumn seemed to have acted like a wetstone and a wash in the case of the Sun and the Moon, respectively for they both shone now with increased brightness and splendour.[19] On the advent of the Autumn season rose the brilliant Agastya star. Due to this star, the waters were cleared of their muddy condition. The poetess compares this to the mind of men becoming clear after receiving instruction from a merciful teacher.[20]

Further, she describes the rivers, also which due to the effects of the Autumn season, were rid of their impurities and looked slimmer. And by uniting them with swans, their lovers, the season really enacted the role of a dear female friend effecting reconciliation between angry lovers.[21]

This autumn season resembled a lion in dispersing the elephant like clouds. His face was the Sun. The Kāśas were his manes and the blossoming China roses-his red eyes. In fact, it was no empty saying that the Sun and the Moon are the eyes of Viṣṇu. Now, he has woken up from sleep, hence these two, the Sun and the Moon opened in their proper splendour.[22] As the autumn season sets in, the white clouds lined the sky and lightning disappeared. In that state, the sky resembled the watery expanse of the sea with clusters of foam here and there and coral reefs gone.[23] Due to the arrival of Autumn season, everywhere there heard the sweet sounds of swans resembling the music of Lakṣmī's feet wandering on the lotus-beds, or the auspicious sounding of Cupid's musical instrument *i.e.*, turīya.[24]

Moreover, elephants in rut, often pulled the chains with which they were fastened, as forest-winds liaden with the smell of blossoming Saptaparṇa trees blew over their bodies. Everywhere the forest grounds were adorned with blossoming China roses. And as the latter stirred in the wind, it seemed as if by the orders of the king, they were waving auspicious flame to his victorious horses before any others did.[25] The young women guarding the rice fields sang the spotless fame of the-king, decked as their persons were with garlands of pearls that had come out of the bursting of ripe red sugarcane. Also, the king Kampaṇa enjoyed the autumnal nights fully, for in their contents they resembled his ladies in every respect; blue water-lilies had the beauty of their eyes, the moon of their face, white water-lilies of their smile and stars of the pupil of their eyes.[26]

Winter Season

The poetess Gaṅgādevī does give equal importance to the description of Hemanta Ṛtu *i.e.*, winter season. Though there are only five verses describing the Hemanta Ṛtu, yet they depict this season in a brief but precise and comprehensive manner. The poetess describes the influence of the Hemanta on the royal young ladies. It follows that Lotus clusters were hit by snow and the moon became pale in colour. Only the faces of the king's beloved consorts gained usual charm. The royal ladies as they shivered in cold seemed to be in an uninterrupted state of love, passion, the hairs in their breasts always standing on end, and their mouths always uttering murmuring sounds. The king's beloveds made him fancy that they were decking their hair with pearls, in season and out of season, as the cluster of their curls were always dressed with white blossoms of jasmine. The king loved to remain in his inner apartments sweetly scented with Agaru fumes, in company of his beautiful consorts whose breasts were warm and painted with saffron paste. The poetess distinctly displays her knowledge about natural phenomena like the days becoming shorter and night becoming longer during the winter season. The poetess fancies very beautifully the reason for nights becoming longer in the following words: 'The winter season makes the nights longer as if to please the amorous king who loved very much to enjoy the night sports.[27]

Cold Season (Śisīra Ṛtu)

As the cold season sets in the king Kampaṇa who incarnated Cupid in point of his personal charm, enjoying the comforts of the winter season, desired to sport with his ladies in the nights in spite of the chilly weather.[28] The ladies of the harem presented a particularly attractive appearance to the king, with their faces white with the dust of lodhra flowers and with their foreheads annointed with musk paste. Those young girls who had horripilation due to their proximity to their royal lover ascribed it, to cold. But they felt ashamed, as beads of sweat, suggestive of their unmistakable love passion, began to collect on their persons. The breasts of his ladies warm with blossoming youthfulness drove away the cold of the season when the king cast longing looks on them; they were very attractive also in their semi-covered state with marks of nail scratches, and without the strings of pearls on them.[29]

Summer Season

As has been described by the poetess Gaṅgādevī, during the Summer season, the days enjoy bright and long sun-shine; and the nights are short. Young ladies love to enjoy water-sport. Gentle winds, fragrant with the smell of full bloomed pāṭala flowers, blow. The poet fancies that the days become longer and longer to the delight of the Cakravāka birds. In the unbearable heat of summer even the horses of the Sun may get tottered and have to move with less speed. The elephant cupid, getting scorched in the Sun, found shelter in the breasts of beautiful ladies which were wet with pastes of Sandal and had the cooling contact of pearl string. Day by day, waters in the pleasure—lakes in the palace grounds of the king were found raceding further and further from the shores. This made one fancies that they were getting more and more afraid of receiving knocks from the breasts of Kuntala damsels who delighted in sporting in those lakes. Further, it is described that the king was delighted with the unadorned faces of his beautiful ladies with the Śirīṣa wreaths placed on the ear and pearl like drops of sweat appearing on the faces. The king got over the heat of the day by retiring with the choicest lads to his summer house where water particles sparkling like the stars were being sprayed incessantly.[30] Thus, ends the song of description of the seasons in the Madhurāvijayaṁ.

Sunset and Moonrise

Gaṅgādevī's descriptions of such natural phenomena as sun-set and moon rise are also very impressive. She has given vivid picture of both these phenomena in her Madhurāvijayaṁ. The description of sun-set and moon-rise provides a proper atmosphere for the sentiment of Śṛṅgārarasa.

Sunset

The description of the sun-set appears in the seventh canto. Here Gaṅgādevī has beautifully depicted the various stages of the sun-set and the subsequent night and moon-rise. Giving a fascinating picture of the setting sun, Gaṅgādevī imagines that though the setting sun submerges into the waters of the ocean as if to replenish his heat from the submarine fire there-heat which had been spent in the day in making lotuses blossom.[31] When the sun started moving away. from east to west, the poetess states that the sun at one stage seemed to be afflicted with the heat of separation from the eastern quarter but now he was seen enjoying himself in the company of the opposite quarter his heat gone, on reaching her. The minds of lovers are certainly inscrutable.[32] Further she describes the orb of the sun moving in the waves of the ocean in the following words :

The orb of the sun, with its lustre gone, rolled, scattered by the ocean waves, sea-fishes licked it often mistaking it for the broken remains of a fruit.[33] Casting her imaginative eyes on the trees, birds, evening twilight etc., the poetess gives some charming picture At the close of the day when the birds return to their nests, she states : Taking a warning as if it were from the fall of one Khaga (the sun, also a bird) because of his (its) over stepping Viṣṇupāda (the feet of Viṣṇu also sky), the other Khagas (birds) quietly hid themselves in their nests in trees.[34] In the next verse she refers to the evening twilight which immediately followed the sun-set when the sun slipped down. The sky studded with stars, was reddened by the spread of evening twilight. The poetess imagines here that the evening twilight was fancied by people as the screen of the stage where the dancer Time, was about to act the part of night, having taken off his disguise as day.[35] Referring to the falling of the night she describes that the darkness began to set in obscuring trees, the sky, the regions and it gave rise to such various fancies, that they were tender leaves of Tamāla with which the regions decorated their ears, or that they were musk - paste drawings on the face of the lady called night or that they were smokes emanating from the quenching of the sun's heated surface, or that they were black bees disguised as darkness filling regions after leaving the closing lotuses, or the black waters of the Jamuna rising up-tall as trees, when disturbed by Śrīkṛṣṇā.[36] Further she describes darkness with twinkling stars and imagines that Lord Śiva was letting go his elephant skin clothing dotted with drops of blood (after his dance was over).[37]

Moon rise

Gaṅgādevī then proceeds to describe the moon-rise and the moon. She has portrayed the various phases of the rising moon in a touching way. The various phases of the gradually rising moon are also colourfully depicted. The moon first appeared as if filled with red colour (passion). She imagines that a portion of the reddish orb of the moon appeared on the eastern region like the mark on the forehead of a beautiful maiden whom that region might be imagined to inearnate.[38] Further she states that the reddish globe of the rising moon looked like the victorious patākā or flag of cupid made of red sandhyaka flowers.[39] After the rising of the moon, darkness gets dispersed. Here the poetess wants to know as to why that thick darkness dispersed. She states that the lord night hugs the eastern region to his bosom in an ardent embrace and with his nail-like rays unties her braid of hair which incarnates darkness.[40] After the rising of the moon, the moon-light spread in the vast area and the poetess imagines this to be a damsel called the eastern region who draws out her white-silk garment of moon light presented to her by night from the conch like white box of moon globe and dresses herself with it and looks so splendid.[41] During the night, lotuses do not bloom and they do not raise their heads. The poetess compares this phenomenon to virtuous women in the following words. Due to moon-light lotuses do not bloom and do not look up to the moon nor return the greetings and this proves how virtuous women are firm in their vow of chastity.[42] According to the general view, moon light increases the ardour of love in separated lovers. The poetess describes why the moon intensifies the ardour of love in separated lovers. She states that the sun enters the moon every new moon-day and so the latter is also endowed with the heating quality of the former and his, the sun exhibits in the case of lovers in separation.[43]

Male Personality

Most of the Sanskrit poets have given more attention to describe the female personality. But Gaṅgādevī is an exception to this. She has tried her best to describe the male beauty effectively. Bukka, the king of Vijayanagara, and his son Kampaṇa are the two male characters on whom the poetess has focussed her greater attention. The various limbs of the male body such as the long arms, broad chest, strong shoulders scintillating eyes, gracious glances etc., are described with a realistic touch. In the very beginning of the first canto while describing the greatness of Kampaṇa's father, the poetess suggestively throws light on the personality of king Bukka and describes him as a Śeṣa among the serpants, Himavān, among the mountains and Viṣṇu among the gods. He occupied the first place among the lords of the earth.[44] She further describes him as severer than the sun and more pleasant than the moon. In depth (of qualities) he has excelled the ocean, and in firmness, the mountain Sumeru.[45] Again she describes the special character of the king Bukka. She states that he was discernment alone for his minister, and the bow alone for his army. He counted on his army, of his only ally in the heart of the battle.[46] Bukka was religious minded. She states that the tree of Dharma which had withered away by the scorching heat of this Kali age sprouted again by the water that flowed (from his hands) while making gifts of charity.[47] In the beginning of the third canto, the poetess presents a beautiful description of Kampaṇa's pleasing personality. The poetess fancies his youthful personality. She states that his waist was shapely, and slender, which greatly a enchanced the beauty of his personality and suggested the idea of the lions having yielded their monopoly, as a sort of hush-money in his favour, as they were extremely afraid of his strength.[48] The poetess states that Kampaṇa was having a broad chest. She states that his paneral like chest shone just as broad as to be able to hold in its expanse the breasts of beautiful women which could well compare with the frontal globes on an elephant's head.[49] His stout shoulders were always a sight for people to see.[50] His face with beard was looking like the black spot of the moon.[51]

Further she describes his eyes: The redness that appeared in the corner of his lotus like eyes suggested anger against the ears that set a limit to the freedom of their (eyes) expansiveness.[52] Then the poetess imagines about his long and lofty nose like this "the world thought of his long and lofty nose as a demarcation on the province of the other.[53] Then she describes hiss hair-dressed". She states his hair dressed with red blossom which looked like emblems expressing red hearts of beautiful women.[54]

Thus, it can be said that Gaṅgādevī is rather an exception to give attention to describe the male personality.

Description of the City

The description of Vijayanagar follows in the wave of that of the king. Except in the Rāmāyaṇa and in the works as Bhatti, in Sanskrit literature this description is always separately dealt with. Some Kāvyas have ended with the description of either the city, or the king very rarely, rather incidentally, there are a few that took up this description of the capital. In the Kumārasambhava, the Himālayas are described in the beginning, only incidentally a little description of capital Oṣadhiprasthamu is given in sixth canto. Lord Śrī Kṛṣṇa and the city Dvārakā are described in a few verses of the third canto of the Śiśupālavadha. Naiṣdham starts with the description of Nala. In the Naiṣadha, description of the capital city, is not at all to be found. Telugu Kāvyas have observed the tradition of describing both the king and his capital just in the beginning of the works. The same pattern is adopted here also. Essentially this epic resembles the 'Kādambarī' and the

Śiśupālavadha' in wealth of imagination and in metaphoric descriptions.

The description of the city is found in the beginning of first canto of the Madhurāvijayaṁ. Vijayanagara, the capital city of king Bukka, is described in detail running into twenty three verses. Beautiful palaces, sky-kissing storyed buildings, royal roads, pleasure parks city gates moats, ramparts, sporting lakes etc., are described in such a way as to reveal the prosperity of the empire. The poetess keenly observes the sophisticated culture of the citizens and presents the same in a splendid manner.

At the very outset, it is described that the king Bukka who had augmented his riches by conquest, had the famous Vijayanagar for his capital city. This capital city had won the approbation of knowing men as Indra's Amarāvatī won that of the gods. The river Tuṅgabhadrā, which encircled the Vijayanagara as a formidable moat, appeared as if in rivalry with the heavenly Ganges that flowed around the borders of Svargaloka.[55] The city is described as having natural protection. It was surrounded by ramparts on all sides which were as high as the Cakrācala mountains. And it had the beauty of a water-trench round the creeper Lakṣmī and looked like the navel of goddess Earth. The city was very beautiful with lofty and gem-set towers like the peaks of the Sumeru emitting rainbow colours. There were many pleasure groves which looked like the abodes of spring and which were full of flowering trees like Campaka, Aśoka, Nāga and Kesara.[56] The pleasure-hillocks were frequented by the musk deer that sought the shade of the plantains and Karpūra plants in them. These hillocks looked like the vertable hiding places of the god of love. There were sporting-lakes with gem-set steps, fragrant with the smell of lotuses, and as such were always inhabited by beautiful swans. The elevated portions of the city had multi-storied palaces which were white like the clouds of the Autumn. One wondered if they were so many shapes which the fame of the king's conquest of world-cities itself had taken. The Vijayanagara City looked like the stage set for flowering beauty to display its charms; or it may even be pictured as the mark of fashion and loveliness adorning the forehead of the lady known as Earth's southern quarter.[57] Further Gaṅgādevī describes that, the city was full of virtuous brāhmins, and armies of musicians ever strode its expansive grounds. Thus, like the full-moon light, or the world of celestial bords, serenity and music a reigned unceasingly all round. The Bhujaṅgas or the youths of fashion made that city their favourite haunt, even as bhujaṅgas or serpents make the crown of Lord Śiva their chosen abode. Good hearted people at large, loved to wander in its precincts like gods in the regions of the Sumeru. The city was just an abode of all good fortunes. Prosperity in all its aspects delighted to live in its saloons. Thus, the city looked like a garland of precious stones on the shores of the sea of virtue.[58]

The disc of the sun caught in the heights of the city-palaces produced on the on-lookers the illusion of a golden jar. The damsels playing on the grounds of the top floor of the mansions often laid their hands on the rounded body of the moon, mistaking it for their play-ball of pearls. Further it is described that, hearing the sound of the drum accompanying the music played in palaces, the peacocks began to dance even in the absence of any appropriate occasions. The clouds that hung about the sides of the palaces with the colour of Padmarāga gems reflected in them, always looked brown like evening clouds.[59] The clouds of smoke that rushed through the crevices in the buildings of the city at the evening-time appeared like darkness effecting its escape afraid of being caught in the effulgence of approaching lamp-light inside. As the lustre of the gems with which the steps were paved in the lakes always drove darkness away, the Cakravāka birds were not separated even at night fall. The moon, as if ashamed by reason of the shining beauty marking the lotus-like faces of the lovely women in the city, ever wore a mourning black on her body known as Kalaṅka. The god of love never thought of resorting to his flower-arrows to effect his conquests in the face of the lovely glances shot from the eyes of beautiful women thereto subdue the hearts of youth. As if to take their lessons in graceful walking the swans ever sought the company of women there, attracted by the sweet jingling of their foot-ornaments. The blooming breasts of the maidens of the city were beautifully set off by their slender waists even as thick clouds in the void above. There was no hardness there in the city–except in the breasts of beautiful damsels, nor crookedness except in their curly locks, nor thinness except in their waists. Pampā was the branch city of Vijayanagara. Many a Kubira (lords of wealth) were there so much so that God Virūpākṣa (Śiva) who was enshrined there never spent a thought about his original home at Alakā.[60]

Description of the Pregnency and Morning Sickness

The description of the pregnancy and morning sickness of Devāyī is analogous with the descriptions of such sickness of Sudhakṣiṇa and of Raghu in Raghuvaṁśa.[61] She describes the morning sickness of Devāyī which is quite natural. During the pregnancy time, Devāyī expresses her desire to eat particles of earth, which are tasty to her. Gaṅgādevī imagins that she was the beloved consort of the lord of this earth, indulged in tasting particles of it as if to teach the responsibility of reining over the world to the infant in her womb.[62] The very nature of her longings in her pregnancy which always took a daring turn, suggested that her son would be wedded to heroic accomplishments.[63] Without caring for the Tuṅgabhadrā which flowed near by and which was easily fordable, she desired to sport in the Tāmraparṇī in company with her army of elephants that would raise waves in its waters (while they submerged with their huge bodies).[64] Though she was physically unable to walk as far as the pleasure-hill where the deer were quietly grazing, she, in her mental flights, was on the tops of the Malaya mountain inhabited by (ferocious) lions.[65] As time advanced the limbs of her body began to put on flesh, her face regained its sweet and lazy eye-looks, her belly began to show its folds distinctly, and this change in his beloved filled the king with delight.[66] The auspicious line of hair that was on her abdomen looked like a black serpent on guard in order to protect the infant within.[67] Her breasts, with black nipples, surpassed in their attractiveness the Cakravāka couple with a bit of blue Utpala flower in their beaks.[68]

Aquatic Sports

The description of aquatic sprots are amorously introduced in Sanskrit literature. For instance Kālidāsa, in his Raghuvaṁśa describes the water sports of Kuśa and the women of his royal harem.[69] Bhāravi describes the aquatic sports of Gandharvas and Apsarās in his Kirātārjunīya.[70] Māgha depicts the water sports of Yādavas and their wives in his Śiśupālavadha.[71] In the sixth canto of the Madhurāvijayaṁ we find a beautiful description of aquatic sports of Kampaṇa and the women of his royal house-hold.[72]

At the commencement of the description of watersports of Kampaṇa, the poetess states that Kampaṇa and the ladies of his royal harem went to the pleasure garden. Referring to the pleasure garden, the poetess says that the Indra's moving to Nandana with celestial nymphs.[73] It was covered with their jewelled girdles sounding the sight of it was like a line of humming bees moving in the wake of the southern gale.[74] Kampaṇa entered into the garden-pond and sprinkled water on the group of ladies. The poetess imagines that the pond was looking like a Vāruṇāstra of Kāmadeva.[75]

The path which the ladies took, was lined with red lac-dye dripping from their feet, and it seemed as if a cover of tender leaves, laid on the ground. The glances of ladies, radiating blue, white and red hues, seem to line the sky with blue lilies, white lilies and red lotuses, the sounds of jewelled anklets of ladies, as they fell on the king's ears, produced the impression in his mind, that it might be the noise of the stringing of Cupid's bow. Mutual conversation held by the ladies as they followed the king, was heard in varying notes of sweetness.[76]

Aquatic sports of Kampaṇa create jealousy in the minds of some ladies. The poetess states that the king splashed water on a lotus in the pleasure lake, and this made a lady cast on him angry, looks of jealousy, the fringes of her eye-lashes wet with tears.[77] Further, she describes very beautifully the embraces under the water. She states that Kampaṇa touched nicely (delicately) the upper part of a lady's thigh underneath the water. She feigned fish bite and embraced her lover even when her companions were looking on.[78] The poetess described how the water sheet touched the whole body of the ladies.[79] She states the sheet of water, first touched the feet; then the thighs; then the garment;[80] as they emerged out of the lake, with nail marks on their persons distinctly visible, with their thighs revealed through the waving cover of wet clothing, and water particles dripping from their long braids of hair.[81] While describing the aquatic sports of Kampaṇa and his beloveds, Gaṅgādevī has referred to all the important features of aquatic sports, such as swimming in the water, as also the different strokes of swimming, splashing the water on each other, embracing under the water, snatching away the under-garments, all the amorous frivolities in the waters are described colourfully with the magic-touch of her imagination.

Description of Battle Scenes

This has been presented in two contexts *viz.*, war with Śambuvarāya and with the muslim king. These have been described not alike but very differently. This shows richness of the poetess's imagination. Those descriptions unlike in the Purāṇas, proceed with much emphasis (the outlook of) on Rasa and thus maintain the traditions of the Kāvya. The description of battles in this Kāvya appears to be, to some extent, inspired by the descriptions of battles between Raghu and Indra, of Aja with his enemy kings, of Rāma with Rāvaṇa, in Raghuvaṁśa. In some places, the shadows of the descriptions of warfare in the Rāmāyaṇa to a little extent are found. In some others, in elephant warfare, the shadows of description of battle in Śiśupālavadha are visible. Yet in some others, the shadows of the descriptions in the Champū Bhārata are traceable to us. These descriptions are found to be full of thought, and consistent with Rasa delineation.

As per the requirement of the theme of this Mahākāvya (*i.e.*, victory of the Nayaka), Gaṅgādevī has concentrated her attention on describing important battle scenes in the Madhurāvijayaṁ. The main battle-scenes as has been said already, are,

1. Kampaṇa versus Śambuvarāya–of Tundiramandalam,
2. Kampaṇa versus Turuṣka king–of Madhurā.

1. While describing the terrible war of Kampaṇa vs Śambuvarāya, Gaṅgādevī presents numerous dreadful pictures of the battle. The poetess referring to the Kampaṇa's army and Camparāja army states, how they attacked each other. She states that they attacked each other, like two oceans brought against each other by stormy winds at the time of the great deluge.[82] Further the poetess highlights how the weapons of the warriors generated sparks in the darkness and how it was looking. She says that sparks generated in large numbers by the clashing of the weapon on either side and bore a close resemblance to a collection of glow worms in the darkness of the dust.[83] Then she describes how during that war the sharp pointed arrows knocked down the soldiers even she fancied side-glances of the amorous goddess of fight, the sharp pointed arrows let fly against one another by bow men-fell to the ground.[84]

She describes the blood-stained sword blades. She imagines that the blood-stained sword blades waving in the hands of heroic warriors appeared like the rolling tongue of Yama, eager to make a meal of them.[85] Due to that war, countless rivers of blood began to flow.[86] The poetess then describes the fight between Kampaṇa and Śambuvarāya, in sixteen verses.[87] This is one of the instances where the imaginative power of the poetess is superb. King Kampaṇa then converted the Tamil king's town into an encampment for his own forces, and from there began to lay seige to the hill fortress named Rājagambhīra in which the enemy had sought asylam.[88]

The last part of the Madhurāvijayaṁ *i.e.*, the ninth canto is fully devoted to describe the battle scenes of Kampaṇa and Turaṣka king. The fighting scene is very dreadful and loathsome. The major fight taking place between Kampaṇa and Turaṣka king is described with all its details in the space of twenty verses.[89]

While describing the meeting of Kampaṇa and Turaṣka in the battle-field, she states that the Turaṣka forces were routed in the battle. The Yavana king met king Kampaṇa, even as Vṛtra did the king of the gods.[90] Again referring to the valour of the Turaṣka king, the poetess states that the brave king Kampaṇa was delighted in having an opponent like the Suratrāṇa (Sultan) who had by his valour reduced the Colas and Pāṇḍyas, and despoiled the wealth of Vīra Ballāla (the third).[91]Again referring to the valour of the two mighty men (Kampaṇa and Sultan), the poetess states that the two proud opponents fought in a manner befitting the respective might of their arms, by showering arrows on each other with their bows bent up to their ears.[92] Finally, the fall of the Turaṣka king also is described with great valour. The poetess says the head of the Suratrāṇa fell on the ground, the head that never knew the art of cajoling servant, like, the head that had borne the royal burden of the Turaṣka Sāmrājya (Supremacy) and had not bowed down even to gods.[93]

Kampaṇa was astonished to see that even after the head had fallen, the trunk on the horse back, still held the reins, checking the horses course with one hand while the other was uplifted to return the blow of the adversary.[94]

Thus an account of the various descriptions in the Madhurāvijayaṁ, may be seen. As it is evident from the above account, Gaṅgādevī is not strictly conventional in her descriptions. Although Gaṅgādevī has used certain poetic conventions, she has flashes of originality in presenting the different aspects of the objects of her description. The description pertaining to Śṛṅgāra, are noted in the Chapter on the Rasa delineation. Other descriptions are exhaustively presented in this chapter. The descriptive power of Gaṅgadevī is thus evident. It may be observed that she is surprisingly brief in the narration of the story, leaving some most significant incidents by a mere reference to give a vivid picture of the seasons, the phenomena of sun-set moonrise, and every twilight city, water-sports, battle scenes etc., in all their fullness. The descriptions are perfectly set with original refreshing images of the beauty in nature and the beauty in human life. Due credit should be given to the poetess Gaṅgadevī for her extra-ordinary imaginative ability and poetic skill in using the poetic conventions and Alaṅkāras.

REFERENCES

1. उपाहरन् कुसुमानि महीरुहा किसलयैः कलितांजलिबन्धः।
   मधुरकोविलकूजितभाषितो मधुरथैनमुपासितुमासदत्।। *MV*. V-62
   मधु सुगन्धिरजः सहकारजं मलयशैलसमीरणमान्त्रिकाः।
   प्रणयरोष पराङ्मुखमानिनीहृदयसंवननार्थमिवाकिरम्।। *Ibid.*, V-63
2. उपवनेष्वगमन्नुपमेयतां स्फुटरुचो नविकंशुककुड्मलाः।
   मथितान्थमृगक्षतजारुणैर्मदनकेसरिणः कुटिलैर्नखैः।। *Ibid.*, V-64
3. चटुलषट्पदकज्जलपातिनी विरुरुचे नवचम्पकमंजरी।
   प्रकटितेवहिमापगमश्रिया स्मरमहोत्सवदीपपरंपरा।। *Ibid.*, V-65
4. क्वणितनूपुरकुन्तलकामिनी चरणपंकजसङ्गवशादिव।
   मुखरभृङ्गमशोकमहीरुहैस्तदनुरूपमधार्यते पल्लवम्।। *Ibid.*, V-67
5. वरवधु परिरम्भरसोल्लसल्ललितकुड्मलकण्टकिताकृतिः।
   कुरबकः कुसुमेषु अचेतनेष्वपि विश्रृंखलवृत्तिमसूचयत्।। *Ibid.*, V-68
6. पथिकसार्थ पराक्रमणोत्सुकप्रसवकार्मुक काहलनिस्वनः।
   मधुर पंचमरागरसांचितो जगदरंजयदन्यभृतध्वनिः।। *Ibid.*, V-69
7. अधिगताविभनवार्तवसम्पदः स्तबकसंजनिजस्तनविभ्रमाः।
   भ्रमरकामुकसंवननक्षमा वनलतालिलतां दधिरे दशाम्।। *Ibid.*, V-70

8. सुतनवः फलकेषु मधूत्सवे रतिपतिं परिलेखितुमुत्थताः।
हृदयगोचरतामनिशं गतं हरिहरात्मजमेव समालिखन्।। *MV.*, V-71-75
मदनबेरनिभां निभृन्तपुरः क्षितिपतिं कृतचन्दनचर्चिकाः।
अधिकधर्मपयोभिरवागमन् मृगदृशो विकसत्पुलकैः करैः।। *Ibid.*, V-72
मुखरकङ्कणमाकुलमेखलं चरितहारलतां लुलितालकम्।
अधिगतश्रममस्य वधूजनो रतिविशेषमाशिक्षत डोलया।। *Ibid.*, V-73
उचितरागविशेषमनोहरे रतिपतेरूपगानविधौ स्त्रियः।
नृपतित्रोकृतम्खलना ययुः प्रियसखीसविधेषु विलक्षताम्।। *Ibid.*, V-74
क्षितिपतिं किल कुङ्कुममुष्टिना समभिताऽयितुं धियमादधौ।
सपदिधर्मपयः प्रसरणे तं विगलितं न विवेद वधूजनः। *Ibid.*, V-75

9. अथ दलन्निचुलद्रुममंजरीनिचयदर्शितचामरविभ्रमः।
कृतनुतिः किल चातकयाचकैर्नृपतिमन्वगमज्जलदागमः।। *Ibid.*, V-24
तत इतो विहरत्तृटिदङ्गनाललितलास्यहरिन्मणिमण्डपैः।
पटुमृदङ्गरवोपमगर्जि तै र्निबिडमाविरभूयत वारिदैः।। *Ibid.*, V-25

10. स्फुटितटित्तपीयगुणोज्ज्वलै पृथुपयः कणमौक्तिकसङ्गिभिः।
अलिकदम्बकसच्छविभिर्दिशामसितकंचुलिकायितमम्बुदैः। *Ibid.*, V-26

11. हरितलोहितपाण्डुरराजत त्रिदशराजशरासनलेखिका।
मरतकोपलविद्रुममौक्तिकैर्विरचिता रशनेव नभश्श्रियः।। *Ibid.*, V-27

12. अभिमते सति वारिधरोदये मधुरषड्जमनोहरगीतिभिः।
गिरितटीषु मुहुः परिमण्डलीकृतकलापममनिर्त शिखण्डिभिः।। *Ibid.*, V-30

13. पटुतटिद्गणकोणहताः पुरो रतिपतेः पटहा इव दिव्यका।
निशमिताः स्फुटसाहसमध्वगैर्जलधरा वियदध्वनि दध्वनुः।। *Ibid.*, V-31
दलितकन्दलमुच्छ्वसदर्जनं स्फुटकदम्बमुदंचितकैतकम्।
मुदितचातकमुन्मुखबर्हिणं कतिचिदास दिनानि वितान्तरम्।। *Ibid.*, V-32
करतलैरिव गन्धवहैघनाः प्रहितकैतकपांसुविभूतयः।
स्तनितहुंकृतिभिःनिरकासयन् नृपतियौवनमानमहाग्रहम्।। *Ibid.*, V-33

14. पटुपुरः पवनाधिगतभ्रमा जलमुचः करकोपलकैतवात्।
सलिलराशिपयस्सहचूषितामुदवमन्निव मौक्तिकसंहितम्।। *Ibid.*, V-29

15. रुधिरबिन्दुनिभच्छविरन्वगात् क्षितितले हरिगोपपरम्परा।
घनधरट्टपरस्परघट्टनक्षरतिरम्मदवह्निकणावलिम्।। *Ibid.*, V-28

16. नववधू परिरम्भणदोहलान्यनुपदं निनदैः प्रतिपादयन्।
अलभत क्षणदासु घनागमो नरपतेः किल नर्मसुहृत्पदम्।। *Ibid.*, V-37

17. चलितबर्हिणचन्द्रक्वचितत्रितैः सुरभिगन्धिशिलामदशालिभिः।
विकचनीपवनैर्नृपतेर्मनो मुहरहरि विहारमहीधरैः।। *Ibid.*, V-34
तमहरन्नहरत्ययमालतीकुसुमदन्तुरकुन्तलकान्तयः।

परिहितागरुधूपतिवाससः सुतनवो मृगनाभिसुगन्धयः।। *MV*. V-35
मणिमयानि गृहाणि समीरणाः कुटजकैतकसौरभवाहिनः।
मदकलाश्च गिरः प्रचलाकिना क्षितिपतेः स्मरदीपकतां ययुः।। *Ibid.*, V-36

18. विकचपद्मविलोचनमात्मनो मुखमवेक्षितुंमात्तकुतूहला।
नियतमभ्रनिचोलक गर्भतः शरदकर्षदहर्पतिदर्पणम्।। *Ibid.*, V-46

19. नियतमम्बुदशाणनिघर्षणादतिमहस्क महस्करमण्डलम्।
अजनि वर्षविधोरपिवार्षिकैर्जलधरैः परिधौतमिवौज्ज्वलम्।। *Ibid.*, V-43

20. कलशजस्य मुनेरुद्रयाज्जहुः कलुषता सलिलानि महौजसः।
सदुपदेशवशादिव शासितुस्तनुभृता हृदयानि दयानि दयानिधेः।। *Ibid.*, V-41

21. जलदकालकलिस्फुरितां शनैः कलुषतां प्रशमय कृशाः पुनः।
घटयति स्म शरत् तटिनीसखीरूपनतैः कलहंसविलासिभिः।। *Ibid.*, V-44

22. विद्युत्काशसटाभरभासुरः प्रकटितोरूजपारुणलोचनः।
व्यघटयद् घनदन्तिघटाः स्फुरद्रविमुखः शरदागमकेसरी।। *Ibid.*, V-39
अवितथं रजनीदिवसाधिपौ मधुरिपोर्नयने इति भाषितम्।
स्फुटममुष्य यतः स्वपनात्ययादजति तादृशमुन्मिषितं तयोः।। *Ibid.*, V-40

23. विशदशारदनीरदशारितं वियदलक्ष्यत वीततटिद्गुणम्।
प्रकटफेनवदम्बककर्बुरं जलभिवाम्बुनिधेर्गतविद्रुमम्।। *Ibid.*, V-43

24. सरसिजाकरसंचरदिन्दिराचरणहंसकनिक्वणमन्थरः।
मदनमङ्गलतूर्यरवाऽभवन्मदकलः कलसंसकुलध्वनिः।। *Ibid.*, V-45

25. दलदयुग्मदलोदरसौरभ प्रसरपक्ष्मलिता वनवायवः।
मुहुरधः कृतयन्तृनिवारणानकृणत क्षितिभृन्मदवारणान्।। *Ibid.*, V-49
वनभुवः परितः पवनेरितैर्नवजपाकुसुमैः कृतदीपिकाः।
प्रथममेव नृपस्यनिदेशतो विजयिनस्तुरगान् निरराजयन्।। *Ibid.*, V-48

26. परिणतेक्षुपरिच्युतमौक्तिकग्रथितहारमनोहरमूर्तिभिः।
विशदमस्य यशो नृपतेः कलं कलमगोपवधूभिरगीयत।। *Ibid.*, V-48
विलसदुत्पललोचनशालिनीः स्फुरितचन्द्रमुखीः कुमुदस्मिताः।
नरपतिः स्फुटताकहारिणीर्निविशद् दयिता इव यामिनीः।। *Ibid.*, V-47

27. अथ नृपस्य समुत्सुकवेतसो मदनकेलिकलासु विलासिनः।
प्रियामिवाचितरं समुपागमत् प्रणदयन् क्षणदास्तुहिनागमः।। *Ibid.*, V-51
हिमभरैर्विहितः कमलाकरो मृदितकान्तिरभून्मृगलांछनः।
वदनमेव नरेन्द्रनतभ्रुवामभजत श्रियमप्रतिशासनाम्।। *Ibid.*, V-52
पुलककंचुकितैः कुचमण्डलैः स्फुरितसीत्कृतिभिश्च मुखेन्दुभिः।
अविरतं स्मरतन्त्रमिवान्वभूदवनिपालविलासवतीजनः।। *Ibid.*, V-53
विकचकुन्दकलापपरिष्क्रियाविरचितालकजालकविभ्रमम्।

अशमयेऽपि समौक्तिकमण्डनं प्रभुरमस्तं निजं प्रमदाजनम्।। *MV*. V. 54
बहुलकुङ्कुमपङ्कविलेपनप्रसृमरोष्मपयोधरमण्डलैः।
अरमताविरतं रमणीजनैरगरूगन्धिषु गर्भ गृहेषु सः।। *Ibid.*, V-55

28. इति सुखान्युचितानि हिमागमे समनुभूय मनोभवसन्निभः।
शिशिरयामवतीष्वपि रागवान् रमयितुं रमणीरुदयुङ्क्त सः।। *Ibid.*, V-56

29. परिलसन्नवलोध्ररजोभरच्छुरणपाण्डरगण्डतलैर्मुखैः।
मृगमदद्रवचारुविशेषकैर्मृगदृशो नृपतेहरन् मनः।। *Ibid.*, V-58
अपदिशच्छिशिरानिलमङ्गकैः पुलकितैर्नृपतेः सविधगतः।
मदनसम्भृतधर्मपयः कणैर्भृशमलज्जत मुग्धवधूजनः।। *Ibid.*, V-59
विकलकंचुकलक्ष्यन(वख)व्रणं विगतमौवितकहारमनोहरम्।
तरुणि–मोष्मनखम्पचमङ्गनास्तनयुगं हिमहारि विभोरभूत्।। *Ibid.*, V-61

30. विकचपाटलगन्धिसमीरणैः सलिलकेलिपरायणयौवनैः।
रजनिदैर्घ्यहरैरधिकोल्लसद्रविमहोभिरहोभिरभूयत।। *Ibid.*, V-16
परुषतापविशेषपरिस्खलद्रथतुरङ्गममन्दगताविव।
अहिमधाम्नि रथाङ्गसुखावहामहरगाहत दैर्घ्यवर्ती दशाम्।। *Ibid.*, V-18
सलिलकेलिकुतूहलकुन्तलीकुचतटाहतिजातभयैरिव।
अपसृतैरजनि प्रतिवासरं नृपतिगेहविहारसरोजलैः।। *Ibid.*, V-20
प्रचुरधर्मपयः कणजालिकागुणितमौवितकमण्डनशालिभिः।
नवशिरीषवन्तसमनोहरैः सुवदना वदनैस्तममोदयन्।। *Ibid.*, V-21
हिमगृहेषु निरन्तरशीकरप्रकरदर्शितातारकपंक्तिषु।
दिवसतापं महापयदायतं वरवधु सूहितो वसुधाधिपः।। *Ibid.*, V-23

31. परिचूषितदीप्तिरम्बुजैः पुररूष्माणमिवाप्तुमौर्वनैः।
रयवल्गितवाहनो रविः पयसाराशिमिवापि पश्चिमम्।। *Ibid.*, VII-2

32. प्रथमां हरितं प्रभाकरो विरहय्यात्मनि तापमाप यम्।
अपरामुपगम्यं तं जहौ हृदयं कः खलु वेत्ति रागिणाम्। *Ibid.*, VII-6

33. गतदीप्तिगभस्तिमालिनो विलुठद्वीचिषु बिम्ब मम्बुधेः।
शफराः फलखण्डशङ्कया रसनाभिर्लिलिहुर्मुहुर्मुहुः।। *Ibid.*, VII-13

34. खामेकमवेक्ष्य तादृशं पतितं विष्णुपदातिलङ्घनात्।
निभृतं चकिता इवाखिलास्तस्त्रीडेषु विलिल्यिरे खगाः।। *Ibid.*, VII-16

35. दिनवेषमपास्य यामिनीवपुषा कालनटस्य नृत्यतः।
ददृशे जगता पितृप्रसूर्दिवि नेपथ्यपटीव पाटला।। *Ibid.*, VII-23
किमु धूमभरः प्रशाम्यतो द्युमणिग्रावगतस्य तेजसः।
प्रससार दिशस्तमोमिषात् किमु मीलत्कमलालिसंचयः।। *Ibid.*, VII-24
हलिहेतिदलत्कलिन्दजालहरीकन्दलकालिमद्रुहः।
परितस्तरुरम्बरस्थलीं परितः स्थूल तमास्तामोभरः।। *Ibid.*, VII-25

37. तदमंसत मांसलं तमस्तनुतारागण बिन्दुजालकम्।
दिवसात्ययचण्डताण्डवच्युतमीशस्य गजाजिनं जना:।। *MV*. VII-27

38. अथ किंचिददृश्यतैन्दवं वपुरार्द्रोदयरागलोहितम्।
बलशासनदिग्विलासिनीमुखसिन्धूरललामकोमलम्।। *Ibid.*, VII-36

39. परिपिण्डितयावकारुणं प्रचकाशे हिमरश्मिमण्डलम्।
रचितं नवरक्तसन्ध्यकैर्विजयच्छत्रमिवात्मजन्मन:।। *Ibid.*, VII-37

40. परिरभ्य दृढं चिरागम: प्रथमाशासुदृशा निशापति:।
श्लथयत्यय मंशुभिर्नखैस्तिमिरश्रेणिमयीं प्रवेणिकाम्।। *Ibid.*, VII-43

41. शशिमण्डलशङ्खपेटकादवकृष्य क्षपया समर्पितम्।
कुमुदच्छवि कौमदीमयं दधती क्षौममभाद् दिगङ्गना।। *Ibid.*, VII-46

42. मुहुरामृशदेव पद्मिनीमपि रागी क्षणदाकर: करै:।
यदमुं प्रति नेयमुन्मुखी प्रभवत्यत्र पतिव्रतागुण:।। *Ibid.*, VII-48

43. अनुदर्शमनुप्रवेशतस्तपनाच्छवितमवाप तापिनीम्।
नियतं हिमदीधितिर्यत: क्षमते तापयितुं वियोगिन:।। *Ibid.*, VII-49

44. य: शेष इव नागानां नगानां हिमवानिव।
दैत्यारिरिव देवानां प्रथम: पृथिवीभुजाम्।। *Ibid.*, I-27

45. तिग्मांशोरपि तेजस्वी शीतांशोरपि शीतल:।
सागरादपि गम्भीर: सुमेरोरपि य: स्थिर:।। *Ibid.*, I-28

46. विवेकमेव संचितं धनुरव वरूथिमीम्।
बाहुमेव रणोत्साहे य: सहायममन्यत।। *Ibid.*, I-29

47. कलिकालमहाधर्म प्लुष्टो धर्ममहीरुह:।
यस्य दानाम्बुसेकेन पुनरङ्कुरितोऽभवत्।। *Ibid.*, I-37

48. अधारयत् दर्शितदेहसौष्ठवां स राजसूनुस्तनुवृत्तमध्य(मा?ता)म्।
पराक्रमत्रासितचित्तवृत्तिर्भिमृगाधिराजैरूपदीकृतामवि।। *Ibid.*, III-9

49. व्यराजतोर: स्थलमस्य तावता विशालभावेन कवाटबन्धुरम्।
करीन्द्रकुम्भप्रतिमं मृगीदृशां कुचद्वयं याति न यावता बहि:।। *Ibid.*, III-10

50. धनांसपीठौ कठिनारुणाङ्गुली पटुप्रकोष्ठो परिधानुकारिणौ।
महौजसस्तस्य मनोहरौ भुजावपश्यदाजानुविलम्बिनौ जन:।। *Ibid.*, III-1

51. विहाय मध्यं यदि लक्ष्मरेखया बहि: प्रसार्येत सुधांशुमण्डलम्।
दरोदितश्मश्रु (धृ?कु)तश्रियस्तदा तदाननेन्दोरूपमानतां व्रजेत्।। *Ibid.*, III-12

52. विनिद्रपङ्केरुहदाम दीर्घयोर्दृशोरूपान्ते जनितोऽस्य शोणिमा।
अनर्गलस्वप्रसरप्ररोधकश्रुतिद्वयीदर्शितरोषयोरिव।। *Ibid.*, III., 13

53. अनल्बणामायततुङ्गबन्धुराममंस्त लोकः स्फुटमस्य नासिकाम्।
विशृङ्खलव्याप्नुवदीक्षणद्वयी परस्पराक्रान्तिनिवारणार्गलाम्।। *MV*. III-I

54. अधारयत् गर्भितरक्तसन्ध्यकं नृपात्मजः केशकलापमायतम्।
दृढानुरागच्छुरितैर्मगीदृशामनुप्रविष्टं हृदयैरिवान्तरा।। *Ibid*., III-15

55. तस्यासीद् विजया नाम विजयार्जितसम्पदः।
राजधानी बुधैः श्लाघ्या शक्रस्येवामरावती।। *Ibid*., I-43
सुरलोकान्तसङ्क्रान्तस्वर्णदीमत्सरादिव।
परिखाकारतां यान्त्या परीता तुङ्गभद्रया।। *Ibid*., I-44

56. लक्ष्मीलतालवालेन क्षमावधूनाभिशोभिता।
चक्राचलप्रकारेण प्राकारेण परिष्कृता।। *Ibid*., I-45
उत्फुल्लचम्पकाशोकनागकेसरकेसरैः।
वसन्तबासभवनैरारामैरभितो वृता।। *Ibid*., I-47

57. कस्तूरीहरिणाक्रान्तकर्पूरकदलीतलैः।
मनोभवमहीदुर्गैर्महिता केलिपर्वतैः।। *Ibid*., I-48
कमलामोदमधुरैः कलहंसकुलावुलैः।
क्रीडासरोभिः सहिता मणिसोपानमंजुलैः।। *Ibid*., I-49
यशस्तोमैरिवाशेषनगरीविजयार्जितैः।
सौधेः प्रकाशितोत्सेधा शरदम्भोदपाण्डरैः।। *Ibid*., I-50
द्वनितावल्लीविलासवनवाटिका।
दक्षिणाशा सरोजाक्षीफलाललीलाललाटिका।। *Ibid*., I-51

58. द्विजराजसमुल्लासनित्यराकानिशीथिनी।
गन्धर्वगणसानिध्यनव्यदिव्यवरूथिनी।। *Ibid*., I-52
भुजङ्गसङ्घसंवासभूतेशमुकुटस्थली।
सुमनस्तोम संचारसुवर्णगिरिमेखला।। *Ibid*., I-53
लीलेव दिष्टिवृद्धीना शालेव सकलश्रियाम्।
मालेव सर्वरत्नानाम् वेलेव सुकृताम्बुधेः।। *Ibid*., I-54

59. यस्या प्रसादशृङ्गेण लग्नं मार्ताण्डमण्डलम्।
संधत्ते वीक्षमाणानां सौवर्णकलशभ्रमम्।। *Ibid*., I-55
यत्सौध चन्द्रशालासु विहरन्त्यो मृगेक्षणाः।
शशां कमवलम्बन्ते मुक्ताकन्दुकशङ्कया।। *Ibid*., I-56
यत्र सौधेषु सङ्गीतमृदङ्गप्रतिनादिषु।
अकाण्डे ताण्डवारम्भं वितन्वन्ति शिखण्डिनः।। *Ibid*., I-57
पद्मरागोपलोत्कीर्ण प्रसादप्रान्तवर्तिनः।
सन्ततं यत्र दृश्यन्ते सन्ध्या इव बलाहकाः।। *Ibid*., I-58

60. सन्ध्यासु यत्र निर्यान्ति जालेभ्यो धूपराजयः।
अन्तः प्रदीपिकालोक चकितध्वान्तसन्निभाः।। *MV.* I-59
यद्दीर्घिकासु माणिक्य सोपानचारिभिः।
क्षणदास्वपि चक्राह्वैर्विरहो नानुभूयते।। *Ibid.*, I-60
यदङ्गनामुखाम्भोज लावण्यालाभलज्जितः।
कलङ्कच्छद्मना चन्द्रो व्यनक्ति हृदयव्यथाम्।। *Ibid.*, I-61
यत्र स्त्रीणां कटाक्षेषु यूनां हृदयहारिषु।
पुष्पास्त्रसंचये वांछां मुंचते पंचसायकः।। *Ibid.*, I-62
मरालैर्मजुमंजीरशिंजिताकृष्टमानसैः।
लीलागतिमिव प्राप्तुं सेव्यन्ते यत्र योषितः।। *Ibid.*, I-63
यत्रावलग्नसादृश्य वांछाविमतमम्बरम्।
प्रायः पयोधरोत्सेधैनिरुन्धन्ति पुरन्ध्र्यः।। *Ibid.*, I-64
यत्र वामभ्रुवामेव काठिन्यं स्तनमण्डले।
कौटिल्यं कबरीमारे कार्श्यं मध्ये च दृश्यते।। *Ibid.*, I-65
यच्छाकानगरीं पम्पामनेकधनदाश्रिताम्।
अधितिष्ठान् विरूपाक्षो न स्मरत्यलकापुरीम्।। *Ibid.*, I-66

61. *Raghuvaṁśa* III. 1-10.

62. गर्भस्थितस्येव शिशोर्विधातुं वसुन्धरामण्डलभारशिक्षाम्।
अचोरयत् पार्थिवधर्मपत्नी मन्ये मृदास्वादरसानुबन्धम्।। *Ibid.*, II-3

63. अनन्यसामान्यभुजापदानमुत्पत्स्यमानं तनयं नृपस्य।
अनारतं वीररसानुबन्धे न्यवेदयद् दौहृदमेव देव्याः।। *Ibid.*, II-4

64. सा तुङ्गभद्रां सविधे वहन्तीं सुभ्रूरनादृत्य सुखावगाहाम्।
विहर्तुमैच्छन्निजसैन्यनागैस्तरङ्गिते वारिणि ताम्रपर्ण्याः।। *Ibid.*, II-5

65. अपारयन्ती चरितैणशावं क्रीडाचलोपान्तमपि प्रयातुम्।
आखेटरागादधिरोदुमैच्छन्माद्यन्मृगेन्द्राम्मलयाद्रिकूटान्।। *Ibid.*, II-6

66. क्रमाज्जहद्भिः क्रशिमानमङ्गैर्मुखे न मुग्धालसलोचनेन।
मध्येन च त्यक्तवलित्रयेण नरेश्वरं नन्दयति नन्दयति स्म राज्ञी।। *Ibid.*, II-9

67. सौभाग्यगन्धद्विपदानलेखा रराज तस्या नवरोमराजिः।
तेजोनिधिं गर्भतले निगूढं कालोरगी रक्षितुमागतेव।। *Ibid.*, II-10

68. श्यामायमानच्छविना मुखेन स्तनद्वयं तामरसेक्षणायाः।
सन्दष्टनीलोत्पलयोरभिख्यां रथाङ्गनाम्नोरधरी चकार।। *Ibid.*, II-11

69. *Raghuvaṁśa* XVI. 57-71.

70. Bhāravi, *Kīrātārjunīyaṁ*, VIII. 168-188.

71. *Śiśupālavadha* VIII. 1-71.

72. *Madhurāvijayaṁ* 1-69.

73. अथ वरतनुभिः समं कदाचित् विरचयितुं कुसुमापचायलीलाम्।
प्रमदवनममर्त्यकामिनीभिर्हरिरिव नन्दनमासदन्नरेन्द्रः।। *MV.* VI-1

74. मुखरितमणिमेखलाकलापाः प्रचलितमन्वचलंस्तमायताक्ष्यः।
उपवनलतिकाइवोपगीतभ्रमरकुला मलयाद्रिगन्धवाहम्।। *Ibid.*, VI-2

75. अविरतमवनीशहस्तमुक्तप्रवितटदीर्घपयांसि पतन्ति।
मदनसुभटवारुणास्त्रशङ्का मनसि चचार चकोरलोचनानाम्।। *Ibid.*, VI-55

76. परिवहदनुरागपूरकल्पैः पदगलितैरथ याचकैर्वधूनाम्।
सरणिरणतामिव नीता समजनि नूतनपल्लवास्तृतेव।। *Ibid.*, VI-3
विविधविलसितैर्विलासिनीनामसितसितारुणकान्तिभिः कटाक्षैः।
कुवलयकुमुदारविन्दमालाखचितमिवामलमम्बर बभासे।। *Ibid.*, VI-4
अजनयदवनीश्वरस्य चेतस्यसितदृशा मणिनूपुरप्रणादः।
सहपरिचलितप्रसूनकेतोरवनमदैक्षवचापघोषशङ्काम्।। *Ibid.*, VI-5
अवनिपतिमनुप्रतथुषीणां हरिणदृशामितरेतरप्रसक्ताः।
मधुरसमधुरा गिरस्तदार्नीं बहुविधभङ्तिरङ्गिता बभूवुः।। *Ibid.*, VI-6

77. अवनिपतिरसिक्त दीर्घिकाया मुखकमलं सलिलेन साभिलाशम्।
किमपि समदिकार्द्रपक्ष्मलेखं वदनमभूदरुणेक्षणं परस्याः।। *Ibid.*, VI-57

78. प्रणयिनि सलिलापवारितेन स्पृशति करेण सलीलमूरुमूलम्।
प्रकटितशफराभिधातभीतं भिषति जनेऽप्यमुमा लिलिङ्गिगकावित्।। *Ibid.*, VI-58

79. चरणविलुठितो विलङ्घितोरुः परिगतनीविरवाप्तनाभिचक्रः।
स्नततटलुलितः क्रमेण तासां मुखराशिबिम्बमचुम्बदम्बुपूरः।। *Ibid.*, VI-60

80. विषदमधरमक्ष्यनंजनाभं विगतललाम वितन्वती ललाटम्।
रतिरिव जलकेलिरङ्गनानामवनिपतेः स्पृहणीयतामयासीत्।। *Ibid.*, VI-62

81. परिमुषितपटीरलेपनेष्व(प्य)विरललग्नसरोजकेसरेषु।
कुचकलशतटेषु कुन्तलीनां नखरपदानि न लक्षितान्यभुवन्।। *Ibid.*, VI-63
विहृतिरयपरिच्युतान् वतंसानसितदृशामनुदद् बहिः प्रवाहः।
नहि जडिमसमन्वितोऽपि कोऽपि श्रुतिविषयात् पतितैः करोति मैत्रीम्।। *Ibid.*, VI. 64
अपि दयिततमेन वारिताभिर्गृहसरसो विजहे न वारि ताभिः।
परिलुलितललामचर्चिकाभिर्विहृतिरसान्महिलामचर्चिकाभिः।। *Ibid.*, VI-65
अथ विहरणखेदमन्थराभिः सह निरगाद् सरसो नृपः प्रियाभिः।
कलशजलनिधेरिवाप्सरोभिर्विबुधतरुर्मथनश्रमालसाभिः।। *Ibid.*, VI-6
स्फुटनखरदनाङ्गमङ्गनानां परिलगदार्द्रदुकूलदर्शितोरु।
वपुरनुकलमैक्षत क्षितीशो जलकणदन्तुरदीर्घकुन्तलाग्रम्।। *Ibid.*, VI-67

82. संवर्तमारुताक्षिप्त समुद्रद्वयंसन्निभौ।
व्यूहौ द्रमिडकर्णाटनाथयोः सन्निपेततुः।। *MV*. IV-52

83. रजस्तमसि वीरास्त्र सङ्घसङ्घट्टनोत्थितैः।
बभ्रे स्फुलिङ्गसंघातैः खद्योतनिवहद्युतिः।। *Ibid*., IV-55

84. सङ्ग्रामदेवतापाङ्गविभ्रमभ्रान्तिदायिनः।
मिथो धनुर्धरैर्मुक्ताः पेतुःशातमुखाः शराः।। *Ibid*., IV-56

85. क्षतजार्द्राः प्रवीराणां प्रेङ्खन्त्यः खड्गलेखिकाः।
जिघत्सतः कृतान्तस्य जिह्वा इव विरेजिरे।। *Ibid*., IV-57

86. आस्त्रापगासु परितो निस्सृतासु सहस्रशः।
भटानां भललनिर्लूने रम्भोजायितमाननैः।। *Ibid*., IV-58

87. *Madhurāvijayaṁ* IV. 67-83.

88. अथ तस्य पुरीमेव नीत्वा शिबिरतां नृपः।
अचलं राजगम्भीरमरुन्ध द्विशदाश्रितम्।। *Ibid*., IV-67

89. *Madhurāvijayaṁ* IX. 21-40.

90. ततस्तुलुष्कान् युधि(कान्दिशी)कानालोक्य विस्फारितघोरशाङ्गः।
कम्पक्षितीन्द्रं यवनाधिराजः प्रत्यग्रहीद् वृत्र इवामरेन्द्रम्।। *Ibid*., IX-23

91. पराक्रमाघः कृतचोलपाण्ड्यं वल्लालसम्पल्लतिकाकुठारम्।
रणोन्मुखं कम्पनृपोऽभ्यनन्दीद् वीरः सुरत्राणमुदग्रशौर्यः।। *Ibid*., IX-27

92. आकर्णमाकृष्टशरासनौ तो मिथः किरन्तौ विशिखानसङ्ख्यान्।
वीरौ स्वबाहुद्रविणानुरूपमायोधनं मानघनो व्यघाताम्।। *Ibid*., IX. 28

93. अज्ञातसेवोचितचाटुवादं तुरुष्क साम्राज्यकृताभिषेकम्।
दिवौकसामप्यकृतप्रणामं भूमौ सुरत्राणशिरः पपात।। *Ibid*., IX-38

94. च्युतेऽपि शीर्षे चतिशववल्गानियन्त्रणव्यापृतवामपाणिम्।
प्रतिप्रहारप्रसृतान्यहस्तं वीरः कबन्धं द्विषतोऽभ्यनन्दीत्।। *Ibid*., IX-39

Chapter-5

Alaṅkāras in the Madhurāvijayaṁ

The excellence of a poem lies mainly in its richness of sentiment. But it is not proper to look upon the poem in this manner at every stage, since figurative language reflects only the playful working of the poet's imaginative mind. Infact rhetoricians have included Alaṅkāras among the constituents of poetry.

हारादिवदलंकारः तत्र स्युपमादयः ।।

The figures of speech like Upamā etc., adorn the poetry just as the golden ornaments like necklace etc., adorn an young woman.

So, the poets have made ample use of them.

The poetic figures embellish the body of poetry constituted by Śabda and Artha. Bhāmaha and Daṇḍin, the Alaṅkārikas of the old school, have considered the Alaṅkāras as the invariable elements of charm in poetry.[1] Vāmana states that 'beauty' is Alaṅkāra[2] and a poem appeals to the mind of a reader only if it has Alaṅkāras.[3] But the excessive use of the figures of speech with special efforts would amount to artificiality as rightly observed by Ānandavardhana. He says that Alaṅkāras should be used with great discretion in such a way as to subserve the delination of Rasa. Alaṅkāras should be such as evolved without special effort on the part of the poet.[4] Subservience to Rasa and spontaneity in evolution, are the special requirements of Alaṅkāras, which, when fulfilled, give a stamp of greatness to a poet. Kālidāsa, among the classical poets, has this stamp of greatness in using Alaṅkāras. Poets after him have shown greater fascination for Alaṅkāras to the extent of degenerating them into more and more artificiality.

Now a word about the place of Alaṅkāras in a piece of poetry, would not be out of place here. The word Alaṅkāra literally means अलङ्करोतीति अलङ्कारः *i.e.*, that which decorates. In every day life, Alaṅkāras mean ornaments which decorates person. In rhetorics, the word Alaṅkāra means poetic embellishments which add charm to poetry as necklaces, bangles etc., add charm to the beauty of a lady. Bhāmaha and Daṇḍin hold that Alaṅkāras are very essential in a piece of poetry. Bhāmaha opines that an unornamental poem, thoughtful of poetic sentiments, does not attract a reader like a beautiful but unornamented face of a lady.[5]

Daṇḍin also felt the importance of Alaṅkāras, as a means of adding charm to poetry.[6] Agnipurāṇa also has ascribed the same importance to Alaṅkāras and has added that a poem devoid of Alaṅkāras is like a widow.[7] Though Vāmana laid more emphasis on Rīti, he did accept the importance of Alaṅkāras. He also says beauty is Alaṅkāra and a poem appeals to the mind of a reader, if it has Alaṅkāras, "काव्यं ग्राह्यमलंकारात्, सौन्दयम् अलङ्कारः".[8] He opines that although the *guṇas* make a poem charming, Alaṅkāra too add[9] to the poetic charm. To quote him again:

काव्यशोभायाः कर्तारो धर्माः गुणाः।
तदतिशयहेतवस्त्वलंकाराः ॥

By the time of Vāmana Alaṅkāras were regarded as very important in a Kāvya. Ānandavardhana was the first rhetorician who strongly opposed the importance, ascribed to them. He asserted that Alaṅkāras should not pre-dominate in a Kāvya[10] but they should be used only if they are suitable in the culmination of Rasa. Otherwise they should be avoided. He says:

काले च ग्रहणत्यागौ नातिनिर्वहणैर्विता ।।[11]

A poetic composition has its two aspects.

(a) Words which constitute its outer figure and

(b) The connotations of these words *i.e.*, meaning. Both of these should be well-arranged and ornamental in a composition of high poetic value. Thus, the Alaṅkāras which add charm to any poetic piece, can be of two types :

(1) Decorating the words *i.e.*, Śabdālaṅkāra.

(2) Decorating the sense *i.e.*, Arthālaṅkāra.

These which decorate the words entirely depend upon the words for their existence, for they cease to survive, as soon as a word is replaced by another on the other hand, the Alaṅkāras based on meaning continue to exist even with the change of letters and words.

Gaṅgādevī may be said to be equally well-versed in the Science of Rhetorics, as can be seen from copious examples of various figures of speech. A perusal of the Madhurā-vijayaṁ makes it evident that Gaṅgādevī has employed more than forty figures of speech in appropriate contexts to adorn the narrative part of the text and to attract the hearts of the readers. As a matter of fact, Gaṅgādevī is no lesser than Kālidāsa.

Both the Śabdālaṅkāras and the Arthālaṅkāras consist in a big group of figures of speech that have been used by Gaṅgādevī. To be more precise, Gaṅgādevī's use of 'Śabdālaṅkāras' is considerably scanty comparing to the use of the Arthālaṅkāras. Yet, all the three important varieties of a 'Śabdālaṅkāras' have been brought in beautifully. Those three are — Anuprāsa, Yamaka and Śleṣa.

Śabdālaṅkāras

1. Anuprāsa : It is that, where the same sound is repeated for a number of times, in the same order, no matter, if their vowels differ in such repetitions.[12]

The first benedictory verse[13] of the Madhurāvijayaṁ itself, exemplifies the Anuprāsa. The word 'Kalpa' is repeatedly used thrice in the latter part of the verse. A sort of Vṛtti is used; hence, this may be called an example of Vṛttyanuprāsa.

When writing on literary criticism, Gaṅgādevī describes the qualities of a good work; yet all good qualities like sense, idea, sentiment etc., do not exist simultaneously in a single work[14] when it is said so, the poetess uses 'Kvacit' four times which forms a beautiful Vṛttyānuprāsa.

Similarly, the word "Samasta-Sāmantamastakanyasta-śāsanaḥ" describing the greatness of Bukka,[15] forms the Vṛttyānuprāsa.

Like-wise, another verse[16] describing the beauty of the city of Vijayanagar does point to Vṛttyānuprāsa when it is read; Phāla-līla-lalāṭikā.

So also, the thirty seventh verse from third canto, forty-seventh verse from the fourth canto[18] are the instances of Vṛttyanuprāsa.

2. Yamaka : Yamaka is repetition of a group of consonants along with the vowels in the same order but the repeated words give different meaning Gaṅgādevī uses Yamaka as follows:

In the context of describing the water-sports of king Kampaṇa, an example of Yamaka type of Śabdālaṅkāra is seen in its fulness of meaning. It runs thus:

अपि दयिततमेन वारिताभिर्गृहसरसो विजहे न वारिताभिः।
परिलुलितललामचर्चिकाभिर्विहृतिरसान्महिलामचर्चिकाभिः।।

MV. VI-65

The first two pādas end with the word 'Vāritābhiḥ' and the latter two pādas, with the words 'Carcikābhiḥ'.

These two repeated words contain different meanings. That is, 'varitabhiḥ' in the sense of "removal" and in the second pāda this word should be understood with splitting it as 'vāritabhiḥ', of which the meaning is altogether different.

In the latter two padas, "carcikabhiḥ" is repeated. This word gives the meaning of the application of sandal-paste on the forehead. In the fourth pada the same word appeals as an adjective of Mahilā which means "fair ladies".

This is how, Yamaka is conspicuous in the example above.

3. Śabdaśleṣa : When more than one sense is conveyed by distinct words coalescing into identity, it is termed as paranomasia (Śabdaśleṣa).[19] A pause between two words or letters may be dropped and read with one effort. And the meaning may be understood accordingly. But it is always combined with other *alaṅkāra* like Upamā or Rūpaka or Atiśayokti etc., it seldom occurs as an independent *alaṅkāra*. One beautiful illustration of this figure of speech can be cited from the description of Gaṅgādevī's obeisance to the poets who influenced her. She says:

वैयासिके गिरा गुम्फे पुण्ड्रेक्षाविव लभ्यते।
सद्यः सुहृदयाह्लादी सारः पर्वणि पर्वणि।।

MV. I-6

Just as there is delicious juice in every joint of red Sugar-cane, there is sweet essence in every section of Vyāsa's string of expression the Mahābhārata.

In this verse, both Arthaśleṣa and Śabdaśleṣa are seen "Sahṛdayāhlādi" illustrates Śabdaśleṣa, and the rest of the portion as the verse which illustrates Arthaśleṣa. The phrase mentioned above when read with one effort as 'Sahṛdayā-hlādi' gives the sense of its being an adjective of 'Essence' which may be analysed as *Sahṛadayāna rasajñāna āhlādayituṁ, silam asya iti i.e.*, one whose nature is of giving to men as poetic taste. Further when the phrase is read with splitting, the pronoun 'sa' refers to 'Essence' and *'hṛdayāhladī'* become its adverb, which means 'the Sweet essence which imparts enjoyment to the good-men."

Gaṅgādevī's poetic skill can also be seen from her apt method of employing a number of Arthālaṅkāras throughout the Madhurāvijayaṁ. Of the figures of speech she has brought in, it is evident that she has given more preference to Utprekṣā, Rūpaka, Upamā and Kāvyaliṅga. There are more than sixty examples of Utprekṣā, about forty examples of Rūpaka, about thirty of Upamā and about twenty-five of Kāvyaliṅga. The other Alaṅkāras she has employed, are Śleṣa, Apahnuti, Atiśayokti, Vastudhvani, Bhrāntimān, Arthāntaranyāsa, Vyatireka, Virodhābhāsa etc. Gaṅgādevī has another skill of employing two or three figures of speech in a single example. A selective approach to the elucidation of these Alaṅkāras is attempted here as to highlight Gaṅgādevī's knowledge of Alaṅkāras.

Utprekṣā

Gaṅgādevī being fond of Utprekṣā, has used it freely in her Mahākāvya in all its varieties and shades. She employs the word *iva* more often than not to express poetic fancy. Other words expressing fancy are also used here and there. She has given some instances of Gamyotprekṣā also with such poetic fancy. She is able to portray the various aspects of the objects of her description. She analyses and displays the various shades of their look and location with the flights of imagination which very few poets have reached. Her success as a descriptive poet lies in her efficient use of Utprekṣā. Her description of city, water sports, battle scenes, the supernatural feats of her characters etc., abound in poetic fancies which often come in competition one after the other.

Utprekṣā or poetic fancy is the representation of an Upameya as probably identical with a similar object *i.e.*, with an Upamāna[20] words like manye, śaṅke, dhruvaṁ, prāyaḥ, nūnam, ūhe etc., reveal the presence of Utprekṣā *Iva* is also included among the words of denoting Utprekṣā when Upamāna is such as is specially imagined by the poet, *Iva* suggests probability in Utprekṣā. Following are some of the examples illustrating Utprekṣā.

(a) यत्रावलग्न-सादृश्य-वाञ्छविमतमम्बरम्।
प्रायः पयोधरोत्सेधैर्निरुन्धन्ति पुरन्ध्रयः।।

MV. I-64

"The blooming breasts of the maidens of the city were beautifully set off by their slender waists even as thick clouds in the void above."

A thin fine garment on the breasts of the ladies is slowly slipped down to the waist. Thus, the plumpy breasts with a thin fine garment is fancied as water-laiden clouds in the sky, the word *prāyaḥ* in this verse reveals the presence of Utprekṣā.

(b) मित्राभ्युदयदानिन्या भूत्या नीत्या प्रसूतया।
मनुमेव पुनर्जातं तममन्यन्त मानवाः।।

Ibid., I-68

"By contemplating on his prosperity that was at the service of friends, and his politics that was wide comprehensive, his subjects imagined that Manu himself had in him his second birth."

This verse gives the description of king Bukka. Here king Bukka is fancied to be Manu. This fancy is suggested by the word *eva* in the verse above. Hence, it is also a good example of Utprekṣā.

(c) सौभाग्यगन्धद्विपदानलेखा रराज तस्या नवरोमराजिः।
तेजोनिधिं गर्भतले निगूढं कालोरगी रक्षितुमागतेव।।

Ibid., II-10

"When the queen Devāyī is conceived suddenly she finds a change in her body. The auspicious line of hair that was seen on her abdomen looked like a black serpent guarding and protecting the infant within."

In this verse, the poetess supplies a beautiful fancy which in fact recalls the heroic character of Kampaṇa who is expected to born in short future. It is quite biological fact that a pregnant woman bears a line of hair on the abdomen. As such queen Devāyī too possesses it, the child within the womb is in fact a great treasure as the kingdom itself, such treasure of the kingdom needs to be protected. This act of protection is accomplished by the auspicious line of hair in the form of female black serpent. Here, *iva* is a word revealing Utprekṣā. Thus line of here is fancied to be a female black serpent.

(d) ज्ञात्वा वशे तस्य भुवं भवित्रीं भयादिवास्पृष्टपरागलेशः ।
आकृष्टकल्पद्रुमपुष्पगन्धो मरुद्ववौ मन्दममन्दशैत्यः ।।

MV. II-16

"When Kampaṇa was born, cool breeze with the flower-dusts from heavenly trees began to blow gently as if being afraid of the new-born infant who was soon to attain the mastery of his earth."

Just as, a servant, who entertained a guilty consciousness, moves slowly before the king and obediently serves to gain his favour; at the time of Kampaṇa's birth cool breeze from the heaven started blowing being untouched with anything else, in its own incessent velocity. This is in fact, a good omen. On the way, that cool breeze came in contact with the dust of the Kalpavṛkṣa flowers; hence that wind entertained a sort of fear, and with such guilty consciousness, it started blowing very slowly on the earth to gain the favour of the lord of the earth *i.e.*, infant Kampaṇa. This is how Gaṅgādevī reveals the fancy, through the use of *iva* in the verse above.

Broadly speaking, Utprekṣā is of three kinds, *viz.*, Svarūpotprekṣā, Hetūtprekṣā and Phalotprekṣā. These three varieties arise according to the thing which is fancied, either the nature of an object, or the motive, or the fruit. There is no want of examples illustrating these three kinds of Utprekṣā in the Madhurāvijayaṁ.

Svarūpotprekṣā

अधारयत् दर्शित-देहसौष्ठवां स राजसूनुस्तनुवृत्तमध्यमाम्।
पराक्रमत्रासितचित्तवृत्तिभिर्मृगाधिराजैरुपदीकृतामिव।।

MV. III.9

"Kampaṇa's waist, shapely and slender, which greatly enhanced the beauty of his person suggested the idea of the lions having yielded their monoply, as a sort of hush money in his favour, as they were extremely afraid of his strength."

Here, the very nature of Kampaṇa's waist is described. He is not only beautiful to look at, but also his heroic personality speaks of his prowess, as is revealed by the fancy of his waist to be more frightful than that of lions. Gaṅgadevī says, even the lions were afraid of Kampaṇa's heroic personality. Here *iva* is used in the sense of *Sambhāvanā*. Hence, it is Svarūpotprekṣā.

Phalotprekṣā

गर्भस्थितस्येव शिशोर्विधातुं वसुन्धरामण्डलभारशिक्षाम्।
अरोचयत् पार्थिवधर्मपत्नी मन्ये मृदास्वादरसानुबन्धम्।।

Ibid., II-3

"During the pregnancy she expresses her desire to taste particles of earth as if to teach the responsibility of the earth's sway to the infant in her womb."

As a matter of fact, Devāyī's desire of eating the particles of earth which indicate teaching the responsibility of earth's sway to the infant is, fruit, of Devāyī's eating the particles of earth. And this fancy of the furit is revealed by the use of the word *iva* in the verse above.

Another example of Phalotprekṣā is found in the description of the sun-set.

The example is:

परिचूषितदीप्तिरम्बुजैः पुनरूष्माणमिवाप्तुमौर्वतः।
रथवल्गितवाहनो रविः पयसा राशिमवाप पश्चिमम्।।

MV. VII-2

"Sun submerged into the waters of the western ocean is if to replenish his heat from the submarine fire, the heat which had been spent in the day in making lotuses blossom."

Here, it is said that the sun sets in the waters of the ocean to procure heat from the submarine fire. Really this can never be possible. Yet, fruit in this form of obtaining heat from the submarine fire is here fancied. And this fancy is also revealed by the word *iva* in the verse above.

Kriyotprekṣā

In Kriyotprekṣā, the very action of the object is fancied. Another example of Sun's setting illustrates this kind of Utprekṣā as below :

अथोरगाणामधिपाय भाविन भुवो भरस्यापगमं दिनेश्वरः।
निवेदयिष्यन्निव गाढ-रंहसा रथेन पातालगुहामगाहत।।

Ibid., III-46

"The sun, as is anxious to inform the serpent king who bore this earth (Śeṣa) that his burden would soon be lightened, sank in haste into the nether regions."

The actions of setting of the sun is fancied here. The sun being happy within himself to know that Kampaṇa will be born and will lessen the weight of the earth borne by the serpent king Śeṣa, went down to the Rasātala in haste to inform this happy news. Then the sun's going down to Pātāla is fancied. Thus, it is an apt example of Kriyotprekṣā.

There are some other types of Utprekṣā figure of speech like Dravyotprekṣā, Vastūtprekṣā etc. The examples illustrating such types of Utprekṣā, also are available in the Madhurāvijayaṁ. We find one example in the context of the description of rainbow occuring in the fifth canto. The verse runs as below:

हरितलोहितपाण्डुरराजत त्रिदशराजशरासनलेखिका।
मरतकोपलविद्रुममौक्तिकैर्विरचिता रशनेव नभश्श्रियः।।

MV. V-27

"The rainbow with its colours, green, red and white, shone like the girdle, set with emerald, coral and pearl of the beauty of the Goddess sky."

In this verse, it is said, the sky is very beautiful to look at owing to the rainbow seen in it. This sky is personified as Goddess of sky; and this goddess has adorned the beautiful girdle set with emerald coral and pearl. Hence, the rainbow is fancied to be the girdle. Thus, we find here *tādātmya sambhāvanā* or fancying the oneness of the objects of Upameya and Upamāna. This fancy of oneness is suggested by the word *iva*. Therefore, it is an apt example of Dravyotprekṣā.

Another example from the third canto in the context of the description of Kampaṇa's bodily charm, illustrates the Vastūtprekṣā.

अनुल्बणामायततुङ्गबन्धुराममस्त लोकः स्फुटमस्य नासिकाम्।
विश्रृङ्खलव्याप्नुवदीक्षणद्वयीपरस्पराक्रान्ति निवारणार्गलाम्।।

Ibid., III-14

"The world thought of this long and lofty nose as a demarcating line that prevented each one of the eyes from encroaching on the province of the other."

In this verse, the very object *i.e.*, nose of Kampaṇa is fancied as a bar obstruction the province of the eyes. This fancy is revealed by the word Sphuṭaṁ in the sense of *nūnam*. Hence, this is Vastūtprekṣā.

There are many exmaples wherein we find the combination of Utprekṣā with other figures of speech like, Upamā, Atiśayokti, Parikara, etc. This combination may be seen in the following examples:

Utprekṣā with Atiśayokti and Upamā:

असाधारणसार्वज्ञं विलसत्सर्वमङ्गलम्।
क्रियाशक्तिगुरुं वन्दे त्रिलोचनमिवापरम्।।

Ibid., I-4

"I bow to Guru Kriyāśakti, unparalleled in wisdom and resplendent with auspiciousness like another Trilocana (Śiva) with Sarvamaṅgala (Pārvatī) shining (by his side)."

Here, poetess offers salutation to her preceptor Kriyāśakti. In this verse, the combination of Utprekṣā with Atiśayokti may be known from only phrase *i.e.*, "Trilocanamivāparaṁ" the use of the word *Aparā* and *iva* make the formation of Utprekṣā as it gives the idea of fancy. And when, only *iva* is read with Trilocana, it forms Upamā as it points to similitude; so also, the use of *Apara* only with Trilocana begets Atiśayokti as it describes the Upameya *i.e.*, Kriyāśakti preceptor as an extraordinary.

Utprekṣā with Upamā and Parikara

महौजसस्तस्य निजैर्यशोभिस्द्वेलदुग्धोदधि पूरगोरैः।
प्रक्षालितानीव तदा बभूवुर्धृतप्रसादानि दिशां मुखानि।।

MV. II-15

The quarters then shone with spotless lustre as if they had been newly washed by royal fame which was fit to be likened to the whiteness of milk that filled the milky ocean.

This verse describes the birth of Kampaṇa. It expresses that the brightness emerged out of fame at the time of Kampaṇa's birth pervaded the quarters around.

The pervasion of the lustre throughout all the quarters is fancied that the quarters have been newly washed with royal fame. This fancy is revealed by the word *iva* in the verse above. And, यशोभिः दुग्धोदधिपूरगौरैः developes the idea of Upamā in the shade of *iva;* because "fame" is compared with the milky ocean. So also, the word महौजसः — playing the role of objective of Kampaṇa, is all significant. Hence, this forms the Parikara figure of speech.

Thus, there are many more examples of Utprekṣā, and its combination with other figures of speech, throughout the Madhuravijāyaṁ. The numbers of such examples may be seen as below:

I. 11, 44, 54, 63;
II. 3, 10, 15, 16, 17, 18, 20, 23, 27, 32, 39;
III. 3, 6, 9, 13, 14, 15, 46;
IV. 2, 5, 10, 21, 25, 29, 40, 41, 46, 53, 72, 73, 81;
V. 2, 5, 8, 18, 20, 27, 37, 42, 43, 50, 51, 65, 66;
VI. 56;
VII. 2, 19, 21, 22, 28, 29, 44, 51;
VIII. 10, 19, 21;
IX. 2, 4, 15, 25, 32;

This frequent use of Utprekṣā indicates that Gaṅgādevī is fond of Utprekṣā, as Kālidāsa is of Upamā.

Rūpaka

Gaṅgādevī has made much use of Rūpaka figure of speech throughout the Madhurāvijayaṁ. There are more than forty examples of the figure of speech. Also there are some examples illustrating the sub-divisions of Rūpaka.

Rūpaka or Metaphor is the identification of the Upamāna and the Upmeya. This identification must spring from extreme resemblance between the two. Another point to note is that the Abheda in Rūpaka is āhārya or volitional. Though we identify the face with the moon, we are quite conscious of the difference between the two.[21] This definition may be seen reflected in the following examples:

महाकविमुखाम्भोज मणिपंजरशारिकाम्।
चैतन्यजलधिज्योत्स्ना देवीं वन्दे सरस्वतीम्।।

MV. I-3

"I make obeisance to goddess Sarasvatī who lives in the lotus-like mouths of great poets, as a sārikā bird in a Jewelled cage and who acts like moon-light on the ocean of Universal Intelligence."

In this verse, Gaṅgādevī extols the goddess Sarasvatī. Rūpaka is seen in the word "चैतन्यजलधिज्योत्स्नाम्".

Buddhi is identified with Jaladhi or ocean and goddess

Sarasvatī with Jyotsnā or moonlight. And this identification is volitional. Hence, it is an apt example of Rūpaka.

विवेकमेव संचितं धनुरेव वरूथिनीम्।
बाहुमेव रणोत्साहे यः सहायममन्यत।।

MV. I-29

With discernment alone for his minister, and the bow: alone for his army, he counted on his arms as his only ally in the heart of battle.

This verse describes the greatness of Bukka, the father of Kampaṇa. Here, Viveka or discernment, bow and arms of Bukka are the Upameyas. These Upameyas are identified with the minister, army and his ally are the Upamānas. The former ones are identified with letters ones, respectively. The identification between the two is volitional. Hence, it is faithful example of Rūpaka.

ततः सेनागजेन्द्राणां कर्णतालनिलोद्धता।
अवार्यत रजोराज्ञिः करशीकर दुर्दिनैः।।

Ibid., IV-43

"Particles of dust fanned out by big war elephants flapping their ears were kept back by the rain of spray from the trunks of elephants."

This example suggests : appearance of flow of ichor from the temples of the elephants in the army of Kampaṇa. When ichor is about to flow from the temples, elephants usually flap their ears. And due to the flapping of their ears, particles of dust started spreading around. And this spreading of the dust particles was kept back by rain or spray from the trunks of the elephants. Here, rain of spray means sprinkling of ichor-drops. करशीकरः is Upameya and दुर्दिन (*i.e.* the day on which sky is covered with water laiden clouds)— is Upamāna. And the identification between the two forms Rūpaka.

समस्तवस्तुविषय type of Rūpaka is one of its divisions. It comes under सांगरूपक where there is one principal metaphor and one or more subordinate metaphors. When all the

Upamānas are expressed by means of Upameyas, समस्तवस्तुविषय variety of Rūpaka arises.[22]

This may be exemplified as below:

विरोधिवाहिनीनाथ विक्षोभणपटीयसा।
भुजेन भूभृता यस्य प्राप्ता कीर्तिमयीसुधा।।

MV. I-32

By (the might of) his arm which confounded the army generals of his enemies, fame was won by him, even as nectar (by the gods) by using the Manthara mountain with which was churned the boundless lord of the rivers (*viz.*, Ocean).

This verse supplies a beautiful identification of the fame (of Bukka) and the nectar produced from churning of the milky ocean. There are three metaphors in the verse:

Upameyas	**Upamānas**
1. विरोधिनः शात्रवः विक्षोभण	समुद्राः
2. भुजः	भूमृत् मन्दरपर्वतः
3. कीर्तिः	सुधा

The first metaphor is the principal one, and rest are subordinate ones. There are as many Upamānas as Upameyas. Thus, the fame acquired by strength of Bukka's arms in the battle between Bukka and his enemy kings, is identified in the light of extreme resemblance, with the nectar acquired in the event of churning the milky ocean, by the gods with demons.

Hence, it is a good example of समस्तवस्तुविषय type of Rūpaka.

Another example of the kind is as below:

सहस्त्रशस्तुङ्गतुरङ्गवीचयो मदद्विपद्वीपविशेषितान्तराः।
भवन्तमुग्रायुधनक्रराजयो भजन्ति नित्यं बहला बलाब्धयः।।

Ibid., III-39

"You know you are surrounded now by an Ocean — like

army. Horses in thousands act as its waves, elephants in ruff appear in its midst like huge islands, and destructive weapons like sharks abound in its waters."

This verse deals with pregnant words of advice of Bukka to his son, Kampaṇa. Here, we find four metaphors:

Upameyas	Upamānas
1. बलः (Army)	अब्धिः (Ocean)
2. तुरङ्गः (Horses)	वीचयः (Waves)
3. मदद्विपः (Elephants)	द्वीपाः (Islands)
4. आयुधानि (Weapons)	नक्रराजयः (Crocodiles)

There are four Upameyas and four Upamānas respectively. The extreme resemblance between army and Ocean, horses and waves, elephants and islands weapons and crocodiles — leads to their identification. The first metaphor *i.e.*, Bala — Abdhi is the principal one and the rest three are subordinate ones.

Besides, Paramaparita is another kind of Rūpaka. Paramparita is developed when there are two metaphors which are related to each other as cause and effect.[23] Following are the examples illustrating the Paramparita types of Rūpaka.

द्विजराजसम्मुल्लासनित्यराकानिशीथिनी।
गन्धर्वगणसान्निध्य - नव्यदिव्यरूथिनी।।

MV. I-52

"The city was full of virtuous Brāhmaṇas, and armies of musicians ever strode its expansive grounds. Thus, like the full-moon light, or the world of celestial birds, serenity and music reigned unceasingly all round."

This verse gives the description of the city of Vijayanagar.

द्विजराजयुक्तशकानिशीथिनी समल्लासं करोति (कारण)

द्विजराजयुक्तनगरी समुल्लासं करोति (कार्य)

The former is in the form of cause and the latter of the effect. The former Rūpaka gives rise to the latter. Since, there is pun on the word द्विजराज; this stanza therefore forms the श्लिष्टपरम्परित-रूपक।।

> स पंचबाणाद्विपकेलिदीर्घिकां धनानुरागद्रुमपुष्पमंजरीम्।
> नितिम्बिनीनेत्रचकोरचन्द्रिकामवापदास्कन्दित शैशवां दशाम्।।

MV. III.4

"He now attained his youthfulness which could be described as the sporting lake of the elephant called Manmatha, as the bunch of flowers called love, as the moon-light for the Cakora birds called women's eyes."

This stanza describes the youthfulness of Kampaṇa from one Rūpaka *i.e.*,आस्कन्दितशैशव नवयौवन-पंचबाणद्विपकेलि।

i.e., youth-hood — Sporting lake of the elephant called Manmatha.

From this Rūpaka, other two Rūpakas are formed:

नवयौवन - अनुरागद्रुमपुष्पमंजरी।।

i.e., youth-hood — the bunch of flowers called Love.

नवयौवन - नितम्बिनीनेत्रचकोरचन्द्रिका।।

i.e., youth-hood — the moonlight for the Cakora birds called women's eyes.

Thus, Kampaṇa's youthfulness (Upameya) is identified with three objects (Upamānas) in all, *viz.*, — Sporting lake, bunch of flowers and moon-light. Here, since one Upameya is identified with three Upamānas (or the three Upamānas are enlaced). This stanza is an example of the मालापरम्परितरूपक।।

Thus Gaṅgādevī has made use of Rūpaka figure of speech in many descriptions, as she belongs to a period prior to the development of the niceties of this figure of speech. She makes appropriate use of this Alaṅkāra sometimes with other figures of speech like Utprekṣā, Kāvyaliṅga, Upamā, Bhrāntimān etc. Such examples illustrating the combination of Rūpaka with other Alaṅkāras may be noted as — 1.51; V.17; VII. 32, 36, 19; VIII. 21; IX.27 etc. Other examples of Rūpaka from the Madhurāvijayaṁ are:

I. 1, 7,10, 12, 29, 34, 38, 45, 53, 68;
II. 11. 4, 24, 25, 34;
IV. 12, 13, 60, 25, 69;
V. 19, 25, 38, 39, 69, 70;
VI. 60;
VII. 5, 33, 43, 45, 46;
VIII. 28, 32, 33, 36;
IX. 14, 17.

Upamā

Upamā figure of speech has been the foundational of all other Alaṅkāras, Upamā is formed where there are all four constituents in the given example. Those are: Upameya, Upamāna, Sādhāraṇa dharma and Upamā pratipādaka śabda. Upamā with all these constituents is called Pūrṇopamā; and when there is an absence of one or two or three constituents mentioned above it is called Luptopamā. Upamā is based on the resemblance between Upameya and Upamāna, through which the common property or the Sādhāraṇa Dharma is understood. The resemblance is known by the Upamā Pratipādaka words like yathā, iva, vā, vat etc.[24]

Gangādevī's use of Upamā may be seen from the examples below:

सत्स्वप्यन्येषु दारेषु तामेव मनुजाधिपः।
वह्वमंस्त निशानाथो नक्षत्रेष्विव रोहिणीम्।।

MV. I-74

"Though the king had other wives also, she alone became the object of his and regard, even as Rohiṇī to the moon among celestial luminaries."

This verse tells us that Devāyī was the dearest of all the wives of the king Bukka. This is compared with the Rohiṇī's being the dearest to the Moon though he is surrounded by many star-wives. Here, Bukka, Devayī, and other wives (Upameyas) are respectively compared with the Moon,

Rohiṇī and other stars (Upamānas). This comparison is possible due to the resemblance between them. Through the resemblance of her/their being wife/wives, the common property or Sādhāraṇa Dharma, *i.e.*, "dearness" is known. And the resemblence in this verse may be understood by the word *iva*. Hence, this stanza illustrates Upamā figure of speech.

प्रायो भयदुतामित्रपदविध्वंसनोत्सुकः।
स जगाहे प्रतिध्वाननिभादवनिभृद्गुहाः।।

MV. III-5

"His body shone distinctly in its full contours, now that boy-hood had entirely passed away and youth-hood had asserted itself, even as the sun shines in his total brilliance after the passing away of the devy season. This stanza speaks of the assertion of youth-hood in the body of prince Kampaṇa."

This assertion of his youth-hood is compared with the arrival of the brilliant sun during the Vasanta. Just as the brilliance of the sun is asserted by Vasanta, so too, the youth-hood is asserted by the age factor after his boy-hood. Here, Kampaṇa and his youth-hood are compared with the sun and his brilliance respectively. *Iva* is the Upamā Pratipādaka word suggesting the resemblance of lustre. *Janarañjana* or delighting (the subjects) is the Sādhāraṇa dharma. Thus, both the examples above illustrate the Pūrṇopamā, as all constituents are present in them. This is in fact an effective portrayal of Upamā. Gaṅgādevī often employs this figure as speech with special charm.

प्रबन्धमीषन्मात्रोऽपि दोषो नयति दूष्यताम्।
कालागरुद्रवभरं शुक्तिक्षारकणो यथा।।

Ibid., I-18

"Even as a single particle from an oystershell spoils the liquid essence of black sandal, so too, even the smallest flaw found in poetic work renders it censurable."

This verse speaking on literary criticism gives the nature of Kāvya. Due to a contact of smallest error or calamity, any object sentient or insentient, of purest quality becomes, censurable. Here Upameyas ईषदोषः : (smallest flaw) and प्रबन्ध (a poetic work) ; and शुक्तिक्षारकणः as well as कालागरुद्रवः are respectively the Upamānas. यथा is the word denoting the resemblance between the Upameyas and the Upamānas. And the common property suggested here is दूषण or censure.

कलशजस्य मुनेरुद्रयाज्जहुः कलुषता सलिलानि महौजसः।
सदुपदेशवशादिव शासितुस्तनुभृता ह्दयानि दयानिदयानिधेः।।

MV. V-41

"By reason of the brilliant Agastya star, the waters were cleared of their muddy condition and shone as clear as the minds of men that had received proper instruction from a merciful guru."

This stanza describes beauty of Nature during the autumn season. During autumn season water in lake rivers usually is very clean. Here water is cleared of muddy condition due to a mere appearance of Agastya star. And this is compared with pure wind of good men, at the instruction of competent preceptor.

Thus, Upameyas are सलिल अगस्त्य and the Upamānas are ह्दय तनुभृत्. *Iva* is the Upamāpratipādaka śabda. कलुषराहित्य or free from blemish is the common property. Thus it is an apt example of Pūrṇopamā.

अथ प्रशस्ते समस्तैर्मौहूर्तिकैः साधितपुण्यलग्ने।
असूत सुनुं नरनाथ पत्नी देवी महासेनमिवेन्दुमौलेः।।

Ibid., II-14

"Then on auspicious day, at the hour pronounced as auspicious by astrologers, the queen presented her lord with a boy, as a Goddess Pārvatī bore to Śiva the child Subrahmaṇya." This stanza gives the description of the birth of Kampaṇa. Here, Kampaṇa's birth from Bukka and Devāyī is compared with the birth of god Subrahmaṇya from Śiva and Pārvatī. Kampaṇa is *Upameya* Mahāsena or Subrahmaṇya is *Upamāna. Iva* is the word denoting resemblance between the two. Since Sādhāraṇadharma or the common property is not available here, this example illustrates Dharmaluptopamā.

कल्पान्तोद्भ्रान्तचण्डीशडमरुध्वानडामरः।
उदजृम्भत गम्भीरो वियदध्वनि तद्ध्वनिः।।

MV. IV-4

The sound grew louder and louder, and filled the skies as if it emanated from Caṇḍīśa's ḍamaru at the time of the great Deluge. This is another example illustrating the Luptopamā. This example deals with the preparation for the march on the Śambuvarāya territory. In the beginning of the war, drums were beaten. The sound arose from the beating of the war-drums is as frightful as that of the sound of Ḍamaru beaten by Lord Śiva at the time of dissolution of the world. Thus, sound of war drums is Upameya; and sound of Ḍamaru of Śiva, Upamāna The common property denoted here is frightfulness. But *iva*, the word denoting resemblance is absent here. Hence, it is an example of luptopamā.

This is how Gaṅgādevī makes use of Upamā figure of speech throughout the Madhurāvijayaṁ. She suggess even the Paurāṇic allusious, as has been seen in the fourth example given above. Her method of employing the similes is a unique nature. Other examples of this figure of speech may be noted as below:

I. 27, 60;

II. 12, 25, 33, 35;

III. 8, 23, 26, 35, 40;

IV. 19, 52, 77;

V. 28, 41, 47; VII. 17, 32; VIII. 6, 18;

XI. 3, 18, 31, 41.

Kāvyaliṅga or Poetical Cause

The name Kāvyaliṅga is significant. It means that the

reason that is to be dealt with in this figure is a poetical one and not the logical one, with rigid requirements of five characteristics. This figure of speech arises when the reason for a certain thing is contained in Vākyārtha or the sense of a sentence, or in Padārtha or the sense of words or a word.[25] Thus, as समर्थ्यसमर्थकभाव in the अर्थान्तरन्यास..... too, it in Kāvyaliṅga proceeds from Kāryakāraṇabhāva. Here the two sentences are inter-dependent and the sense of the one is not properly understood without that of the other. And a productive cause in Kāvyaliṅga is understood from the sense of the sentence.

Such important figure of speech has been profusely made use of by Gaṅgādevī in her own inimitable style. We find more than twenty-five examples of Kāvyaliṅga in the Madhurāvijayaṁ. Some important examples may be illustrated as below.

न प्रार्थनीयः सत्काव्यश्रुत्यै सहृदयो जनः।
स्वादुपुष्परसास्वादे कः प्रेरयति षट्पदम्।।

MV. I-24

A connoisseur of learning needs no invitation to listen to good poetry, who urges the bee to taste the sweetness of honey. The Sahṛdayas or good men of poetic taste need not be invited to listen to a good poetry as the bee need not be urged to taste the sweetness of honey from the flowers. This sense of the sentence becomes clear when the latter is read. Former and the latter sentences are interdependent. Good men need not be invited; why? because Kāvya is sweet. Thus, sweetness of Kāvya becomes the reason for 'not inviting' or 'प्रार्थनाभाव' And this reason of sweetness is contained in the sense of a single word "*Svādu*". Hence, this stanza is an example of काव्यलिङ्ग।

यद्दीर्घिकासु माणिक्यमयसोपानचारिभिः।
क्षणदास्वपि चक्राह्वैर्विरहो नानुभूयते।।

Ibid., I-60

As if the lustre of the gems with which the steps were

paved in the lakes always drove darkness away, the Cakravāka birds were not separated even at night.

This verse runs in the context of the description of the capital city — Vijayanagar. It describes that gem-steps were paved in the lakes of the city. And the lustre of those gem-steps had driven the darkness away. As a result, Cakravāka birds did not get separated from each other at night. Thus, "Viyogabhāva" is produced from the lustre of gem-steps. In other words "the lustre of gem-steps" is the cause; and this is contained in the word "माणिक्यमयसोपानचारिभिः". Hence, it is an example of पदार्थहेतुक-काव्यलिङ्ग।

क्रमाज्जहार्द्भः क्रशिमानमङ्गैर्मुखेन मुग्धालसलोचनेन।
मध्येन च त्यक्ततवलित्रयेण नरेश्वरं नन्दयति स्म राज्ञी।।

MV. II-9

"As time advanced, the limbs of her body began to put on flash, her face regained its sweet and lazy eye-looks, her belly began to show its folds definitely and this change in his beloved filled the king with delight."

This stanza supplies the description of the advancement of Devāyī's abdomen. All marks of a lady in advanced pregnancy appeared distinctly; this made the king Bukka filled with joy. Thus, the cause of King's joy is understood from the sense of the words in the first three lines of the verse above.

Hence, this stanza is an example illustrating अनेकपदार्थ हेतुक Kāvyaliṅga figure of speech.

भवादृशास्तु स्वत एव शुद्धया गुरूपदेशैर्गुणितप्रकाशया।
धिया निरस्तव्यसनानुबन्धया विलोक्य कार्याणि विधातुमीषते।।

Ibid., III-36

"But youth like you who have their intelligence duly shaped and purified by instruction received from proper Gurus know how to keep away from vices and act always in the proper manner."

This stanza tells about Bukka's advice to Kampaṇa before he marches against Śambuvarāya at Tamil Country. A person of pure-intellect by nature, attends to his work only after observing the work closely whether it is good or bad. Thus, the accomplishment understood from the sentence कार्याणि विधातुमीषं is possible only through "pure intellect". The cause or reason "pure intellect" is understood from the sense of the words — "शुद्धया धिया निरस्तव्यसनानुबन्धया"।

Hence, this stanza is an example of अनेक पदार्थ हेतुक काव्यलिङ्ग.

Another example of the same figure of speech can be cited here in the description of the water sports of the prince — Kampaṇa. When Kampaṇa moved to his pleasure of garden, women also followed him with their jewelled girdles making tinkling sounds. They then started mutual conversations which were heard in the varying notes of sweetness:

शशिमुखि! शशिकान्तकुट्टिमेषु स्खळनभिया न पदात् पदं प्रयासि।
इयमिह वदनानुबिम्बराजिस्त्व न पुनर्नवपङ्कजोपहारः।।

MV. VI-10

"You, moon faced dear, move not a step lest you knock against the moon stone wall. But the reflection of your lotus like face has already entered it." Here, young lady's having close resemblance with the moon, created a sort of fear in the mind of her friend. Thus, the cause or reason here consists in the sense of the word *Śaśimukhī*. Therefore, it is an example of एकदार्थहेतुक Kāvyaliṅga.

Two examples of Kāvyaliṅga are found in the description of song of Varṣārtu or rainy season:

चलितबर्हिणचन्द्रकचित्रितैः सुरभिगन्धिशिलामदशालिभिः।
विकचीनपवनैर्नृपतेर्मनो मुहरहारि विहारमहीधरैः।।

Ibid., V-34

तमहरन्नहरत्ययमालतीकुसुमदन्तुरकुन्तलकान्तयः ।
परिहितागरुधूपितवाससः सुतनवो मृगनाभि सुगन्धयः।।

Ibid., V-35

"The mind of the king was very much attracted by pleasure-hillocks. Eyes in the tails of dancing peacocks rendered them very picturesque and camphor deposits in them excluded the most agreeable odour. The numberless Kadamba trees there were in full blossom. The king was always attracted by his beautiful ladies whose curling locks were decorated with the vening bloosoming *mālatī* flowers. Their cloths were scented with agaru fames, and they were sweet-smelling like musk."

The first stanza above says that Kampaṇa is very much attracted by pleasure hillocks. The reason or the cause of his attraction is the picturesque view of the peacocks, agreeable odour of camphor and the Kadamba trees with full of flowers. Thus, the cause is here understood from the words of the first three lines.

So too, in the second verse, Kampaṇa's attractions is due to curling locks with *mālatī* flowers. Clothes scented with agaru fumes of this young beautiful ladies. This reason is understood from the words of latter three lines of the stanza. Hence, both verses exemplify अनेकपदार्थ हेतुक Kāvyaliṅga figure of speech.

Bhrāntimān or Error

The figure Bhrāntimān consists in the comprehension of the Upameya as identical with another. And Bhrāntimān arises when the Upameya is mistaken for the Upamāna. Thus, there are three points of consideration —

1. There is a mistake or error of one thing for another.
2. The error is due to similarity between the two things.
3. The error is not intentional, but real or honest.

The last point is expressed by saying that while in Rūpaka and Atiśayokti, there is no real delusion; but in Bhrāntimān as the very name indicates, real delusion is quite distinctly comprehended as being present. Another point of consideration is that Bhrānti or illusion is a characteristic of the mind :

as such can belong to a sentient being. It cannot belong to the non-sentient or inanimate figure. The name applied to the figure is therefore, metaphorical, because the figure contains a description of the illusion of same sentient being.[26]

There are more than fifteen examples of Bhrāntimān figure, in the Madhurāvijayaṁ. A few of them are explained as below:

यस्यां प्रासादशृङ्गेषु लग्नं मार्ताण्डमण्डलम्।
संधत्ते वीक्षमाणानां सौवर्णकलशभ्रमम्।।

MV. I-55

"The disc of the sun caught in the heights of the city's palaces produced on the on-lookers the illusion of a golden jar."

This stanza describes the beauty of the city of Vijayanagara. The disc of the Sun caught in the heights of lofty mansions, is mistaken for a golden jar. The mistaken object is the sentient being *i.e.*, the Sun. This mistake is due to the similarity between the Upameya and Upamāna *viz.*, the Sun and the golden jar. And this real delusion is distinctly comprehended as being present by the use of the word "Bhramaṁ" in the verse above. Hence, this stanza is an example of Bhrātimān.

तस्य दिक्षु प्ररोहन्त्याः शतधा कीर्तिवीरुधः।
विततान रजस्स्तोमः करीषनिकरभ्रमम्।।

Ibid., IV-38

"The aggregate of dust caused the illusion of a huge heap capable of manuring the creepers of (Kampaṇa's) fame that had begun to sprout out in all the quarters."

This stanza occurs in the context of the description of Kampaṇa's orderly march of the Karnata forces against Śambuvarāya territory. As the Karnata forces marched ahead, the heap of dust arose and spread all over the ether. This aggregate of dust is here, mistaken for a huge heap of dry dung of cow, which is capable of manuring the creepers of Kampaṇa's fame. This mistake is due to the close similarity of black colour between dust and cow-dung. The mistaken object i.e., dust though is insentient, yet action of spreading is seen in it. Hence, the characteristics of Bhrāntimān are well in tune with the stanza quoted above. Hence, it is Bhrāntimān.

अजनयदवनीश्वरस्य चेतस्य सितदृशा मणिनूपुरप्रणादः।
सहपरिचलितप्रसूनकेतोरवनमदैधवचापघोषशङ्काम्।।

MV. VI-5

"The sounds of jewelled anklets of ladies, as they fell on the king's ears, produced the impression in his mind, that it might be the noise of the stringing of cupid's bow.

This stanza occurs in the context of the description of water-sport of Kampaṇa with lovely women.

Here the tinkling sounds of jewelled anklets of ladies is mistaken for the noise of the stringing of cupid's bow.

कमलोदरसम्भ्रतं करैर्मधु पीत्वा रविरुज्झिताम्बरः।
स्पृशति स्म दिशं प्रचेतसो न मदः कस्य विकारकारणम्।।

Ibid., VII-5

"The glow of the setting Sun, as it touched its own reflection in the waves of the Western Ocean, raised one's in mind the idea of the Golden cymbals, for the evening dancer, Śiva."

This stanza occurs in the contest of the description of the Sun-set. Here Upameya is the disc of the setting Sun, and Upamāna is the golden Cymbals for the evening dancer, Lord Śiva. Due to the close similarity of golden lustre and circular form, the former is mistaken for the latter. Hence, it is an example of Bhrāntimān.

In this manner, all the examples of the figure of Bhrāntimān have added much significance to the respective contexts and descriptions in this poem. Other examples of the figure Bhrāntimān, may be cited below:

IV. 54, 56, 59, 66, 71;

VI. 9, 55;

VII. 8, 9, 11, 27;

IX. 7, 31.

Atiśayokti or Hyperbole

Atiśayokti means the statement of excellence. The figure is so called, because here the excellence of the Upameya is brought out on account of its complete identification with Upamāna. Atiśayokti arises:

1. When the matter under description though the same, is represented or ascertained as another or different; or
2. When there is a supposition or assumption of an impossible thing as a result of expressing or bringing in the sense of *yadi*.
3. When there is an inversion of the order or sequence of the effect and the cause *i.e.*, when the effect is mentioned first in order to bring out the capacity of the cause to produce its result very quickly.[27]

This figure of speech has been used not as often as the figure Bhrāntimān. We find some twelve examples of this figure. More often, this figure is used in combination with some other figures of speech like *Sandeha, Bhrāntimān, Vibhāvanā, Kāvyaliṅga* etc. A few of the examples may be seen as below:

तस्मिन् विसर्पति त्रासमीलिताशेषलोचनः।
शेषो युगपदज्ञासीदान्ध्यवाधिर्ययोर्दशाम्।।

MV. IV-6

"As the uproar entered the bowels of earth Śeṣa closed his eyes (which were also his ears), and he became, both blind and by a single."

Here, poetess wants to impress the height of the terrifying uproar caused by Kampaṇa's march on Śambuvarāya territory. Therefore, she makes an assumption of an impossible result *i.e.*, making Śeṣa both blind and deaf.

क्षितिपतिं किल कुङ्कुममुष्टिना समभिताडयितुं धियमानधौ।
सपदिधर्मपयः प्रसरेण तं विगलितं न विवेद वधूजनः।।

MV. V-75

"They desired to splash on the kind paste of Saffron, but they were not aware that the substance had already leaked out of their sweat-bathed hands."

This stanza occurs in the context of the description of the spring season. Leaking out of paste of Saffron is in Kāraṇa form. And "the ladies desired to splash the paste of Saffron on the king" is Kārya form. The stanza should have been described the Kāraṇa first and the Kārya then. But the order of these two is inverted. Therefore, it is an exmple of Atiśayokti figure.

यत्सौधचन्द्रशालासु विहरन्त्यो मृगेक्षणाः।
शशाङ्कमवलम्बन्ते मुक्ताकन्दुकशङ्कया।।

Ibid., I-56

"The damsels playing on the grounds of the top floor of the city's mansions often laid their hands on the rounded body of the moon, mistaking it for their play-ball of pearls."

This stanza occurs in the description of the city of Vijayanagar. The Stanza describes that the mansions there were so lofty that they could touch the orb of the moon. As such, the damsels playing on the grounds of the top floor of such mansions used to lay their hands on the orb of the moon, as they were mistaking it for their play-ball.

Touching the Orb of the moon is impossible; yet that impossibility is supposed and the relation is shown between those two. Hence, it is Atiśayokti. So also, 'mistaking the Orb of the moon for the play-ball' forms Bhrāntimān. Thus, we find here the combination of Atiśayokti with Bhrāntimān, figure. In like manner there are some examples which may be cited below:

I. 42, 58, 62;

IX. 14, 15, 36, 42, 80;

IX. 8.

Apahnuti or Concealment

The denial of the real nature of a thing and ascription of an alien or imaginary, character, constitute the figure of concealment or Apahnuti.[28]

This figure of speech has been rarely used, yet such examples add much beauty to the poem. We may find about 7-8 examples in the poem, of which a few are as below:

यदीयो दक्षिणः पाणिः कृपाणिग्रहणच्छलात्।
अशिक्षत विपक्षश्रीः वेणीकर्षणकौशलम्।।

MV. I-35

"This right hand which to all appearance seemed to be drawing the sword was in fact practising the art of drawing, by her braided hair, the goddess of prosperity of his cover of slough."

This stanza describes the greatness of Bukka, the father of Kampaṇa. As this verse describes, holding or drawing the sword is unreal; and drawing the goddess of prosperity of his enemies is real nature. The former is *upamāna* and the latter *upameya*. Here the content of *upameya* denied and *Upamāna* is established. This is served by the word *Chala* in the verse above. Hence, it is Apahnuti.

Other few examples are:

I - 15, 62; IV - 39; VI - 61; VII - 45, 50.

Vyatireka or Distinction

The name Vyatireka is significant. Vyatireka means excellence or superiority owing to some characteristic feature. In this figure, the Upameya is stated to be superior to the Upamāna owing to the former's possessing some special characteristics.[29]

There are some five examples of this figure in the Madhurāvijayaṁ. An instance may be seen below:

तिग्मांशोरपि तेजस्वी शीतांशोरपि शीतलः।
सागरादपि गम्भीरः सुमेरोरपि यः स्थिरः।।

MV. I-28

"Severer than the Sun and pleasanter than the Moon was he. In depth he excelled the ocean, and in firmness, the mountain Sumeru."

In this stanza, King Bukka is Upameya; the Sun (Tigmāṁśu) the moon (Śītāṁśu), the Ocean (Sāgara) are Upamānas. Lustre, pleasance and depth — these are the three qualities of the respective Upamānas, which indicate the similarity. In order to show the excellence of Kampaṇa, he is described more than the Sun, the Moon and ocean. Hence, it is Vyatireka.

तथा न कर्पूरभरैर्न हारैर्न चन्दनैर्नाप्यमृतांशुपादैः।
यथाभवन्निर्वृतमस्य गात्रं सुताङ्गसंस्पर्शभुवा सुखेन।।

Ibid., II. 38

"The pleasurable feeling which the King had while embracing his cherub boy, was not to be matched by the contact or camphor, pearl, sandal paste or moon beams."

In this verse, the embracing of his (Bukka's) son is compared with the contact of camphor, pearl, sandal paste or Moon beams. No doubt, contact, of camphor etc., cause much joy; yet the joy experienced by embracing his son is much more pleasurable than the contact of camphor etc. Thus, the excellence of Upameya *i.e.*, Bukka's embracing (his) cherub boy, is indicated here. Hence, it is an example of Vyatireka.

स सत्यवाग् भूरिबलो धनुर्धरस्तुरङ्गमाराहणकर्ममर्मवित्।
कृपाणविद्यानिपुणः पृथाभुवामदर्शि सङ्घात इवैकतां गतः।।

Ibid., III. 3

"He spoke the truth, had immense bodily strength and was an expert in handling the bow. A fine horseman and a master in sword-play, he possessed all — accomplishments for each of which were the Pāṇḍavas separately noted."

This stanza expresses excellent qualities of the prince, Kampaṇa. All good qualities which a competent hero should possess, have made their home, in Kampaṇa. In particular, this stanza brings out the comparison of Kampaṇa with all the five Pāṇḍavas collectively. Pāṇḍavas are here Upamāna and Kampaṇa is Upameya. Kampaṇa excels all the five Pāṇḍavas collectively, in so far as the best qualities of a hero, is concerned.

The similarity between the two is directly expressed owing to the presence of the word *iva* in the verse above. Hence, it is an example illustrating Śabda-sāmya-Vyatireka figure.

Similarly other examples may be understood; they are: I-30, V-52.

Nidarśana or Illustration

Nidarśana is so called, because there is in it the citing of illustration. In this figure, the impossible connection between the things, (the Upamāna, the other being Upamāna) leads to comparison.[30]

Some three to four examples of this figure are found in the poem. One example may be seen below:

हृदये चन्दनालेपैः कर्णे मौक्तिककुण्डलैः।
सतामुखे च कर्पूरैर्यस्याभावि यशोभरैः।।

MV. I-31

"This immense fame displayed its existence among his subjects as sandal paste on their chests, as pearl earrings in their ears, and camphor powder on their faces."

This stanza describes the immense fame of Bukka. The pervasion of fame of Bukka is Upameya; sandal paste on the chest, pearl ear-rings in the ears and camphor powder on faces — these are the objects of Upamāna. The connection between the Bukka's fame and sandal-paste on the chest etc., is impossible. But, through this impossibility, comparison is brought out. Hence, this stanza is an example of Nidarśana.

रजस्तमसि वीरास्त्रसङ्घसंघट्टनोत्थितैः।
बभ्रे स्फुलिङ्गसंघातैः खद्योतनिवहद्युतिः।।

MV. IV-55

"Sparks generated in large number by the clash of the weapons of the warriors on either side bore a close likeness to a collection of glow-worms in the darkness of the dust."

This stanza occurs in the context of the description of the sieze of Paḍaividu, the stronghold of the Śambuvarāyas. In the uproar of battle, there arose the darkness of dust around. At the sametime, the sparks generated by the clash of the weapons of warriors on either side, just like glow worms, spread the light and made the warriors of either side seen. The connection between the sparks and glow-worms here is impossible; yet, it causes comparison between those two, the Upameya and Upamāna.

Virodhābhāsa or Contradiction

When two things are stated to be as though opposed or contradictory to each other though there is really no contradiction between them, the Virodhābhāsa arises. Because the figure contains apparent contradiction, this figure is called Virodhābhāsa.

This is clear from the following example:

लक्ष्मीश्चिराज्जगद्रक्षाजागरूकमुपेत्य यम्।
योगनिद्राजडं विष्णुं कदाचिदपि नास्मरत्।।

Ibid., I-36

"Having after a long time, come to him who was ever wakeful in protecting this universe, Goddess Lakṣmī never again remembered Viṣṇu. who was insensible, wrapped up in Yogic sleep."

This stanza describes Bukka's being engaged always in the work of protecting his kingdom; as such, even goddess Lakṣmī having abandoned Lord Viṣṇu who has become jaḍa or insensible due to His continuous yogic sleeping, goddess

Lakṣmī came to Bukka. This apparent contradiction is removed by the use of the word "Lakṣmī" which also means "wealth in the form of kingdom". Hence, this stanza is an example of Virodhābhāsa. Other instances are: I-66, 69; IX-13.

Udātta or Exalted

Udātta occurs in two ways, *viz.*, (1) when there is a description of the prosperity of abundance (Sampat) of a certain thing and (2) when the great is subordinated to the object which is to be indicated *i.e.*, which is the matter under description and which hence is principal.[32] Following example illustrates this figure:

नरपते प्रतिहारमहीं मुहुर्विजयदन्तिमदोदकपङ्किलाम्।
क्षितिभुजां भुजभूषणघट्टनप्रसृतरो मणिरेणुरशोषयत्।।

MV. V-7

"The threshold of his palace was ever thronged with elephants, and also kings waiting for audience. The former made it muddy with their flowing ichor, while the latter made it dry with gem-dusts falling down from ornaments broken as a result of jostling."

Here, the stanza describes that all kings were receiving or serving Kampaṇa with great honour. Thus, we exalt here the greatness of Kampaṇa.

Other instances of this figure-Udātta are : I-48, 49; IX-16.

Arthāntaranyāsa or Corroboration

That is corroboration, where a general proposition or a particular proposition is corroborated by a proposition other than that, either through similarity or dissimilarity.[33] Following is an example:

हरितं परिरभ्य वासवीं हरिणाङ्कः करपातलीलया।
स्पृशति प्रणयात् कुमुद्वतीं बत विश्वासपदं न कामिनः।।

Ibid., VII-47

"The Moon embraces with his hands of rays the damsel of Eastern Region, and the same time, also touches another called Kumudvati (bed of might lotuses). This shows, that lustful men ought not to be trusted."

This stanza brings out a general proposition that lustful men ought not to be trusted. By this general proposition the lustfulness of the Moon is corroborated.

कुन्तेन कश्चित् द्विषता विभिन्नस्तथैव संश्लेषममुष्य यातः।
भिंदन्नुरस्तेन चमत्कृतोऽभूद् गुणेषु को मत्सरमादधाति।।

MV. X-12

"Some royal warriors, like lions wandered in the field of battle, and bore the heads of their adversaries with their sharp nails as if the latter were opposing elephants."

This stanza shows a general proposition that 'who is there that is not moved by real exhibition of daring qualities'. By this general rule, particular contact of the condition of a certain warrior in battle, is substantiated.

Parikara or Significant

The figure Parikara arises when a certain thing (or substantive) is described by mans of significant adjectives.[34] "Significant adjectives" means adjectives which possess two senses: One expressed and the other suggested. Thus, Parikara arises when a certain substantive is qualified by many adjectives that express our sense and suggest another.

Following example illustrates this figure:

इतीरयित्वा विरते नरेश्वरे प्रवृष्टपाथोधरसाम्यधारिणि।
कृतप्रणामः शिरसा प्रतीष्टवान् गुरूपदेशं गुणिनां पुरस्सरः।।

Ibid., III-44

"Having delivered this speech, the king stopped, even as the cloud does after pouring down its watery contents. The prince bowed low and took to heart, like the good son by the advice of his father."

This stanza expresses that Kampaṇa receives humbly the advice of Bukka. And it suggests through the sense of the words "गुणिनां पुरस्सरः" that, always virtuous men receive the advice of their preceptor and that advice promotes them to their future prospects. Hence, it is Parikara.

Asaṅgati or Incongruity

The figure Asaṅgati occurs when two properties, the cause and the effect, which are usually found in one place, are described as residing in two different places.[35] This figure is illustrated in the following example:

वीराः कुंजरकुम्भेषु शायिनः शत्रुसायकैः।
प्राबुध्यन्ते सुरस्त्रीणां कुचकुम्भेषु तत्क्षणात्॥

MV. IV-61

"Brave fighters sent to (everlasting) sleep by enemy arrows on the protrusion of their elephants, soon woke up on the pot-like breasts of divine damsels."

The purport of this stanza is that the warriors being incapable of facing the enemies, die in battle and obtain heaven and remain enjoying with heavenly damsels therein: This is described figuratively: The warriors being hit by the weapons of enemies have slept permanantly on the protrusion of their elephants; and woke up on the potpot-like breasts of divine damsels. Usually sleeping and waking up are found in one place; but they are described as residing in two different places. Hence, it is Asaṅgati.

Another example of this figure of speech may be seen in the same context *i.e.*, IV-64.

Besides these many figures of speech, the other figures like Svabhāvokti (IV-79; V-16), Gūḍhokti (VI-7, 8), Samāsokti (I-59, VI-60), Nirukti (II-7), Prauḍhokti (II-8), Sahokti (III-16, II-21, IV-49), Paryāyokta (IV-82, VIII-34), Dṛṣṭānta (III-17; VIII-26), Nāma (VII-41), Aprastutaprasaṁsā (1-17), Preya (V-72, 74), Prativastūpamā (I-19, 21; III-31, 42), Vastudhvani (I-4, 44, 66; III-10), Anumāna (III-7), Tadgunaṅkāra (I-58), Ullekha (III-22), Arthāpatti (II-22), Yathāsāṅkhya (II-36), Sasandeha (VII-24), and Vibhāvanā (IV-45)—have been used rarely to create poetic charm. Gaṅgādevī in fact, is not head-strong in their use. She has not stuck to any one figure, but she has used different Alaṅkāras and left them according to the occasion. The use of these many Alaṅkāras no doubt has added much in the expression of ideas and culmination of Rasa. Though the poetess has frequently used the Alaṅkāras, it is not the centre of her concentration. They have been used by her fit to the purpose. With Gaṅgādevī, the use Alaṅkāras is only means to bring additional charm to the Madhurāvijayaṁ, but never to display her knowledge of Rhetorics. Thus, Gaṅgādevī stands as a good poetess.

REFERENCES

1. Bhāmaha's *Kāvyalaṅkāra*. I-13.
2. Vāmana's *Kāvyālaṅkāra Sūtravṛtti*.-I.
3. *Ibid.*
4. अलंकारान्तरस्यापि प्रतीतौ यत्र भासते।
   तत्परत्वं न वाच्यस्य नासौ मार्गो ध्वनेर्मतः।। *Dhvanyāloka*. II-27
5. न कान्तमपि निर्भूषं विभाति वनितामुखम्। *Kāvyālaṅkāra*. I-13
6. काव्यशोभाकरान् धर्मानलङ्कारान् प्रचक्षते। *Kāvyādarśa*. II-1
7. अलङ्काररहिता विधवेव सरस्वती। *Agni Purāṇa*. 34. 13
8. *Kāvyalaṅkāra Sūtra*. I-12.
9. *Ibid.*, I-3.
10. निवेक्षातत्परत्वेन नाङ्गित्वेन कदाचन। *Dhvanyāloka*. II-19
11. *Ibid.*, 2. 18. 19.
12. अनुप्रास शब्दसाम्यं वैषम्येऽपि स्वरसाम्यात्। *Sāhityadarpaṇa*. X-3
13. कल्याणाया सतां भूयात् देवो दन्ताकलाननः।
    शरणागतसङ्कल्प कल्पना कल्पपादपः।। *MV*. I-1
14. क्वचिदर्थः क्वचिच्छब्दः क्वचिद्भावः क्वचिद्रसः।
    यत्रैते सन्ति सर्वेऽपि स निबन्धो न लभ्यते।। *Ibid.*, I-17
15. आसीत् समस्तसामन्त मस्तकन्यस्तशासनः।
    बुक्कराज इति ख्यातो राजा हरिहरानुजः।। *Ibid.*, I-26
16. विकसद्वनितावल्लीविलासवनवाटिका।
    दक्षिणाशा सरोजाक्षी फाललीलाललाटिका।। *Ibid.*, I-51

17. तदादनं तस्य सुगन्धि जिघ्रन्नालक्ष्यदन्ताङ्कुरदर्शनीयम्।
न तृप्तिमासादयति स्म राजा नवोदयं हंस इवारविन्दम्।। *Sāhityadarpaṇa*. III-37

18. अथ लङ्घितकर्णाटः पंचषैरेव वासरैः।
प्रापत्कम्पमहीपालः कण्टकाननपट्टनम्।। *Ibid*., IV-47

19. शिष्टै पदैरनेकार्थाभिधाने श्लेष इष्यते। *Ibid*., X-11

20. सम्भावनमथोत्प्रेक्षा प्रकृतस्य समेन यत्। Mammaṭa's *Kāvyaprākash* Bombay, 1959, p. 45.

21. तद् रूपकामभेदो य उपमानोपमेययोः। *Ibid*., p. 48

22. समस्तवस्तुविषयं श्रौता आरोपिता यदा। *Kāvyaprakāśa*. X, p. 48

23. नियतारोपणोपायः स्यादारोपः परस्य यः।
तत् परम्परितं श्लिष्टे वाचके भेदभाजि वा।। *Kāvyaprakāśa*. X, p. 51

24. उपमानोपमेययोरेव, न कार्यकारणादिकयोः, साधर्म्यं भवतीति तयोरेव समानेन धर्मेण सम्बन्धः उपमा। एकस्य द्वयोस्त्रयाणां वा लोपे लुप्ताः। यथेववादिशब्दाः यत्पराः तस्यैव उपमानताप्रतीतिः।। *Ibid*., X. p. 83

25. काव्यलिङ्गि हेतोर्वाक्यपदार्थता।। *Ibid*., X. p. 83

26. भ्रान्तिमानन्यसंवित् तत्तुल्यदर्शने।। *Ibid*., X. p. 110

27. निगीर्याध्यवसानं तु प्रकृतस्य परेण यत्।
प्रस्तुतस्य यदन्यत्वं यद्यर्थोक्तौ च कल्पनम्।। *Ibid*., X. p 63

28. प्रकृतं यन्निषिध्यात् साध्यते सा त्वपह्नुति।। *Ibid*., X. p. 53

29. उपमानाद् यदन्यस्य व्यतिरेकः स एव सः।। *Ibid*., X. p. 68

30. अभवन् वस्तुसम्बन्धः उपमा परिकल्पकः। *Ibid*., X. p. 56

31. विरोधः सोऽविरोधेऽपि विरुद्धत्वेन यद्वचः।
वस्तुवृत्तेनाविरोधेऽपि विरुद्धयोरिव यदभिधानं स विरोधः।। *Ibid*., X. p. 76

32. उदात्तं वस्तुनः सम्पत्, महतां चोपलक्षणम्।। *Ibid*., X. p. 86

33. सामान्यं वा विशेषो वा तदन्येन समर्थ्यते।
यत्र सोऽर्थान्तरन्यासः साधर्म्येणेतरेण वा।। *Ibid*., X. p. 75

34. विशेषणैर्यत् साकूतैरुक्तिः परिकरस्तु सः। *Ibid*., X. p. 92

35. भिन्नदेशतयात्यन्तं कार्यकारणभूतयोः।
युगपद् धर्मयोर्यत्र ख्यातिः सा स्यादसङ्गतिः।। *Ibid*., X. p. 1

Chapter-6

Rasa Delineation in the Madhurāvijayaṁ

Indian literary critics consider Rasa as the soul of poetry. Rasa literaly means taste, relish, or flavour. That is called Rasa which is relished. "*Rasyatīti Rasaḥ*". It is the emotional element which fall into an organised pattern. It is as Prof. M. Hiriyanna has put it in his book "The Problem of the Rasavadālaṅkāra," integral aesthetic experience. The ultimate appeal of any poem depends upon this theme. Bharata, the celebrated author of the Nāṭyaśāstra and the founder of Rasa theory, points out very clearly that no Kāvya can be fully enjoyed without Rasa.[1] The later rhetoricians from Bhāmaha to Jagannātha follow Bharata in this respect. Admitting the predominance of Rasa in poetry, the literary critics deal with various topics such as Guṇas, Rītis, Alaṅkāras etc., as these topics subscribe to the delineation of Rasa.

Literary critics have highlighted two objectives of poetry *viz.*, creating delight in the hearts of Sahṛdayas (*Vigalita-vedyāntara ānanda* or *Sahṛadayāhlāda*), and inculcating the ideals and morals of life in the manner of a wife (*Kāntāsammitopadeśa*).

A Mahākāvya is a literary composition of some length. It has enough scope to carry out both these purposes through a variety of events and descriptions coming as the constituent parts of a well organised and well executed theme. It has a capacity to create delight through the delineation of Rasa. In its various constituent parts, it delineates various Rasas.

In their explanation of the characteristics of Mahākāvya Bhāmaha and Daṇḍin maintain that the main feature of a Mahākāvya is its repleteness with Rasa. However, Ānandavardhana and his followers maintain that Rasa is the soul of poetry.[2] In general, it may be stated that all the factors of poetic charms should contribute to Rasa realisation. The rhetoricians mentioned above have also stated that one of the Rasas such as Śṛṅgāra, Vīra, Karuṇa or Śānta should be predominant in a Mahākāvya, while other Rasas should be introduced as subordinate to the main sentiment.[3] These observations of the literary critics regarding Rasa delineation in a Mahākāvya have been inspired by the example of the Rāmāyaṇa, Mahābhārata, the Mahākāvyas of Kālidāsa, Aśvaghoṣa, etc. This literary tradition is meticulously followed by Gaṅgādevī in the Madhurāvijayaṁ.

In keeping with that objective and the events of the story, whether major or minor, contributing to it, Vīrarasa alone may be regarded as the central Rasa of the Madhurāvijayaṁ. It pervades the entire poem from the beginning to end. Other Rasas like Śṛṅgāra, Hāsya, Karuṇa, etc., are delineated as subordinate Rasas in the constituent parts of the poem. On account of this, we find the unity of the theme in the poem. A critical account of the main and subsidiary Rasas as expounded in the Madhurāvijayaṁ is given below.

Vīrarasa

According to Bharata, Vīrarasa is constituted of supreme natures and consists of Energy (Utsāha). This is aroused by the determinants such as presence of mind, perseverance, diplomacy, discipline, military strength, power reputation of mighty influence and the like, and it is to be represented by firmness, patience heroism, charity, sacrifice, diplomacy and the like.

This heroic sentiment undoubtedly is the predominant sentiment of the poem Madhurāvijayaṁ. Since the theme of this epic is Kampaṇa's victory over Śambuvarāya and the Sultana of Madurai, Kampaṇa is the *Ālambana Vibhāva* of *Utsāha*. Kampana's Utsaha to subjugate the enemy, leads the march on Śambuvarāya territory and the Karnātaka forces and arriving at Virinchipuram for fighting, etc. Since it is expressed in these ways they can be considered as Anubhāvas. Kampaṇa's conquest of Madhurai and Kāñchi to punish the culprit may be treated as a development of that Utsāha.

It may be noted here that literary critics mention four kinds of heroic sentiments, *viz.*, Dānavīra, Dharmavīra, Dayāvīra, Yuddhavīra. It is possible to find in Kampaṇa the combination of all these four types. But Yuddhavīra type of Kampaṇa's personality is predominantly noticeable and it pervades the whole epic.

Kampaṇa's heroic action comes to light first in his protecting Kāñchi from Śambuvarāya. His administration thus provides a preparatory ground for his ultimate success, namely, the Sultana-Vadha. At the very outset of the fourth canto narration of the compaign of prince Kampaṇa, accompained by the Cola, Kerala and Pāṇḍya kings on the Śambuvarāya territory, suggests that the predominant sentiment of the poem is *Vīra*. At the time of the campaign, Kampaṇa's mounting the horse is described as the personification of his strength and how he felt as if the entire kingdom of the earth had already passed into his hands.[4] Here Vīra-Rasa is combined with *Sthāyībhāva i.e. Utsāha.*

The eighth canto is fully devoted to describe the valour and vigour of the Sultan, the Pratināyaka of this Mahākāvya. His ill-treatment to people who were made to serve him as his slaves, is described in order to highlight the greatness of

Kampaṇa's achievement as a hero, as he is going to kill such a mighty person as the Sultan. Describing Pratināyāka's might and hero's victory over the former one is a favourite method adopted by master poets in Sanskrit. Gaṅgādevī is not an exception. The pitiable condition of Madhurai and affliction of Madhurā-Devatā, the advice of Bukka to Kampaṇa to destroy the Sultan, all these incidents are a sure indication of the Sultan's extra-ordinary valour.

The main thread of heroic sentiment is present every where in the poem. It should be clearly noted that a mere actual war between the rival groups is not an instance of heroic sentiment. That sentiment should be reflected in every deed of the hero. This is what we find in every deed of Kampaṇa which proves that he is a hero of the Dhirodātta type, most worthy of the praise, for which he is born. He is compassionate to render help to a person in need and this indicates the better aspects of his heroic temperament.

Again, while describing Kampaṇa's childhood and boyhood, his sports and practice of wielding the bow and the sword and his ability in using all miraculous weapons, the poetess says that, all these are preparatory to the main cause of the Sultan's downfall.

The advice of Bukka to Kampaṇa for destroying Śambuvarāya and the Sultan, shows that Bukka was in favour of heroism. The advice of Bukka to Kampaṇa contains the seeds of encouragement to foster the spirit of valour in Kampaṇa. The conquest of Madhurai was accomplished and king Kampaṇa guaranteed the safety of the remaining men in his enemy ranks and was crowned with happiness and glory.[5] Here Kampaṇa demonstrated his Dayāvīra and Yuddhavīra qualities.

Yuddhavīra and Dharmavīra Combined

Kampaṇa killed Śambuvarāya in the battlefield and thus fulfilled the decree of his father that she should rule with the fame of his victory duly established in Kāñcī. He inaugurated a just and prosperous rule over Tundiramandalam.[6] Here, Kampaṇa demonstrated his Yuddhavīratā by killing Śambuvarāya and he has demonstrated his Dharmavīratā by removing differences in Castes and religious orders. This has been the first instance. Here we come across the revealation of the ideas of heroism of Kampaṇa and addition of some flashes in the delineation of the heroic sentiment.

Kampaṇa's extra-ordinary strength and heroism or leadership are appropriately exhibited in his administration at Kāñcī. His heroic deed is seen more striking when the poetess introduces the administration of Kampaṇa in an unusual manner as follows:

King Kampaṇa established himself and ruled the earth peacefully. The earth by finding rest on his strong attractive ornamented. liberal hands, lessened the burden of Śeṣa who was her prime support.[7]

The amours of prince Kampaṇa and queen Devāyī conceives Bukka's happiness for his sons. These provide an opportunity for the poet to delineate the heroic sentiment in a more appealing way. Devāyī heard of Viṣṇu's miraculous exploits underneath the earth and wanted to intimate him.[8] This incident highlights Kampaṇa's greatness as a hero once again. Here again Kampaṇa is characterised as an extra ordinary manifestation (औज्वल) of Vāmana.

In the spring festival, ladies wanted to paint different forms of cupid in picture bounds. But they ended up by painting the different forms or poses of king Kampaṇa who was always in their heart.[9] Here also, we can see the manifestation of the charming character of Kampaṇa.

Kampaṇa's extra-ordinary generous nature. was appropriately exhibited at the time of his birth as indicated in the following words: The Kalpavṛkṣa by showering down flowers through clouds looked as if courting in advance the friendship of the royal child who was soon to excel them in the glory of giving.[10]

A great fortune of Kampaṇa is appreciably exhibited the administration of Kāñcī. This is described in the following words:

Every day kings that had cast of their old enemity rubbed their foreheads against his royal foot-stool and their resultant change of fortune suggested the idea that now letters of prosperity were written on their foreheads (in lieu of those that were already there from their birth).[11]

The heroic sentiment has been delineated to a great extent in the great war between the rival armies in general and in a fierce-fight between Kampaṇa and the Sultan in particular. For instance, the King of Yavanas was shattered by the arrows let off by king Kampaṇa which were like the side glances of the Goddess of Heroism, and the king, similarly checked the Farasika's (Persian's) arrows which resembled the eye-darts of Yama's sister.[12]

The Madhurāvijayaṁ further describes in detail the battle, an account of which is given below:

King Kampaṇa let fly against the Yavana king his arrows that had, like serpants, drunk the life-breaths of Keralas, like fire had consumed the lords of the Vanya kingdom, and like the sun had destroyed the dark Āndhras.[13]

The scratches caused by the Yavana king's arrow on the person of the Goddess of Victory that was so passionate to enjoy her privacy.[14]

Here king Kampaṇa who was the glory of the Karnātak race; avoiding the sword blow aimed by Yavana, cut off in an instant the head of the latter.[15]

The head of the Sūratrāṇa (Sultan) fell on the ground the head that never knew the art of cajoling servant like, the head that had borne the royal burden of the Turaṣka Sāmrājya (Supremacy) and had not bowed down even to gods.[16]

The hero Kampaṇa, was astonished to see that, even after the head had fallen, the trunk on the horseback still held the reins checking the horse's course with one hand while the other was uplifted to return the blows of the adversary.[17]

Cantos six and nine have been fully devoted to the delineation of Vīra Rasa. Not only every incident but each and every verse therein is replete with Vīra Rasa.

Thus, all the events of the story major or minor have contributed to the development of the heroic sentiment. In the beginning of the poem, the poetess has successfully delineated Vīra Rasa by describing the greatness of Bukka, the father of Kampaṇa in the following words:

Like Śeṣa among serpents, Himavān among mountains and Viṣṇu among gods, Kampaṇa occupied the first place among the lords of the earth.[18] With discernment alone for his minister, and the bow alone for his army, he counted on his arms as his only ally in the heart of battle.[19] He demonstrated the presence of the (four) guardian deities of the universe even on this earth: Indra by being the over-lord of the waters, Kubera by giving away wealth and Yama by being impartial.[20]

Above all, both the hero and his adversary in the poem have been portrayed beautifully as Yuddhavīras.

Kampaṇa's birth under the circumstances of the Sultan harrassing his subjects, is the starting point of the delincation of the Vīra-rasa whose climax is seen in the killing of the Sultan. In this way, the poetess has depicted the heroic sentiment so predominantly in the whole of her Kāvya with such care and capacity that the main thread of the principal Rasa is never broken.

Śṛṅgāra Rasa

Next to Vīra Rasa Śṛṅgāra finds a prominent place in the Madhurāvijayaṁ. Śṛṅgāra is caused by the durable psychological state of Rati or in other words it proceeds from *Ayoga i.e., Vipralambha* taking place before the consummation of marriage and *Viprayoga*, the separation of the lovers deep in love after marriage.[21] Whatever may be the reason for the separation of lovers, it has ten stages beginning with *Abhilāsā* and ending with what is technically called *Maraṇa.*[22] In a way, all these effects of separation of lovers clearly indicate the psychological insight of the rhetoricians. Without going into the intricacies and complexities of the classification of Śṛṅgāra Rasa, it is proposed to deal with the delineation of Śṛṅgāra Rasa in the Madhurāvijayaṁ in a general way.

Sambhoga Śṛṅgāra, the sentiment of love, is developed in two full cantos (sixth and seventh) of the Madhurāvijayaṁ. It is noteworthy that the delineation of Śṛṅgāra Rasa is used with a view to heighten the effect of Vīra Rasa.

These cantos also protray the different situations of love sentiment.

In the sixth canto of the Madhurāvijayaṁ, the poetess, Gaṅgādevī describes elaborately the aquatic sports of king Kampaṇa as *Uddīpanavibhāva* for the delineation of Śṛṅgāra. In handling this situation, many transitory emotions of the lovers have been attractively expressed by the poetess. For instance, Prince Kampaṇa tries to get the pleasure of an embrace of his beloved under water. As the king touched nicely the uppar part of the lady underneath the water, she feigned fishbite and embraced her lover even when her companions were looking on.[23] Here the subtle anxiety and eagerness of the king to get the pleasure of an embrace of his beloved are effectively suggested.

In another instance, a lady blinded the king by splashing water, as if in sport against his eyes when the other ladies turned to look at the nail-marks on the person of her rival.[24] Here the situation is such as to create jealousy in the hearts of other ladies. In another instance, the king splashed water on a lotus in the pleasure lake, and this made a lady cast on him angry looks of jealousy the fringes of her eye lashes wet with tears.[25] Here also we can see jealousy in the hearts of other ladies. Though their royal lover asked them to stop, his ladies had no mind to do so, as they were very much attracted by the love of the sport and so they did not leave the pleasure-lake though its water had completely washed away their decorative marks.[26] With this eagerness of the water sports of the young ladies Kampaṇa was immensely satisfied.

To enliven and stimulate Śṛṅgāra Rasa, copious description of seasons is given in the Kāvya. For instance, the summer season. The elephant-cupid getting scorched in the sun, found shelter in the breasts of beautiful ladies, which were wet with pastes of sandal and had the cooling contact of pear strings.[27] During the spring season the young ladies were not able to worship and paint the forms of the god Kāma.[28] The rainy season was favourable for Ratikrīḍā of Kampaṇa.[29]

The beauty of the evening twilight adds to the romantic atmosphere in the context. The poetess delineating their love sentiment begins the seventh canto with the description of the evening and the night. In the evening, the sun at one stage seemed to be afflicted with the feeling of separation from the eastern quarter, yet now he is seen enjoying himself the company with the opposite quarter, his heat gone on reaching her. The minds of lovers are certainly inscrutable.[30]

Gaṅgādevī describes very beautifully how night comes after the evening. For instance, the evening twilight was fancied by people as the screen of the stage where the dancer was about to act the part of night having taken off his disguise as day.[31]

In another instance, time was certainly the ploughman, the stars were well washed seeds of grain, the dark skies were fields rendered muddy, wherein those seeds were sown by him in order to raise the crop of moonlight. Such was the fancy in the minds of all.[32] And, these points do contribute to the development of Śṛṅgāra Rasa.

Then Gaṅgādevī gives, a charming description of the moonrise. For instance, the lord of night hugs the eastern region to his bossom in an ardent embrace, and with his nail-like rays unties her braid of hair which incarnates darkness.[33]

In another instance, the moon embraces with his hand of rays the damsel of the Eastern Region, and at the sametime, also touches another lover called Kumudvatī (night lotus). This shows that lustful men ought not to be trusted.[34]

The poetess explains very beautifully how the moon produces heat in the hearts of lovers in separation. The sun enters the moon every new-moon-day and so, the latter also becomes endowed with the quality of heat.[35]

In consonance with the description in the eight canto of the Kumārasambhava, the Madhurāvijayaṁ gives the description of the evening and the moonrise.

The sentiment of love thus is delineated in cantos more than one. In this way, Gaṅgādevī has displayed her skill in giving minute descriptions of the sentiment of love. Though it is subordinate in the Madhurāvijayaṁ, it is presented in all its details, within the scope which she has provided in the poem.

Karuṇa Rasa

The sentiment of pathos (Karuṇa) with sorrow or grief as its *Sthāyībhāva,* is given a proper treatment in some portion of the Madhurāvijayaṁ. Karuṇa is the heartfelt compassion. That is called Karuṇa Rasa when it arises in the heart of the aesthetics. It proceeds from the permanent mental state of sorrow and it arises on account of the loss of a person or an object of one's liking (Iṣṭanāśa) or on account of the befalling of what is underlined (Aniṣṭaprāpti). In the Madhurāvijayaṁ, Gaṅgādevī delineates this sentiment of Karuṇa effectively in her descriptions of the conditions of the Tamil country after the Muslim occupation.

The exhoration and encouragement given to the hero by the Goddess of Madhurā describing her grief at the revolutionary situation in the country, is full of pathetic sentiments. And the Goddess of Madhurā explains the miserable condition of the Tamil country to Kampaṇa in his dream as follows:

Those temples which were once resonant with the sounds of Mṛdaṅga drums are now echoing the fearful howls of jackals.[36] Here the distress of the temples is the *Ālambana Vibhāva* for *śoka*, the administration of Turaṣkas is the *Uddīpanavibhāva*. The lamentations and tears of the shocking state of Madhurā Goddess, constitute the *Anubhāvas; Cintā, Viṣāda* etc., suggested by the *Anubhāva* are the *Sañcārībhāvas.*

The river Kāverī uncurbed by proper bonds or dams, has become reflected very much from her time-honoured course and flows in all sorts of wrong directions as if imitating the Turaṣkas in their actions.[37] Kāverī is the *Ālambanavibhāva* of *Śoka* and the flows of Kāverī in all sorts of wrong directions is *Uddīpanavibhāva*. The sorrow of the Goddess is *Anubhāva*, and *Cintā, Viṣāda*, etc., are the *Sañcārībhāvas.*

In the brāhmin streets where once the sacrificial smoke was ever seen rising and the chanting of Vedas, always greeted the ears, now exude the musty odour of meat, and resound with the lion roars of drunken Turaṣkas.[38] Here the brāhmin streets are the *Ālmbanavibhāva* of *Śoka* and exluding of the musty odour of meat and resounding with the lion roars of drunken Turaskas, is the *Uddīpanavibhāva*. Sorrowful speech of the goddess is *Anubhāva; Cintā, Viṣāda* etc., are the *Sañcārībhāvas.*

Murderous deed of the Turaṣka is described very effectively by the poetess as follows: The coconut trees have all been cut in the upavana of Madhurā, and in their place are to be seen rows of iron spikes with human skulls dangling at the points.[39] Here the upavana of Madhurā is *Ālambana Vibhāva*. The human skulls dangling at the points, are the *Uddīpanavibhāva* and the lamentations of the Goddess, is the *Anubhāva*. Feelings like *Nirveda, Dainya, Moha, Maraṇa*, etc., are the *Sañcārībhāvas*. Thus, the *sthāyibhāva* of *śoka* come to the experience of the Sahṛdayas as Karuṇa Rasa.

Madhurā Goddess explains her own condition to Kampaṇa like this: I am very much distressed by looking at the tearful face of Dravidas, their lips parched by hot sighs, and their hair worn in utter disorder.[40] Here the words of Goddess are full of pathos.

The waters of Tāmraparṇī which were once white with sandal paste rubbed away from the breasts of charming girls, are now flowing red with the blood of cows slaughtered by the miscreants.[41] This point promotes the sentiment of pathos.

Thus, in the Madhurāvijayaṁ, the sentiment of pathos, is delineated effectively in the proper contexts. It is to be noted here that the delineation of this sentiment is not as elaborate as in the works of Kālidāsa and Bhavabhūti. But, the level of sentiment of pathos has been developed more or less similar to that of other works.

Hāsya Rasa

Usually Hāsya is treated in literature as subordinate to Śṛṅgara or in other words, Hāsya is the miming of Śṛṅgāra. Hāsya consists of the permanent mental state of Hāsa *i.e.*, its soul is formed of the *Hāsa Sthāyībhāva*. This is aroused by determinants such as unseemly dress or ornament, impudence, greediness, jugglery, defective limb, use of irrelevant words, mentioning of different faults and similar other things.

Sanskrit dramatists introduce the character of Vidūṣaka, Śaka, for the delineation of Hāsya Rasa, but such a character is conspicuous by its absence in Mahākāvyas. But subtle humour is introduced by master poets like Kālidāsa in their Mahākāvyas. Lord Śiva's self-satire in the fifth canto of the Kumārasambhava is a fine example of the Abhijāta type of Hāsya.[42] Śrī Harṣa delineates Hāsya to a full length while describing the merry-making of Nala's marriage party.[43] Gaṅgādevī reveals a sense of humour mixed with wit. But Vīra, being the principal sentiment of the Kāvya, Hāsya finds very little scope in the Madhurāvijayaṁ. Yet like Kālidāsa,

Gaṅgādevī is capable of introducing 'Abhijāta' type of Hāsya in her epic. While describing the defeat of the Tamil forces, the poetess gets an opportunity of introducing a meaningful humour on the occasions of the fighting between Śambuvarāya and Kampaṇa. Kampaṇa defeated Śambuvarāyas army. Then the army of the Tamils routed by the mighty forces of Kampaṇa took to flight. Some men fleeing in great disorder let fall their weapons in great terror and swore they would never fight again.[44]

Others, feigning death, dropped down, but fearing the presence of jackals, they at once rose up and started running pellmell, affording no small mirth to the Karnāta forces.[45] There were still others who in their flight mistook their own shadows for the pursuing enemy in the extremity of their fright and began to prostrate before them, biting their fingers.[46] While describing the fight between Champarāja and Kampaṇa, the poetess has again hinted at Hāsyarasa. With the forepart of their bodies bent and eyes fixed, the two kings, sword in hand, stood still for a moment like a picture on a piece of painting.[47] In addition to the indication of Gaṅgādevī's sense of humour, it also indicates her knowledge of the graphic art.

In fine, it is beyond doubt that Gaṅgādevī is capable of treating Hāsya Rasa wherever and whenever she finds a proper occasion. The depiction of Hāsya Rasa in the Madhurāvijayaṁ is thus dignified and refined.

Bhayānaka Rasa

The Bhayānaka Rasa has a close relation with Vīra Rasa. Even though this sentiment is generally to be found in the description of the battlefield wherein terrific scenes are usual, yet it is common on any occasion, creating a sort of fear in the mind of a person. Its *Sthāyībhāva* is *Bhaya*. The sight of a wild animal, a serpent or a wicked person, is sufficient to create Bhaya, which is manifested in the shaking of the body, faltering speech, perspiration, change of colour, stupefaction restlessness, death etc.

Gaṅgādevī has delineated this sentiment very appropriately in several situations. When describing the defeat of the Tamil forces, the poetess has delineated Bhayānka Rasa. A few examples are given below:

Some men fleeing in great disorder let fall their weapons in great terror and swore they would never fight again.[48] Others feigning death, dropped down, but fearing the presence of jackals, they at once rose up and starter running Pellmell, affording no small mirth to the Karnātak forces.[49] These examples though quoted earlier under Hāsyarasa are repeated here to indicate the fear with which Tamil forces were fleeing from the battle around indicating the sentiment of Bhayānaka. Yet others, mistaking a mirage for water (river) made futile attempts to cross it with a boat improvised out of the shields which they had forgotten to abandon (in their flight).[50] Again, we find some instances in the nine canto in which the fight between Kampaṇa and Turaṣka king is described. The brave king pounded the turbaned heads of his enemies with his mace it such a way that the eyes which came out of the sockets sand again in their old places.[51] Birds of prey with a view taste the inner flesh entered into the body of a dear elephant making it quiver. Jackals that mistook it for sign of life fled away, though they very much loved to feast on the body.[52]

A certain elephant having seized by the foot, and thrown up a warrior with his trunk, wanted to catch him again, as he fell, with his pair of tusks.[53] A certain warrior was struck with a (double-edged) lance by his opposing foe, and by embracing the latter with the same lance sticking his body, wounded him.[54]

Thus, we can say Gaṅgādevī is capable of handling Bhayānaka Rasa also, wherever and whenever she finds proper occasion.

Bībhatsa Rasa

Bībhatsa Rasa with disgust (*Jugupsā*) as its : Sthāyībhāva

has been depicted to a considerable extent in the Madhurāvijayaṁ. This consists of the durable psychological state of disgust. Anything creating disgust or aversion by mere thought or sight is the *Ālambana Vibhāva*. In general it occurs only in the descriptions of filthy object, obscene sights and load talk:— Flesh, blood, entrails, the disfigure dead body, foul smell (*anitavikasana*) produce disgust in the minds of men. *Bhaya, Āvega, Vyādhi, Apasmāra* etc., are the *Sañcārībhāvas* of this sentiment. Since the Madhurāvijayaṁ is full of terrific fights as a result of which so many deaths take place, the poetess has ample scope for the depiction of Bībhatsa Rasa.

There are many occasions for the delineation of Bībhatsa Rasa on the battle field. The battle-field crowded with many dead bodies with blood flowing out from them creates disgust and aversion in the mind of every reader. In the four canto of the Madhurāvijayaṁ, when describing the battle between Śambhuvavarāya and Kampaṇa, Gaṅgādevī gives some picturesque descriptions conducive to Bībhatsa Rasa. A few examples are given below:

Karnāta forces and the Tamil king attacked each other.

Due to this war, in the battle-field, countless rivers of blood began to flow on all sides, the faces of soldiers cut off by the bhalla and arrows looked like lotuses.[55] It is an example of the Bībhatsa situation, creating a disgusting effect on the minds of the readers. Here Jugupsā, the Sthāyībhāva of Bībhatsa is well depicted. This situation is of course, common in the battle-field. But unnatural with any cultured man and creates disgust and aversion in the minds of readers while listening to or reading its description. Describing the dead bodies of the enemies, the poetess says the arms of the kings severed by swords resembled the trunks of elephants but were mistaken for snakes by the eagles that snatched them away.[56] The blood flowing from human trunks was very much liked by the Rākṣasas who deftly seated themselves on the trunks of elephants as if on tops of palaces.[57]

The blood-stained sword-blades waving in the hands of heroic warriors appeared like the folling tongue of Yama eager to make a meal of them away.[58]

Again, we find a live depiction of Bībhatsa sentiment in canto nine. It is sufficient to quote a typical example of Bībhatsa Rasa, which describes Kampaṇa's final battle with the Muslims. The blood flowing from the wounded frontal globes of elephants was seen being drunk through their trunks by some night prowling demons in great glee, spitting the pearls that also came with the blood stream.[59] One thought, by looking at them, that there was not only one Tāmraparṇī river but several hundreds of Tāmraparṇīs.[60] Thus, in the Madhurāvijayaṁ, Bībhatsa Rasa is delineated side by side with Vīrarasa.

Thus, the eight Rasas accepted in the poetic tradition, have been properly developed in the Madhurāvijayam. As already shown, Vīra Rasa is the ruling sentiment of this Mahākāvya. Other Rasas are given a subordinate position here. They are delineated in such a way as to enhance ultimately the effect of the principal Rasa.

Gaṅgādevī has shown her ability in delineating all the Rasas. Except in the case of Vīra Rasa, the principal sentiment and Śṛṅgāra Rasa, one of the subsidiary sentiments, she has been very brief. In the sentiment of Śṛṅgāra, her depiction of the scenes is in keeping with decourm and propriety. Hāsya is of the Abhijāta type. Since she has given long descriptions, the situations of Rasas other than Vīra and Śṛṅgāra are brief but effective.

REFERENCES

1. न हि रसादृते कश्चिदप्यर्थः प्रवर्तते। *Nāṭyaśāstra* VI-82
2. काव्यस्यात्मा स एवार्थस्तथा चादिकवेः पुरा।
   क्रौंचद्वन्द्ववियोगोत्थः शोकः श्लोकत्वमागतः।। *Dhvanyāloka* I-5
3. एको रसोङ्गी कर्तव्यो वीरः शृङ्गार एव वा। *Daśarūpakaṁ* III-3

4. देहबन्धमिवोत्साहं तमारुह्य महीपतिः।
अमंस्त पृथिवीं सर्वामात्मनो हस्तवर्तिनीम्।। *MV.* IV-29

5. हतावशिष्टानथ वैरियोधान् संरक्ष्यपादप्रणतान् शरण्यः।
कृताभिषेकः प्रशशास मेदिनीं दिवं मरुत्वानिव कम्पभूपतिः।। *Ibid.*, IX-42

6. इत्थं सङ्गरमूर्ध्नि चम्पनृपतिं नीत्वा कथाशेषताम्।
श्रीमान् कम्पनृपेश्वरो जनयितुः सम्प्राप्तवाच्छासनम्। *Ibid.*, IV-33
कांचीन्यस्तजयप्रशस्तिरमिथस्सङ्कीर्णवर्णाश्रमम्।
नीत्यानीत्यनिरत्ययर्द्धिरशिषत् तुण्डीरभूमण्डलम्।। *Ibid.*, IV-34

7. द्रढिमशालिनि भोगमनोहरे कटकधारिणि दानगुणोर्जिते।
नृपतिदोष्णि निवासमुपेत्य भूरलगयत् प्रथमास्पदगौरवम्।। *Ibid.*, V-6

8. सा दैत्यनाथप्रथताय पूर्वं विष्णोरधस्तात्कृतपौरुषस्य।
आकर्णयन्ती कुहनाप्रपंचादासीद् ध्रुवं वामन इत्यमंस्त।। *Ibid.*, II-7

9. सुतनवः फलकेषु मधूत्सवे रतिपतिपरिलेखितुमुद्यताः।
हृदयगोचरतामनिशं गतं हरिहरात्मजमेव समालिखत्।। *Ibid.*, V-72

10. कल्पद्रुमास्तेन हरिष्यमाणां मत्वा निजा त्यगयशः पताकाम्।
पयोधरप्रेषितपुष्पवर्षाः प्रागेव सन्धानमिवान्वतिष्ठन्।। *Ibid.*, II-18

11. अहरहर्नृपतेः पदपीठिकातटसमुल्लिखितैरलिकस्थलैः।
पुनरिवार्पितभाग्यमयाक्षरै रजनि वैरमृचामवनीभुजाम्।। *Ibid.*, V-8

12. बाणा निरस्ता यवनेन तस्मिन्नपाङ्गपाता इव वीरलक्ष्मया।
कम्पेश्वरेणा प्यभिपारसीकं शराः कटाक्षा इव कालरात्रेः।। *Ibid.*, IX-29

13. स केरलप्राणमरुद्भुजङ्गान् वन्यावनीन्द्रद्रुमदाववन्हीन्।
अन्ध्रान्धकारक्षयतिग्मभासो बाणानमुंचद् यवने नरेन्द्र।। *Ibid.*, IX-30

14. क्षतानियान्यस्य शरैः शरीरे चकार वीरस्य तुरुष्कवीरः।
वितेनिरे तानि नखाङ्कशङ्कां जयश्रियो भोगसमुत्सुकायाः।। *Ibid.*, IX-31

15. स वंचयस्तत्तरवारिधारां धाराविशेष प्रवणौपवाह्यः।
अशातयत्तस्य शिरो निमेषादनेन कर्णाटकुलप्रदीपः।। *Ibid.*, IX-37

16. अज्ञातसेवोचितवाटुवाद तुरुष्कसाम्राज्यकृताभिषेकम्।
दिवौकसामप्यकृतप्रणामं भूमौ सुरत्राण शिरः पपात्।। *Ibid.*, IX-38

17. च्युताऽपि शीर्षे चलिताश्ववल्गानियन्त्रणव्यापृतवामपाणिम्।
प्रतिप्रहारप्रसृतान्यहस्तं वीरः कबन्धं द्विषतोभ्यनन्दीत्।। *Ibid.*, IX-39

18. यः शेष इव नागानां नगानां हिमवाहिनः।
दैत्यारिरिव देवानां प्रथमः पृथिवीभुजाम्।। *Ibid.*, I-27

19. विवेकमेव सचिवं धनुरेव वरूथिनीम्।
बाहुमेव रणोत्साहं यः सहाययमन्यत्।। *Ibid.*, I-29

20. जिष्णुना भुवनेशेन श्रीदेन समवर्तिना।
सान्निध्यं लोकपालानां धरणौ येन दर्शितम्।। *Ibid.*, I-30

21. अयोगो विप्रयोगश्च संभोगश्चेति सा त्रिधा। *Daśarūpaka* IV-50

22. अभिलाषश्चिन्ता स्मृति-गुणकथनोद्वेग-सम्प्रलाश्च।
उन्मादोऽथ व्याधिर्जडतामृतिरिति दशाऽत्र कामदशाः।। *Sāhityadarpaṇa* III-218

23. प्रणयिनि सलिलापवारितेन स्पृशति करेण सलीलमूरुमूलम्।
प्रकटितशफराभिघातभीतिर्मिषति जनेप्यमुमालिलिङ्ग काचित्।। *MV*. VI-58

24. विषदनखपदं वपुः सपत्न्याश्चिरामिव पश्यति निनिमेषमस्मिन्।
व्यधित विहृतिवैतवेन काचित् प्रहितजला परिमीलिताक्षमेनम्।। *Ibid.*, VI-6

25. अवनिपतिरसिक्ता दीर्घिकायां मुखकमलं सलिलेन साभिलाषम्।
किमपि सधिकार्द्रपक्ष्मलेखं वदनमभूदरूणेक्षणं परस्याः।। *Ibid.*, VI-57

26. अपि दयिततमेन वारिताभिर्गृहसरसो विजहे न वारिताभिः।
परिलुलितललामचर्चिकाभिर्विहृतिरसान्महिलामचर्चिकाभिः।। *Ibid.*, VI-65

27. सरचन्दनधारिषु मौक्तिकत्रिसरनिर्झरहारिषु सुभ्रुवाम्।
कुचतटेषु निधागनिपीडितो धृतिमधात् कुसुमायुध कुंजरः।। *Ibid.*, V-19

28. सुतनवः फलवेषु मधूत्सवे रतिपतिं पतिलेखितुमुद्यताः।
हृदयगोचरतामनिशं गतं हरिहरात्मजमेव समालिखन्।। *Ibid.*, V-71

29. नववधू परिरम्भणदोहलान्यनुपदं निनदैः प्रतिपादयन्।
अलभत क्षणदासु घनागमो नरपतेः किल नर्मसुहृत्पदम्।। *Ibid.*, V-37

30. प्रथमां हरितं प्रभाकरो विरहय्यात्मनि तापमाप यम्।
अपरामुपगम्य तं जहौ हृदयं कः खलु वेत्ति रागिणाम्।। *Ibid.*, VII-6

31. दिनवेषमपास्य यामिनी वपुषा कालनटस्य नृत्यतः।
ददृशे जगता पितृप्रसूर्दिवि नेपथ्यपटीव पाटला।। *Ibid.*, VII-19

32. अवपत्किमु कालकर्षकस्तिमिराम्भः कलुषे नभस्तले।
विमलामुडुबीचमण्डलीं नवचन्द्रातपसस्यसिद्धये।। *Ibid.*, VII-29

33. पारिरभ्य दृढं चिरागतः प्रथमाशासुदृशा निशापतिः।
श्लथयत्ययमंशुभिर्नखैस्तिमिरश्रेणिमयीं प्रवेणिकाम्।। *Ibid.*, VII-43

34. हरितं परिरभ्य वासवीं हरिणाङ्कः करपातलीलया।
स्पृशति प्रणयात् कुमुद्वतीं बत विश्वासपदं न कामिनः।। *Ibid.*, VII-47

35. अनुदर्शमनुप्रवेशस्तपनाच्छक्तिमवाप तापिनीम्।
नियतं हिमदीधितिर्यतः क्षमते तापयितुं वियोगिनः।। *Ibid.*, VII-49

36. मुखराणि पुरा मृदङ्गघोषैरभितो देवकुलानि यान्यभूवन्।
तुमुलानि भवन्ति फेरवाणां निनदैस्तानि भयङ्करैरिदानीम्।। *MV*. VIII-5

37. अतिलङ्घ्य चिरन्तनीं स्वसीमामपदेप्वर्पित जीवनप्रवृत्तिः।
मुहुरुत्पथगामिनी तुलुष्कानधुता ह्यनुकरोति सह्यकन्या।। *Ibid.*, VIII-6

38. सतताध्वरधूमसौरभैः प्राङ्निगमोद्घोषणवद्भिरग्रहारैः।
अधुनाजनि विस्रमांसगन्धैरधिकक्षीवतुलुष्कसिंहनादैः।। *Ibid.*, VIII-7

39. मधुरोपवनं निरीक्ष्य दूये बहुषः खण्डितनालिकेरषण्डम्।
परितो नृकरोटिकोटिहारप्रचलच्छूलपरम्परापरीतम्।। *Ibid.*, VIII-8

40. श्वयितानिलशोषिताधराणि श्लथशीर्णायतचूर्णकुन्तलानि।
बहुबाष्पपरिप्लुतेक्षणानि द्रमिडायां वदनानि वीक्ष्य दूये।। *Ibid.*, VIII

41. स्तनचन्दनपाण्डुताम्रपर्ण्यास्तरुणीनामभवत् पुरा यदम्भः।
तदसृग्भिरूपैति शोणिमानं निहतानामभितो गवां नृशंसैः।। *Ibid.*, VIII-28

42. *Kumārasambhavam* V. 65-73

43. *Naiṣadhīyacaritam* XVI. 48-112

44. उल्लङ्घ्योल्लङ्घ्य धावद्भिर्भीत्या भ्रशितमायुधम्।
प्रायः प्रथमसंन्यासे शपथः कैश्चिदाददे।। *Ibid.*, IV-63

45. हतानुकारिणः केचित् क्षिप्तौ निपतितास्ततः।
क्रोष्टुर्भयेन धावन्तः कर्णाटान् पर्यहासयन्।। *Ibid.*, IV-64

46. छायामेवात्मनः केचित् धावन्तो भीतिभाविताः।
अराति शङ्कया कष्टं दष्टाङ्गुलि ववन्दिरे।। *Ibid.*, IV-66

47. तौ निकुंचित पूर्वाङ्गौ निश्चलाक्षौ कृपाणिनौ।
उचितस्थानकावास्तां चित्रन्यस्तविवं क्षणम्।। *Ibid.*, IV-79

48. उल्लङ्घ्योल्लङ्घ्य धावद्भिर्भीत्या भ्रंशितमायुधम्।
प्रायः प्रथमसंन्यासे शपथः कैश्चिदाददे।। *Ibid.*, IV-63

49. हतानुकारिणः केचित् क्षिप्तौनिपतितास्ततः।
क्रोर्ष्टुभयेन धावन्तः कर्णाटान् पर्यहासयन्।। *Ibid.*, IV-64

50. विक्षेप्तुं विस्मृतैश्चर्मफलकैर्निमितप्लवाः।
मृषैव केचिदतरन् मृगतृष्णातरङ्गिणीः।। *Ibid.*, IV-65

51. शूरस्तथा प्राहृत मुद्गारेण शिरस्त्रवन्ति द्विषतां शिरासि।
यथा विनिर्यन्नयनानि तानि मङ्क्षुन्यमाङ्क्षुः स्वशरीर एव।। *Ibid.*, IX

52. जिघत्सयान्तः पंतगैः प्रविष्टैः प्रस्पन्दमानं कुपणं द्विपस्य।
समीपमासाद्य सजीवबुध्या व्यसुं सतृष्णोऽपि जहौ शृगालः।। *Ibid.*, IX

53. करेण कंचिद् पदयोर्गृहीत्वा क्षिप्तं दवीयो वियति द्विपेन्द्रः।
पतन्तमाच्छिन्नकृपाणयष्टिः प्रत्यैच्छुच्चैदर्शनद्वयेन।। *MV.* IX.9

54. कुन्तेन कश्चित् द्विषता विभिन्नस्तथैव सर्वंश्लेषममुष्य यातः।
भिन्दन्नुरस्तेन चमत्कृतोऽभूद् गुणेषु को मत्सरमादधाति।। *Ibid.*, IX

55. आस्त्रापगासु परितो निस्सृतासु सहस्रशः।
भटानां भल्लनिर्लूनैरम्भोजायितमाननैः।। *Ibid.*, IV-58

56. कृपाणकृतान् वेतण्डशुण्डादण्डनिवाभितः।
भुजङ्गशार्ङ्गिनो गृध्रा जगृहुर्भूभुजां भुजान्।। *Ibid.*, IV-59

57. वेतण्डशुण्डाहर्म्याग्रमास्थिताः सचमत्क्रियाम्।
आद्रियन्त कबन्धानां रक्तं नवतांचरस्त्रियः।। *Ibid.*, IV-60

58. क्षतजार्द्राः प्रवीराणां प्रेङ्खन्त्यः खड्गलेखिकाः।
जिघत्सतः कृतान्तस्य जिह्वा इव विरेजिरे।। *Ibid.*, IV-57

59. निशाचराः केचन कुंजराणां कुम्भस्थलान्निसृतमास्रपूरम्।
निष्ठ्युतमुक्तामणयः हर्षं चुचूषु रुत्पुष्करनालदण्डैः।। *Ibid.*, IX-6

60. कुम्भेषु भिन्दन् नृपतिद्विपेन्द्रान् मुक्ताफलैः शर्करिलान्तराभिः।
प्रावर्तयद् रक्ततरङ्गिणीभिः परश्शताः संयति ताम्रपर्णीः।। *Ibid.*, IX-1

Chapter-7

Gaṅgādevī's Scholarship

Gaṅgādevī being a gem of poetess, throws the light of her poetic genius (Śakti or *pratibhā*) throughout the Madhurāvijayaṁ. Besides, her proficiency (*nipuṇatā*) in different sciences and practice (*abhyāsa*) of the poetry under the guidance of poets and critics have been found as being the cause of the refinement of the Madhurāvijayaṁ. As Mammaṭa has stated the three requisite factors — Śakti, Nipuṇatā and Abhyāsa, constituting the basic ground of poetry,[1] the author, Gaṅgādevī has collectively displayed all these three, and made the composition of the Madhurāvijayaṁ significant. Gaṅgādevī no doubt all along the delineation of the theme of the Madhurāvijayaṁ generates a poetic delight in the hearts of Sahṛdayas. Moreover, her descriptions do not deviate from the common truth. It is through this excellent skill of interfusing the ideas in the Madhurāvijayaṁ, that Gaṅgādevī has won the admiration of all lovers of poetry.

Profuse materials pertaining to Gaṅgādevī's erudition in the various branches of knowledge, available in her celebrated work the Madhurāvijayaṁ. Gaṅgādevī's scholarship in different branches of learning like knowledge of the world, Dharmaśāstra, Vedas and philosophy, Purāṇas, Political Science, Kalāśāstra, Mantraśāstra, Physical Science, knowledge of warfare, ideals of kingship, poetic imagination, Music, Dance, Palmistry, Religion, Geography, Botany etc., may be exemplified in the following manner :

Knowledge of the World

Gaṅgādevī's close observation of the world points out happy harmony between Realism and Idealism. Her well-acquaintance with the world and different sciences makes the descriptions of the things or expressions of feelings and emotions charming with realistic thought. An element of her knowledge of the world can be witnessed as below.

Time was certainly the plough man, the stars were well-washed seeds of grain, the dark skies were fields rendered muddy, where in those seeds were sown by him in order to raise the crop of moon-light. Such was the fancy in the mind of all.[2]

This verse reflects here knowledge of Agriculture, that is, farmers first plough the field and make wet with the water, then well washed seeds are sown in muddy field, afterwards farmers take all care till they receive the fruit, therefrom. So too, in the verse above, the time has pervaded the moonlight in the dark and made the people happy.

Time	Plough man
Dark sky	Muddy field
Stars	Well washed seeds
Moonlight	Fruit

This description in a poetic style captures the hearts of readers.[3] So also there are many examples in the poetry, illustrations with similar view points are like:

The darkness began to set in, now obscuring trees, now the sky, now the regions, and it gave rise to various fancies such as: that they were tender leaves of tamāla with which the region decorated their ears, or that they were paste drawings on the face of the lady called night, or that they were smokes rising from the quenching of the sun's heated surface, or that they were black bees disguised as darkness filling the regions after leaving the closing lotuses, of the black water of the Jamunā rising up, tall as trees when disturbed by Śrī Kṛṣṇa people eyes suddenly lost their (power of seeing) it seemed as if the burning lamp of the sun was put out, and from the lamp pot of sky, lamp black being scattered all round.[4]

Horses with foaming mouths, and swift as wind, were seer bounding like waves in the army ocean.[5]

This description of animate object *i.e.*, horse appearing the wave in the army ocean, suggests Gaṅgādevi's knowledge animals of nature in various occasion.

Knowledge of the Dharmaśāstra

Gaṅgādevī's profound knowledge of Dharmaśāstras is also reflected in various contexts. Though her Mahākāvya abounds in sentiments like Sṛṅgāra, Vīra (Major sentiments) etc., her ideas as regards the ethical descipline are also presented through some events. For instance, after the birth of Kampaṇa, Bukka (the king) duly bathed and was clad in white silk. After doing this he gave immense riches as gifts to brāhmins with a delighted heart and he came to see the face of his son.[6] Through this description, the poetess has expressed her knowledge of ethics (Dharmaśāstra). It is laid down in the Dharmaśāstra, that soon after the birth of a son or daughter, its father should take holy bath. And after performing due rites in connection with birth, he has to give away the gifts to brāhmins. Then, he can see his offspring. This idea finds its expression even in the earlier treatises on ethics.[7]

Her ideas as regards the moral discipline are also presented through some events. Kampaṇa engaging himself in hunting, cleared the forest by killing hyenas, wounding buffaloes, scattering deer, and slaughtering wild boars. He also subdued rhinoceroses and caught hold of elephants.[8] Killing the elephants except in the case of battle, is prohibited according to the rules of battle.[9] That is why, Kampaṇa was found not killing them, but caught hold of elephants in course of his hunting. Besides, the purpose behind Kampaṇa's hunting is not self-enjoyment but to keep his subjects away from any danger from wild animals.[10] Thus, protecting the subjects from any type of obstacles is one of the moral disciplines for a king.

Knowledge of the Vedas and Philosophy

The reflection of her knowledge of the Vedas and philosophy may be seen in the second benedictory verse of the Madhurāvijayaṁ.[11] The wordings of the verse are quite philosophic. The phrase स्त्रीपुँसनिर्माणमातृकारूपधारिणौ "Who bear the form of the creator's model for making man and woman" reminds of Manu's statement speaking of creatorship of Lord Śiva: "The Lord having assumed Himself two forms within His body, one man and the other being woman, then created the world."[12] This idea finds its expression even in the works of earlier great poets like Kālidāsa.[13]

Secondly, these two forms of Him embody the effulgence of universal consciousness (चित्प्रकाशात्मकौ). This phrase suggests Brahman being self-effulgent. He surpasses all luminaries and He is the source of all luminaries. This line of philosophy is in consonance with the Śvetāśvatara statement. Further she has expressed her knowledge of Vedaśāstra and Philosophy in the description of the ideal king Bukka. Though impartial to all the three puruṣārthas — dharma, artha and kāma—the king who was the ideal of all virtuous people, had a special regard for dharma, even as Viṣṇu, the lord of all, has for Sattva, among his three *guṇas* Sattva, rajas and tamas.[14]

Erudition in the Purāṇas

We can trace her knowledge of Purāṇas in the description of the day and night. Due to night, the birds hid themselves in the trees. This is described in the following words:

"Taking a warning as it were, from the fall on one Khaga (the Sun, also a bird) because of his over-stepping Viṣṇupāda (the feet of Viṣṇu, also Sky), the other Khagas (birds) quietly hid themselves in their nests of trees."[15]

This description reminds us of the reference in the Brahmapurāṇa, which suggests Garuḍa's retaining its inherent power. Once Garuḍa attempted to eat Śeṣa's son, Maṇināga by name. But Lord Viṣṇu commanded him not to eat as he is a devotee of Lord Śiva. Yet, Garuḍa not obeying Viṣṇu's words, ate out Maṇināga. Viṣṇu got enraged at it and cursed him to be desisted from his inherent power. But, due to the favour of Śiva, Garuḍa became free from his sin after taking bath in the holy river Gautama and regained his inherent power."[16]

Further, she describes how darkness began to spread every where. This is described thus: Then darkness began to set in, now obscuring trees, now the sky, now the regions; and it gave rise to various fancies such as that they were tender leaves of tamāla, with which the regions decorated their ears; or that they were musk paste-drawings on the face of the lady called night or that they were smokes rising from the quenching of the suns heated surface or that they were black bees disguised as darkness filling the regions after leaving the closing lotuses, or the black waters of the Jamunā rising up tall as trees, when disturbed by Śrī Kṛṣṇa.[17]

This delineation of Jamunā's divertion from its course is emphatic from the Bhāgavata Purāṇa:[18] Balarāma summoned the Yamunā to come near Him so as to enable Him to sport in her water. Taking him to be intoxicated, the Yamunā however paid no heed to his command and did not come. As a result, Balarāma got enraged, and dragging the river with the point of his plough, said "O Sinful one, since you have disobeyed me and not come even though called, I shall make you taste the fruit of your waywardness. With the end of my plough, I shall split you into a hundred streams."

Scholarship of Political Science

Poetess Gaṅgādevī's knowledge of political science is also evident from the description of the compaign of Kampaṇa on Śambuvarāyas territory. According to Kāmandaka's Political Science, whenever the king was going to war, at that time, the Brāhmins should chant the Atharva Veda for his victory.[19] Gaṅgādevī is quite aware of this, and states the samething in her Madhurāvijayaṁ. When Kampaṇa starts the march on Śambuvarāya's territory, Brāhmins chanted the Atharva Veda and augmented the chances of his victory with their (hearty) blessings just as the sacrificial fire is made to glow by oblations sanctified by hymns. Gaṅgādevī also states that the king must know the चतुरोपाय of Administration. She also describes the unique qualities of Kampaṇa in the following words bringing out Gaṅgādevī's knowledge of Political Science.

"His process was recognised everywhere; his actions were always fruitful. He increased the scope of negotiation among other strategems in achieving his purpose. Highly intelligent and politic he was, there was something original in his statecraft, which showed that he was a real master.[20]

Scholarship of Kalāśāstra

Her knowledge of the Kalāśāstra is also revealed in some verses while describing the song of the seasons especially the description of the Hemanta (Winter season). She states that during that season the royal ladies, as they shivered in cold seemed to be in an uninterrupted state of low (passion), the hairs in their breasts always standing on end and their mouths always uttering murmuring sounds.[21] Again Gaṅgādevī describes very artistically the water sports of the Prince and how the water covered the whole bodies of the ladies. This she states in the following words:

"The sheet of water first touched the feet, then the thighs, then the cloth, then the waist and then the breasts of beautiful ladies as they slowly descended it."[22]

Scholarship of Mantraśāstra

Gaṅgādevī's scholarship of the Mantraśāstra is also displayed in some contexts. While she describes the song of the seasons, she reveals her knowledge of the Mantraśāstra. For instance, in the description of the rainy season, she states that during the rainy season, clouds (like a magician) sprinkled Ketaka dusts resembling holy ashes through winds as if with hands. The murmuring of thunder was like the uttering of hum. And all this was effective in exercising the evil-spirit of love-anger which sometimes possessed the ladies of the harem.[23] Further, we can also see her knowledge of Mantraśāstra in the description of the spring season. Due to the arrival of the spring season all the trees of the forest would get flowers and their leaf-dust is scattered everywhere. But Gaṅgādevī compares this phenomenon to a magician in the following words:

"The gentle southern breezes that blew scattering fragrant mango leaf-dust (the pollen of flowers) seemed like sorcerers sprinkling ashes to turn the mind of anger-ridden damsels that spurned their lovers."[24] This holds a mirror to the scholarship of Gaṅgādevī in regard, to Mantraśāstra.

Knowledge of Arts and Science

She has exhibited her knowledge of science in Madhurāvijayaṁ through some verses. For instance, metal should be burnt in a fire to get white shining silver. This is a scientific process. Gaṅgādevī describes this in the following words as applied to the phenomenon of moon-rise :

"The moon, the lord of miraculous herbs, practises alchemy, as it were by transforming the 'iron' called darkness into the 'silver' called moonlight by subjecting the former to a fire-process called Udayarāga (redness of dawn).[25]

In the discipline of literary criticism she says even the smallest flaw should not be found in a poetic work. She expresses this in the following words:

"Even as a single salt particle from an oystershell spoils

the liquid essence of black sandal, so too even the smallest flaw found in a poetic work renders it censurable."[26] Thus, these verses point to her knowledge of science.

Science of Warfare

Gaṅgādevī was fully acquainted with the science of warfare. In the description of battles she has exhibited her profound knowledge in this field. She has mentioned the three limbs of the army namely:

(1) Cavalary, (2) Elephants, and (3) Infantry.[27]

Besides these she has given a graphic picture of archery (*dhanuryuddha*) sword play (duel) and art of war etc.

Description of Archery

In canto four providing the details of the preparations of the march on Śambuvarāya's territory by Kampaṇa as also the battle that took place between the two, Gaṅgādevī has given a graphic description of archery in her unique poetic language as follows:

"Even like the fancied side-glances of the amorous Goddess of fight, the sharp pointed arrows let fly against one another by bow, men fell to the ground".[28] Further, she describes how the heads of the enemies fell on the ground. Heads severed by arrows resembled palmyra fruits as they fell down from the ramparts and caused an illusion of balls belonging to the deity of war (for playing with).[29] Continuing the description, she states that the hill with the houses lit up by the fire from the missiles of bowmen, looked like holding lamps in readiness for the happy ceremony of ārati to mark the auspicious victory of the king.[30] Like this throughout her work we find good many examples giving a vivid description of the fighting scenes which are testimony to Gaṅgādevī's sense of keen observation and her acquintance with the Science of Warfare."

Mastery on the Science of the Sword Play

In canto four again we can see Gaṅgādevī's mastery on

the Sciences of sword play (duelling). Here the poetess has described the duel between Kampaṇa and Śambuvarāya as follows:

"When they attacked each other with their swords they stood still for a moment. At this moment they were looking like a pictures on a piece of painting with the fore-part of their bodies bent and eyes fixed[31] and the blood stained sword blades waving in the hands of the heroic worriers appeared like the folling tongue of Yama, eager to make a meal of them."[32]

Arms and Ammunitions

Gaṅgādevī's knowledge of various arms and ammunitions is incomparable. In the course of descriptions and narrations she has given quite a few names of the weapons used by the Hindu soldiers. These were the swords, daggers, lances, and bows. There was one more known as Kṛpāṇa.[33]

Ideals of Kingship

In Bukka's advice to Kampaṇa, the poetess speaks of ideals of kingship. Some of these are mentioned below:

"The king should be pleasing in speech. His speech should be very effective. He should not use harsh words to the people or else he will lose his popularity.[34] The king must keep away from gambling.[35] She also mentions how the king should behave with others. The king should not inflict brutal punishment on people, because she says, 'that nobody should climb a tree and apply the axe to its roots.'[36] Then she states how the king should utilise the wealth. The king should not give the wealth to undeserving persons. If he does so, she says, it is like throwing oblations that deserve to be used in holy sacrifices into the fire consuming a dead body.[37] Afterwards she says ignorance-ridden monarchs overcome by vices such as these vices, which like consumption, eat into the body politic become in course of time objects of contempt to their enemies.[38] She states that those fools that are not able to persue by their good qualities, wealth begotten by them on account of merit in previous birth are to be likened to monkeys in whose hands a garland of flowers has been given. The former, like the latter in their unbalanced state, know only to destroy what is given.[39]

Knowledge of Poetic Imagination

Gaṅgādevī's inherent knowledge is enriched with imaginative of poetic taste. Some poetic imaginations are as follows: The flowering of the 'Aśoka' tree, only when kicked by beautiful women, the Cātakas drinking water directly from the clouds, etc. The separation of the 'Cakravāka' birds suffices to mention here that the poetic imaginations have been used by the poetess effectively in her descriptions of the rainy season (*varṣā*). The water sports of the prince and charming body of Kumāra Kampaṇa etc., as a part of the Alaṅkāra likes Rūpaka, Utprekṣā, etc. For instance, she gives a description of the charming body of Kampaṇa, in the following words:

"The lions of the beautiful prince, hard as stone with their golden band, resembled the base of the añjanā hill encircled by a fresh streak of red coloured mineral.[40] One more instance may be read in the description of the song of the seasons. She describes the rainy season wherein thick clouds began to appear here and there, they looked like the sporting pavilions of women called lightnings and the thunder that was heard resembled the sounds of Mṛdaṅgas (drums)."[41] Further she describes the Water-sports of the prince in the following words:

"When Kampaṇa was going for water-sports, beautiful ladies followed him and their glances radiating blue, white and red hues, seemed to line the sky with blue lilies, white lilies and red lotuses.[42]

These descriptions trace to the poetic imaginative power of Gaṅgādevī.

Knowledge of Music

Gaṅgādevī had knowledge of music also. While describing the songs of the seasons, she refers to the musical instruments such as Vīṇā, Mṛdaṅga, etc. Even today, these are the most important and popular musical instruments. In describing the amours of the prince, Gaṅgādevī says that the ladies of the Court played on the Vīṇā with their slim fingers, singing songs that told his world-known acts of glory and the sweet notes of gamaka that wafted from the music made it most attractive.[43] Further Gaṅgādevī also refers to another musical instrument *i.e.*, Mṛdaṅga. In describing the winter season, she says, thick clouds began to appear here and there which looked like the sporting pavilions of women called lightnings and the thunder that was heard resembled the sounds of Mṛdaṅga (drums).[44]

In describing the preparations for the march on the Śambuvarāya territory she refers to musical instruments, known as Koṇa, ḍamaru etc. She described the sound of wardrums in the following words:

"Like the noise of the ocean, churned with the mountain of Mandāra, the sound of war drums beaten by drum-sticks arose at the beginning of the march.[45] Further, she says that the sound grew louder and louder, and filled the skies as if it emanated from Caṇḍīśa's ḍamaru (drum) beaten at the time of the Great Deluge.[46] These descriptions are an indication of the knowledge of music which Gaṅgādevī possessed."

Dance

In the Madhurāvijayaṁ we find some references to dance also. While describing the song of the seasons she states very often that ladies of his harem entertained the king with dancing perfect in every respect, beating time, making gestures and movements.[47] This shows that Gaṅgādevī did possess knowledge of dance also.

Knowledge in Varāhasaṁhitā and Palmistry

Gaṅgādevī had knowledge of Varāhasaṁhitā also. This is evident in the advise given by Bukka to Kampaṇa which is as follows:

"All that a gambler has fruitful earth, valuable ornaments, riches and even his own body, his strength, his wives and his sons — does not belong to him, but belongs to others."[48] Further, she says when the intoxication of youthhood is on, and when wealth is making one falter at every step, who could not think of, getting into the habit of drinking? It would be like getting a bad complication in typhoid fever.[49] In the description of the song of the seasons, we can find out her knowledge of palmistry. She states: "By reason of the rise of the brilliant Agastya, the waters were cleared of their muddy condition, and shone as clear as the minds of men that had received proper instruction from a merciful guru."[50]

Religious Knowledge

Gaṅgādevī reveals her acquaintance with all systems of Indian religion. In particular, she has mentioned the religious system of Śaivism in her work.

Her close acquaintance with Śaivism is reflected throughout her Mahākāvya. There is a definite reference to this effect. For instance, Lord Śiva is invoked in the opening verses of the Kāvya.[51] Besides the existence of the temple of Virūpākṣa in the suburb of Pampā,[52] she hints that Śiva is an adorable deity and Śaivism might have been the faith to which royal patronage was liberally extended.

Sacrifices

Performance of sacrifices on all auspicious occasions is frequently mentioned by Gaṅgādevī in her Kāvya.[53] Priests were the guides of kings and subjects in religious matters.[54] At the time of sacrifices, the atmosphere is said to have been pervaded by the sacrificial smoke and the Vedic mantras were chanted.[55] But with the approach of the Turskas, religion suffered a decline. With the conquest of Mohammedans by prince Kampaṇa, however things changed and the supremacy of the Hindu religion once again came to be established in this kingdom.

Performance of Saṅskāras

Gaṅgādevī was knowing very well how to perform the various saṁskāras. In particular she had a deep knowledge of Hindu saṁskāras like Puṁsavana, Jātakarma Caulakarma etc. These are ceremonies performed before the birth of a child, at the birth and in the grown up age respectively.[56]

Mythology

Gaṅgādevī was equally proficient in the mythological (Paurāṇic) literature, as such her Kāvya abounds in references to many paurāṇic myths. A close study of Madhurāvijayaṁ reveals her wonderful knowledge in the field of mythology. We came accross throughout her Kāvya numerous incidential and pointed references to various Hindu gods. That she was quite familiar with Hindu culture and literature is beyond any shadow of doubt. The following are a few such instances : Her work abounds in mythological references to Rāhu and Mārtaṇḍa (I-41), Kāmadeva (I-62), Śaṅkara and Pārvatī (I-73), moon and Rohiṇī (II-74), Śiva at the time of deluge (VIII-9), demons Madhu and Kaiṭabha (VII-12), Kaṁsa (VIII-29), and Vṛtra and Indra (IX-23). From the various Purāṇas these incidents have been picked up and introduced in the Kāvya (I-42, VI-5, VIII-35, IX-3, 22). Like this, Gaṅgādevī has referred to some popular mythological personages in the Madhurāvijayaṁ.

Geography

Gaṅgādevī's knowledge of Geography of this subcontinent is unquestionable. Her, familiarity with Indian Geography is clearly seen in her Kāvya, Madhurāvijayaṁ. We come accross references to various rivers, forests, cities etc., in her work.

1. Pampā

Pampā is identified with the present Hampī where we find the ruins of celebrated Vijayanagara empire. This was the branch city of Vijayanagara (I-66).

The kings and the chiefs living in the land bounded by the Vindhya Mountains on South by the Udayācala on the east and by the Astācala on west owed allegiance to Bukka I (I-71). This shows that Bukka I had an extensive territory under his rule. But it is to be decided as to what is represented by the terms Udayācla and Astācala. By Udayācala is meant the mountain five miles east of Bhuvaneśvara in Orissa.[57] By Astācala we may take the Western Ghats of the peninsular of the South. Moreover, the Malaya Mountain represents the Southern part of the Western Ghats, south at the river Kāverī, called the Travancore hills (II, IV-34).[58] *Vijayā* : (I- 43-75). It was the capital of Bukka and this appears to be an abbreviation for Vijayanagara. Tondīramaṇḍala[59] : It is known as Tondaimaṇḍalam. In is that portion of Dravida, of which the capital is Kāñchipuram. Pāṇḍya : (IV-32).[60] It is the ancient name of the modern districts of Tinneyelly and Madhurā.

2. Kaṇṭakānanapaṭṭana (Intro. p. 19)

It appears to be an exact rendering into Sanskrit of the vernacular form Malavayapattana. In the inscriptions it is known as Malvāyilu.

3. Viriñcinagara

It is nothing but the name of the same Viriñcipuram (Intro. p. 20)

4. Dramila (IV-51)[61]

It is most probable the same as Draviḍa country of the Pallavas on the east coast.

5. Marataka (V-I)[62]

It appears to be the modified form of *Ma-Yakatanagara*, the city of emeralds. Bates Hindee Dictionary and Platt's

Hindustani Dictionary give both Marakata and Marataka. The form Marataka appears in the Raṅganātha inscription of Sundarapāṇḍya (V-1). It was the new capital of Kampaṇa after the subjugation of Kāñcī.

6. Sevana (V)[63]

The regions that comprised by Nasik and Daulatabad are known as Sevana.

7. Siṁhaḷa (V)

It is understood to be the territory of Ceylon, now known as Sri Lanka.

8. Vyāghrapura (VIII-1)

The city inhabited by the Turuskas has been identified with modern Chidambaram (Intro. p. 10).

9. Madhurā (VIII-8)[64]

It is the name of Madhurai. It was regarded as the second capital of Pāṇḍyas on the river Vaigai, in the province of Madras (the present Tamil Nadu). It is said to have been founded by Kulaśekhara. It was called as Dakṣiṇa Mathurā.

10. Āndhra (IX-30)[65]

It is the country between the Godavari and the Krishna including the district of Krishna. Others regard Telingana the south of Hyderabad as the Āndhra territory.

11. Kṣīrataraṅgiṇī (Intro. p. 20)

It is identified with the river Palar.

12. Sahyakanyā (VIII-6)[66]

It is known as Kāverī. It is the river in a Southern India which rises from the spring called Candratīrtha in the Brahmagiri Mountain in Coorg. It is now known as Koḍagu.[67]

Prosody

Gaṅgādevī was well-versed in the science of Chands.

It is evident from her Mahākāvya where she has used a variety of metres and exhibited her remarkable skill. Like other great poets, she has made use of these metres with ease. And each and every verse of the Madhurāvijayaṁ reveals that Gaṅgādevī has chosen such metres as are quite appropriate enough to the theme depicted.

A break up of the Kāvya metrewise is presented in the table :

Canto No.	Name of Metre
I	Anuṣṭup
II	Upajāti
III	Vaṁśastha
IV	Anuṣṭup
V	Drutavilambita
VI	Puṣpitāgra
VII	Viyoginī
VIII	Malabharini
IX	Upajāti

The concluding verses of the Cantos are composed in different metres such as Vasanta tilakā (I-15), Mālinī (II-42) Hariṇī (III-48), Śikhariṇī (VI-69) and Sārdūlavikrīḍita (IV-83).

Flora and Fauna

Gaṅgādevī was quite familiar with the plant kingdom also. A fascinating description of the botanical world can be found in Madhurāvijyam. To justify her profound knowledge, in this field, she has given the names of various flowers, plants, aquatic plants, creepers, shrubs and herbs plant trees etc., in the Madhurāvijayaṁ.

The following are a few such examples:

Flora: Bakulā (I-9), Mākanda (I-20), Nimba (I-20), Campaka (I-47) , Aśoka (I-48 , V-67) , Nāgakesara (I-47, V-66), Kesara (I 47, V-66), Karpūra (I-48), Kadalī (I-48),

Kamala (I-49), Cintāmaṇi (II-40), Pārijāta (I-49), Candana (V-15), Pātala (V-16), Śirīṣa (V-21), Mallikā (V-22), Nicula (V-24), Nipa (V-34), Mālatī (V-35), Ketaka (V-36), Japākusuma (V-50), Kunda (V-54), Kuṁkuma (V-55), Navalavanga (V-57), Lodra (V-58), Sahakāra (V-63), Navacampaka (V-65), Kuravaka (V-68), Kuvalaya (VI-4), Kumada (VI-4), Aravinda (VI-4), Tamāla (VII-23), and Nārikela (VIII-8).

Fauna : Gaṅgādevī is quite familiar with the zoological world too. We can find numerous reference, to wild beasts as well as domestic animals in her Kāvya. The following are a few such examples:

Kastūri-hariṇa (I-48), Siṁha (II-19), Kuñjara (II-19), Turaṁga (II-20, IX-5), Taraṣku (V-14), Sairibha (V-14), Raṅku (V-14), Śūkara (V-14), Khadgi (V-14), Safarā (VII-13), Ferava (VIII-5), Gaja (IX-5), and Śṛgāla (IX-7), etc. She has mentioned the names of various animals but has also described their nature, their activities etc. Further names of almost all kinds of birds are also mentioned by Gaṅgādevī in her Kāvya. For instance:

Kalahaṁśa (I-49), Maraca (I-63), Cātaka (V-24), Kokila (V-62), Cakravāka (VII-20) etc. The poetess, Gaṅgādevī in the course of her descriptions of these birds refers to their nature, activities and their voice quite perfectly. In short, Gaṅgādevī has displayed her innate skill in different sciences throughout the Madhurāvijayaṁ, in an inimitable but lucid style.

REFERENCES

1. शक्तिर्निपुणता लोकशास्त्रकाव्याद्यवेक्षणात्।
   काव्यज्ञशिक्षयाभ्यास इति हेतुस्तदुद्भवे।। *Kāvyaprakāśa* I-3
2. अवपत्किमु कालकर्षकस्तिमिराम्भः कलुषेनभस्तले।
   विमलामुडु बीजमण्डलीं नवचन्द्रातपसस्यसिद्धये।। *MV*. VII-29
3. उदियाय ततो दिगङ्गना श्रवणाकल्पतमालपल्लवः।
   रजनीमुखपत्रलेखिका रचनारङ्कुमदस्तमोऽङ्कुरः।। *Ibid.*, VIII-23

किमु धूमभरः प्रशाम्यतोद्युमणिग्रावगतस्य तेजसः।
प्रसारदिशस्तमोमिषात्किमु मीलत्कमलालिसंचयः।। *MV*. VII-24
हलिहेतिदलत्कलिदन्दजा लहरीकन्दलकालिमद्रुहः।
परितस्तरुरम्बरस्थलीं परितस्थूलतमास्तमोभरः।। *Ibid.*, VII-25
नयनानि जनस्य तत्क्षणान्निरुणद्धि स्म निरन्तरं तमः।
रविदीपभृताभ्र कर्परच्युतकालांजनपुंजमेचकम्।। *Ibid.*, VII-26

4. समीरणरयोदग्रा वल्गन्तः फेनिलैर्मुखैः।
तुरङ्गास्सैन्यजलधेस्तरङ्गा इव रेजिरे।। *Ibid.*, IV-10

5. स्नातस्ततो धौतदुकूलधारी वितीर्य भूरिद्रविणं द्विजेभ्यः।
महीपतिः पुत्रमुखं दिदृक्षुः प्राविक्षदन्तः पुरमात्तहर्षः।। *Ibid.*, II-24

6. जाते पुत्रे पितुः स्नानं सचेलं तु विधीयते इति।
दानमपि विहितमादित्य पुराणे........। Com. on the *Ibid.*, 1969, p. 115

7. ततो दद्यात्तुवर्णं च भूमिं गां तुरगं रथम्।
छत्रं छागं च मान्यं च शयनं चासनं राहम्।।
तिलपूर्णानि पात्राणि साहिरण्यानि चैव।
शक्षयित्वा तु पक्वान्नं द्विजश्चान्द्रायणं चरेत्।
सूतके तु सकुलयानां न दानो मनुरब्रवीत्।। *Dharmandhu-ch* V

8. हततरक्ष परिक्षतसैरभं मृदितरङ्कु निषूदितसूकरम्।
ग्लपितखड्गि गृहीतमतङ्गज वनमसौ मृगयासु मुहुर्व्यधात्। *MV*. V-14

9. लक्ष्मीकामो युद्धादन्यत्र करिवधं न कुर्यात्–चाक्षुष।
क्रूर मृगास्पदानि प्रजोपद्रवकराणि वनान्यटित्वाटित्वा।
तदुपद्रवेभ्यः स्वप्रजा मृगयाव्याजेन राजा ररक्षेति परमार्थः। Com. on the *MV*

10. स्रष्टुः स्त्रीपुंसनिर्माण मातृकारूप धारिणौ।
प्रपद्ये प्रतिबोधाय चित्प्रकाशात्मकौ शिवौ।। Com. on *MV*. I-2

11. द्विधाकृत्वात्मनो देहमर्धेन पुरुषोऽभवत्।
अर्धेन नारी तस्यां स विराजमासृव्यभुः।। *Manusmṛti* I-32

12. वागर्थाविव सम्पृक्तौ वागर्थ प्रतिपत्तये।
जगतः पितरौ वन्दे पार्वती परमेश्वरौ।। *RV*. I-1

13. रामोऽपि पुरुषार्थेषु स धर्म सम्मतस्सताम्।
बह्वमंस्तपुमानाद्यः सत्त्वं त्रिषु गुणेष्विव।। *MV*. I-69

14. खगमेकमवेक्ष्य तादृशं पतितं विष्णुपदातिलङ्घनात्।
निभृतं चकिता इवाखिलास्तस्त्र नीडेषु विलिल्यिरे खगाः।। *Ibid.*, VII-6

15. पुरा कदाचित् गरुत्मान् मणिनाग इति नागकुमारं शेषतनयं भक्षितुं प्रवृत्तः। स च शिवभक्त इति शिवसदिष्टो हरिर्न तं भक्ष इति गरूडमनुशशास। एवं अनुशिष्टोऽपि भगवता वैनतेयस्तदाज्ञां तृणाय मत्वा अत्र अनुसन्धेया।। *Ibid.*, Com., p. 422

16. हेलिहेतिकलत्कलिन्दजा लहरीकन्दलकालिमद्रुहः।
परितस्तरुरम्बर स्थलीं परितः स्थूलतमास्तमोभराः।। *Ibid.*, VII-25

17. स आजुहाव यमुना जलक्रीडार्थमीश्वरः।
निजवाक्यमनादृत्य मत्तं इत्यापगो बलः।।
अनागतां हलाग्रेण कुपितो विचकर्ष ह।
पापे त्वं मामवज्ञाय यन्नायासि मयाहुता।।
नेष्ये तां लाङ्गलाग्रेण शतधा कामरूपिणीम्।। *Bhāgavata Purāṇa*, 10.65.23-24

18. त्रय्यां च दण्डनीत्यां च कुशलस्यात् पुरोहितिः।
अथर्वविहितं कुर्यान्नित्यं शान्तिक पौष्टिकम्।।

19. अथर्ववेदिनो विप्रास्तं विशेषैः ज्याशिषाम्।
अवर्धयन्मन्त्रपूतै र्हविर्भिरिव पावकम्।। *MV.* IV-19

20. पतित शक्तिरवाप्लफलोदयः प्रगुणयन् पणबन्धमुखान् गुणान्।
निपुणधीर्निरुपायमुपायदित्प्रभुरभुङ्क्त नवां नयसम्प्रदम्।। *Ibid.*, V-3

21. पुलककंचुकितैः कुचमण्डलैः स्फुरतसीत्कृतिभिश्च मुखेन्दुभिः।
अविरतं स्मरतन्त्रमिवान्वभूदवनिपलविलासवतीजनः।। *Ibid.*, V-60

22. द्विगुणयन्नधवृणवेदनां कुतकचग्रहणैः परिचुम्बनैः।
कपठरोषकषयितलोचनं निभृतहासमवेक्ष्यत यौवनैः।। *Ibid.*, V-33

23. करतलैरिव गन्धवहैधनाः प्रहितकैकपांसुविभूतयः।
स्तनितहुंकृतिभिर्निरकासयन् नृपतियौवनमानमहाग्रहम्।। *Ibid.*, V-33

24. मधु सुगन्धि रजः सहकारजं मलयशैलसमीरणमान्त्रिकाः।
प्रणयरोषपराङ्मुखमानिनीहृदयसंवननार्थमिवाकिरन्।। *Ibid.*, V-63

25. अलिनीलमयस्तमोमयं प्रविलाप्योदयरागवन्हिना।
कलयत्ययमोषधीश्वरः कलधौतं शुचि कौमुदीमिषाम्।। *Ibid.*, V-45

26. प्रबन्धमीषन् मात्रोऽपि दोषो नयति दूष्यताम्।
कालाग्ररुद्रवभरं शुक्तिक्षारकणो यथा।। *Ibid.*, V-18

27. आबद्धकुथमातङ्गमात्तपर्याणसैन्धवम्।
संवर्मितभढ सद्यः समनह्यत तद् बलम्।। *Ibid.*, IV-7
विशंकटकटाघाटविगलन्मदनिर्झराः।
परश्शतं जधटिरे विकटाः करिणां घटाः।। *Ibid.*, IV-8
समीरणरयोदग्रा वल्गन्तः फेनिलैर्मुखैः।
तुरङ्गः सैन्यजलधेस्तरङ्गा इव रेजिरे।। *MV.* IV-9
कृपाणकर्पणप्राप्तकुन्तकोदण्डपाणयः।
समगच्छत सहसा नैकदेश्याः पदातयः।। *Ibid.*, IV-10
क्रोधे न योधाः फलकेन केचित्प्रत्यर्थिना वंचितबाणवर्षाः।

अलक्षयपातं युगपत्कृपाणैः कृत्ताखिलाङ्गांस्तुरङ्गान कुर्वन्।। *MV*. IX-1

आसंजिताकङ्कमुखैर्विमुच्य योधाङ्गलानां भुवनेषु पङ्क्तिः।
आराच्चरन्त्या विरराज मृत्योरुत्तम्भिता तोरणमालिकेव।। *Ibid.*, IX-2

कृत्ताश्शशाङ्कार्धमुखैः पृषत्कैर्धनुष्मतां हास्तिक हस्तकाण्डाः।
रक्तह्रदेषु न्यपतन् भुजङ्गाः पारिक्षितस्येव मखानलेषु।। *Ibid.*, IX-3

मुक्ताफलैर्वीरकृपाणलेखा विभिन्नगन्धद्विपकुम्भ मुक्तैः।
रक्तारुणैस्तत्क्षणघट्टनोत्थस्फुलिङ्गसंघातमतिर्वितेन।। *Ibid.*, IX-4

28. सङ्ग्राम देवतापाङ्गविभ्रमभ्रान्तिदायिनः।
मिथो धनुर्धरैर्मुक्ताः पेतुः शातमुखाः शराः।। *Ibid.*, IV-56

29. भ्रश्यत्तालफलाकारैः प्रकाराद् बाणपातितैः।
रणश्रीकन्दुकभ्रान्तिर्विदधे वीरमूर्धभिः।। *Ibid.*, IV-71

30. धातुष्कमुक्तबाणाग्निज्वलितोर्ध्वगृहावलिः।
विजयारात्रिकं तस्य मूर्ध्नेवाद्रिरधारयत्।। *Ibid.*, IV-73

31. तौ निकुंचित पूर्वाङ्गौ निश्चलाक्षौ कृपाणिनौ।
उचितस्थानकावास्तां चित्रन्यस्ताविव क्षणम्।। *Ibid.*, IV-9

32. क्षतजार्द्राः प्रवीराणां प्रेङ्खन्त्यः खड्गलेखिकाः।
जिधत्सतः कृतान्तस्य जिह्वा इव विरेजिरे।। *Ibid.*, IV-57

33. कृपाणकर्पणप्रास कुन्तकोदण्डपाणयः।
समगच्छन्त सहसा नैवदेशः पदातयः।। *Ibid.*, IV-9

34. हितानि कुर्वन्नापि नानुरूवतये जनस्य जल्पन् परुषं रूषा नृपः।
पयांसि वर्षन्नपि किं न भीषणः कठोरविस्फूर्जथुगर्जितो घनः।। *Ibid.*, III-31

35. फलोत्तरा भूमिरनत्ययं बलं महार्हरत्नाभरणं च सम्पदः।
किमन्यदात्मा च कलत्रपुत्रकैः परार्थमेव ध्रुवमक्षदेविनः।। *Ibid.*, III-28

36. दुनोति दण्डेन दुरुत्सहेन यः प्रसह्य राष्ट्रं पदमात्मसम्पदाम्।
स वृक्ष मारुह्य कुठारपातनं करोति मूलोदलनाय दुर्मतिः।। *Ibid.*, III-32

37. मदादपात्रेषु ददाति मन्दधीर्धनानि धर्मादिकसाधनानि यः।
निपात्यते तेन मखक्रियोचितं हविश्चितासद्मनि कृष्णवर्त्मनि।। *Ibid.*, III-33

38. अर्थैभिरैश्वर्यशरारयक्ष्मभिर्हताखिलाङ्गैर्व्यसनैरूपद्रुताः।
तमः पराभूतनिजौजसो नृपाः प्रयान्ति कालाद् द्विषतामुपेक्ष्यताम्।। *Ibid.*, III-3

उपेयुर्षी पुण्यवशेन सम्पदं गुणानुरोधादुपभोक्तुमक्षमाः।
स्वचापलेन श्लथयन्ति दुर्धियो वलीमुखाः पुण्यमयीमिव स्रजम्।। *Ibid.*, III-35

39. शुभाकृतेस्तस्य सुवर्णमेखलं कटिस्थलं स्थूलशिलाविशङ्कटम्।
व्यडमबयन्नूतनधातुपट्टिऽम्का परिष्कृतामंजनभूभृतस्तटीम्।। *Ibid.*, III-8

40. ततो इतोविहरत्तटदङ्गनाललितलास्य हरिन्मणिमण्डपैः।
पटुमृदङ्गरवोपमगजितैर्निबिडमाविरभूयत वारिदैः।। *MV.* V-25

41. विविधविलसितैविलासिनीनामसितसितारुणकान्तिभिः कटाक्षैः।
कुवलयकुमुदारविन्दमालाखचितमिवामलमम्बरं बभासे।। *Ibid.*, VI-4

42. अवैक्षत क्षामशरीरयष्टेः कुमारमुत्सङ्गतं स देव्या।
शरत्कृशाय इव दैवलिन्यास्तरङ्गलग्न कलहंसशाबम्।। *Ibid.*, V-25

43. तरलिताङ्गुलिताडितवल्लकीनिरततानिरन्तरितैः स्वरैः।
जगुरमुष्य जगत्प्रथितं यशोगमकभङ्गितरङ्गितमङ्गनाः।। *Ibid.*, V-12

44. अथ मन्दरसंघ दटक्षोभिताम्भोधिमण्डलम्।
रराण कोणाभिहतो रणनिर्याणदुन्दुभिः।। *Ibid.*, IV-3

45. कल्पान्तोद् भ्रान्तचण्डीशडमरुध्वानडामरः।
उदजृम्भत गम्भीरो वियदध्वनि तद् ध्वनिः।। *Ibid.*, IV-4

46. उचिततालमुदचितविभ्रम चतुरचारिचमत्कृतसौष्टवम्।
मुहुरसाववरोधमृगीदृशा मुखरसोज्ज्वलमैक्षास नर्तनम्।। *Ibid.*, V-13

47. फलोत्तरा भूमिरनत्ययं बलं महार्हरत्नाभरणं च सम्पदः।
किमन्यदात्मा च कलपुत्रकैः परार्थमेव ध्रुवमक्षदेविनः।। *Ibid.*, III-28

48. समग्रतारुण्यमदास्य सम्पदा स्खलद्गतेर्यन्मदिरानिषेवणम्।
स एषदोषत्रयजे महाज्वरे ग्रहाभिभूतस्य भुजङ्गनिग्रहः।। *Ibid.*, III-30

49. कलशजस्य मुनेरुद्रयाज्जहुः कलुषतां सलिलानि महौजसा।
सदुपदेशवशादिवशासितुस्तनुर्भृता हृदयानि दयानि दयानिधे।। *Ibid.*, V-41

50. स्रष्टुः स्त्रीपुंसनिर्माणमातृकारूपधारिणौ।
प्रपथे प्रतिबोधाय चित्प्रकाशात्मनौ शिवौ।। *Ibid.*, I-2

51. यच्छाखानगरीं पम्पामनेकधनदाश्रिताम्।
अधितिष्ठन् विरूपाक्षो न स्मरत्यलकापुरीम्।। *Ibid.*, I-66

52. आगामिनीमध्वरहव्यसिद्धिं निश्चित्य देशेष्वपि दाक्षिणेषु।
प्रदक्षिणीर्भृत शिखाकलापो ननर्त हर्षादिव हव्यवाहनः।। *Ibid.*, II-17

53. ततःपरं तापहरः प्रजानां पुरोहितोक्तया पुरुहूतकल्पः।
व्यधत्त काले विभवानुरूपं पुंसां वरः पुंसवनक्रियां सः।। *Ibid.*, II-13

54. सतताध्वरधूमसौरभैः प्राङ्निरामोदधोषणवन्हिरग्रहारैः।
अधुनाज्जनि विस्रमांसगन्धै रधिकक्षोबतुलुष्कसिंहनादैः।। *Ibid.*, VIII
अथर्ववेदिनो विप्रास्तं विशेषैर्जयाशिषाम्।
अवर्धयन् मन्त्रपूतैर्हविर्भिरिव पावकम्।। *Ibid.*, IV-19

55. ततः परं तापहरः प्रजानां पुरोहितोक्त्या पुरुहूतकल्पः।
व्यधत्त काले विभवानुरूपं पुंसां वरः पुंसवनक्रियां सः।। *MV.* II-13
ततः प्रतीतेऽन्हि पुरोहितेन नरेन्द्रसूनुः कृतजातकर्मा।
समिद्धतेजाः समतामयासीन्मत्रप्रणीतेन मखानलेन।। *Ibid.*, II-33

56. N.L. Dey, *The Geographical Dictionary of Ancient and Medieval Names.* p. 208.

57. *Ibid.*, p. 122.

58. *Ibid.*, p. 205; *JASB* 1838, p. 449.

59. *Ibid., p.* 147.

60. *Ibid.*, p. 57; *BG* Vol. I pt. II p. 281.

61. *EI*, Vol. III; p. 40 fn 5.

62. D.C. Sircar, *Studeis in the Geography of Ancient and Medieval India.* p. 104.

63. N.L. Dey. *The Geographical Dictionary of Ancient and Medival Names,* p. 185.

64. *Ibid.*, p. 128.

65. N.L. Dey, *The Geograhical Dictionary of Ancient and Medival Names.* p. 7.

66. *Ibid.*, p. 171.

67. *Ibid.*, p. 97.

Chapter-8

Conclusion

The foregoing study of the Madhurāvijayaṁ makes it crystal clear that the poetess Gaṅgādevī narrates not only the story of the extension of the Vijayanagar rule into the Tamil country and the circumstances leading to it, but also fills it up all literary charm and grace with literary aspects. The threads of the various aspects developed in the preceding chapters may now be gathered together as a single synthetic whole. The method of the study of the Madhurāvijayaṁ consists in highlighting the historical and literary merits of the Kāvya. A high level of literary honesty and historical earnestenss is often brought out in the heroic deeds of Kampaṇa.

In the beginning of the work, in twenty-two verses, Gaṅgādevī, the foremost among the poetesses of secular classical literature, has paid homage to the real poets, discarded pretenders, Telugu poets like Tikkana etc., and she has explained the features and the characteristics of a classical epic. In fact, no poet or poetess has dealt with the introduction to a work in such a sweet and dignified way.

A general survey of the Classical Sanskrit literature makes it evident that the type of work either prose or poetry or Champū, has not been artistically fullfledged. Some defects in one or the other part may be there, therefore deformed. So, the poetess Gaṅgādevī has indicated at the commencement of the Madhurāvijayaṁ, the elements of words, meaning, loftiness of thought, sentiments etc. Being a dignified poetess, Gaṅgādevī suggested her ideals through this Kāvya.

Gaṅgādevī has a special skill of admixing the historical facts with poetic traditional long descriptions: The poetess suggests lapse of time without specifying the disparity in age between Kampaṇa and his brothers. She indirectly makes it known by describing the boyhood of Kampaṇa as would fit in with the age of three years, and by referring to the birth of Kampaṇa's brother having taken place three years after. Moreover, long descriptions like that of seasons etc., lay down the interval of time between atleast two of his invasions. Such descriptions really add a new attraction to the Madhurāvijayaṁ, just as gold to a diamond in the ring.

The Madhurāvijayaṁ begins with the description of Bukkarāya. Though Hariharay was the king, Bukka is mentioned as the younger brother of Harihara and as having built the kingdom and named it Vijayanagar. Bukkarāya's being Kṣatriya has been described in the first canto of the Madhurāvijayṁ. The royal honours received by Kampaṇa when he started invading the territory of Sambuvarāyas etc., directly indicate that he was the Yuvarāja or the Prince designate.

The Madhurāvijayaṁ has been a lively proof of the historical facts relating to the ancestors and the descendants of the Saṅgama dynasty. At the outset, this epic poem describes that Bukkarāya, the most renowned of all the kings of his race, held sway over Vijayanagar for a very longer period. History undoubtedly supports this point.

This Kāvya makes another note that, the kings of Vijayanagar had followed the custom of having more than one wife, and the children of the first wife alone were entitled to inherit the kingship. Both Bukka and Kampaṇa are so described. Also it is suggested in the poem that Kampaṇa, whom historians refer to as Kumāra Kampaṇadu, was functioning as Yuvarāja even during the life-time of Bukkarāya. Bukkarāya had, no doubt fast affection for Kampaṇa (II-35, III-43 and 36). Even before the invasion, the Madhurāvijayam indicates, Kampaṇa had subdued several enemies and earned repute as a great warrior (III-16, 20).

Kampaṇa was a patron of music and arts (V-13, VII-40). He is described as the conquerer of the kingdoms of Cola, Pāṇḍya, and Kerala (IX-30), a great benefactor engaged in fulfilling the needs of his subjects (II-18), excelled in statecraft (V-3, 4) , considerate in collecting the taxes from his people etc. All this description of Kampaṇa bear close resemblance to the history of Harihararāya II, which runs as follows:

"After Bukkarāya, his son Harihararāya begotten by his wife Gaurambikā, became king. He was very fortunate. He ruled for 27 years with great pomp. From the various inscriptions of his time, it is evident that his empire extended greatly in various places of Mysore, Dharwad, Kanchi, Chengalpat Tiruchinapalli, etc., and so he gave up the titles of Maṇḍaleśvara 'Vadayar' possessed by his prior dependant kings and assumed the titles of 'Mahārājadhirāja', Rājaparameśvara, by which it is to be inferred that he had overlordship over several other kings of his time, and that Vijayanagar had therefore acquired all the splendour and magnitude of an empire. That the Muslims were completely humiliated and subdued by his commanders during his time is also borne out by the inscriptions. Like his father he had the assistance of able and efficient ministers. Of them, Sāyaṇācārya, brother of Mādhavācārya was the foremost a gowda brāhmin, Mādhava Mantri was the second and Muddappa was the third. There is a doubt that this Muddappa was the youngest brother of Harihara Rāya I. There are two inscriptions about Muddappa. In the one at Siddhārthī of 1379 A.D., it is written that Harihararāya got from his father along with the kingdom the reputed minister Muddappa and the latter with his statecraft and diplomacy, imprisoned his enemy kings and even as Rāma obtained Sumantra from his father Daśaratha, so secured minister Muddana from his father, rested all the responsibility of administration on his shoulders and happily be seated himself on the throne like Śrī Mahā Viṣṇu."

Moreover, it is known from the fourth canto of the Madhurāvijayaṁ that Kampaṇa marched against the Śambuvarāya chieftain of Paḍaividu in Tondaimandalam, and defeated him in the battle. It is also concluded that, of the great Śambuvarāya rulers, Venrumankonda Śambuvarāya and his son Rājanārāyaṇa Śambuvarāya, the latter came in combat with Kampaṇa, and was defeated. And this conquest took place between October and December A.D. 1362 approximately.

So also, on the basis of numismatic evidence. Fakruddin Mubrak Shah was the Sultan, defeated by Kampaṇa in A.D. 1371.

These are the points made clear in the second chapter dealing with the History in the Madhurāvijayaṁ.

Since the Madhurāvijayaṁ is of the "Prabandha" type, much importance is given to the narration to keep up the incesscent flow of the story. The narration in fact, has successfully served as a connecting link between what precedes it and what follows it. Bukka's exhortation to Kampaṇa, Kampaṇa's orderly march on the Śambuvarāya territory, Madhurā goddess's speech on the atrocities of the Muslims and her imploring Kampaṇa to save Madhura from them, Kampaṇa's final battle with the Turuṣka king etc., have been explained in detail as they are the main incidents of the Kāvya. It is found, Gaṅgādevī closely follows Vālmīki in the art of narration.

Besides the narration of incidents, Gaṅgādevī essentially brings in the description of city, seasons, water-sport, pleasure-garden, moon-rise, sun-rise, in a grand and charming style. She has given much scope for description in the Madhurāvijayaṁ, so that more number of verses have been devoted to the descriptions than to the narration. This infact, indicates poetess's fondness for description. For the convenience of study and appreciation, the descriptive part runs under three heads: Description of the Nature; Description of the personal beauty and Description of miscellaneous items. A study of these descriptions makes it clear that poetess is no strictly conventional. She has flashes of originality in presenting different objects. Gaṅgādevī's descriptions are perfectly set with original refreshing images of the beauty in nature and the beauty in human life.

The richness of these descriptions is elevated due to the apt use of figures of speech. Gaṅgādevī has made use of more than forty Alaṅkāra. Of these, Utprekṣā, Rūpaka, Upamā Kāvyaliṅga, Bhrāntimān, Atiśayokti, Apahnuti, Vyatireka, Virodhābhāsa have been used frequently. Poetess has used these many Alaṅkāras to increase the beauty of the Kāvya. It is not the centre of her concentration. She is not head-strong in their use. With Gaṅgādevī, the use of Alaṅkāras, is only a means to bring additional charm to the poem. Thus, it is evident Gaṅgādevī is equally well-versed in the science of Rhetorics.

The Madhurāvijayaṁ, in its explanation of events, creates delight through the delineation of Rasa. The poetess has followed the literary tradition of Aśvaghoṣa, Kālidāsa etc., in the delineation of Rasa. The Vīra Rasa has beer regarded as the Principal Rasa of the poem. Other rasas like Śṛṅgāra, Hāsya, Karuṇa, Adbhuta, Raudra have been delineated as subordinate Rasas in the constituent parts of the poem. In all, the eight Rasas have been properly and effectively developed. This speaks of poetess's ability in delineating the Rasas.

A close observation of all these points, shows the light of poetess's poetic genius. Besides, Gaṅgadevī's proficiency in different branches of learning, like, Dharmaśāstra, Kalāśāstra, Mantraśāstra, Rājanītiśāstra, Saṅgītaśāstra-Nṛtyaśāstra, Yuddhaśāstra, Chandas-śāstra, makes it amply clear that she combines in herself a remarkable skill in different sciences.

Almost, the Vaidarbhī style has been employed by Gaṅgādevī, which in fact has made her achieve a great height of artistic excellence in the Mahākāvya. The Madhurāvijayaṁ has the inherence of certain excellences or *guṇas* like Prasāda Śleṣa, Samatā, Samādhi, Mādhūrya, Saukumārya Arthavyakti, and Aujjvalya. These excellences have been regarded as the special features of Vaidarbhī style. A few examples may be given below, illustrating these types of excellences :

Prasāda	:	I-13, 71; 72; VI-2, 7
Śleṣa	:	II-23; VI-43; I-39; VIII-21
Samatā	:	III-38; I-54; V-62; II-12, I-71
Samādhi	:	Ślokas of V and VI cantos
Mādhurya	:	V-41; VI-1, VIII-16
Saukumārya	:	II-32, V-45, 73, VI-2, VIII-16
Arthavyakti	:	III-37; V-43, 61; VI-8
Aujjvalya	:	II-11, 12; IV-57, 58; VI-2; VIII-2

All these excellences have been focussed for the delineation of Rasa more effectively. In this manner, the style, excellences, and sentiments are unique with Gaṅgādevī. Though simple in style, this poetry is deep and dignified in thought.

In short, Gaṅgādevī's descriptions do not deviate from the common truth. Her flow of thought is with ease and simplicity. Her words and ideas are apt and happy. The soft and melodious syllables find place in her style to keep step with the richness of sense. Besides, all these merits, the Madhurāvijayaṁ has gained much popularity now-a-days, as it throws sufficient light on the history of the times. It is through this excellent skill of interfusing the ideas in the Madhurāvijayaṁ, that Gaṅgādevī has won the admiration of all lovers of poetry.

Bibliography

WORKS IN SANSKRIT AND ENGLISH

Ānandavardhana

Dhvanyāloka (Sanskrit Text), Chaukhamba Sanskrit Series Office Varanasi, 1962.

Antoni, B.S.

A Study of Alaṅkāras in Sanskrit Mahākāvyas and Khaṇḍa Kāvyas. Bhāratiya Vidyā Prakashan, Jawaharnagar, Delhi, 1977.

Appayya Dīkṣita

Kuvalayānanda, Nirnaya Sagar Press, Bombay, 1917.

Arnold (Edwin)

Indian Poetry. (A New Edn. of the Indian Song of Songs). London Trubner, 1881.

Bāṇa

Kādambarī (Text and Translation) by R.D. Karmakar. Aryabhushan Press, Poona, 1962.

Bak Kun Bae

Śrīharṣa's Plays. Indian Council for Cultural Relations, Asia Publishing House, Delhi, 1961.

Bhāravi

Kirātārjunīyaṁ (Text). Nirnayasagar Press, Bombay, 1954.

Bhattacharya, S.

The Kāvyamīmāṁsā of Rajaśekhara. P-II, Govt. of West Bengal, 1961.

Daṇḍin

Kāvyādarśa. Madras University, Madras, 1952.

De, S.K.

History of Sanskrit Poetics, Calcutta Oriental Press, Calcutta, 1960.

De, S.K., Hazre, R.C.

Sāhityaratnakośa Vol. 2, Puraṇaitihāsa Saṅgraha (Antology of the Epics and Purāṇas) Sahitya Akademy, New Delhi, 1959.

Dharmasūri

Sāhityadarpaṇa. Sanskrit Academy, Osmania University, Hyderabad, 1972.

Gajendragadkar, A.B.

Abhijñāna Śākuntalam. Popular Book Depot., Surat, 1951.

Gopal Panick

Bharatanāṭyadarśanam, Govt. of India, 1981.

Handique, K.K.

Naiṣadhacaritaṁ of Śrīharṣa. S.M. Katre Deccan College. Postgraduate and Research Institute, Poona, 1956.

Harichandra Sharma

Kāvyaprakāsa. Oriental Book Agency, Poona, 1935.

Hemachandra Acharya

Kāvyānuśāsana. Jain Vidyalaya, Bombay, 1938.

Jalhana

Sūktimuktāvali. Ed. by Embar Krishnamacharya. Oriental Institute, Baroda, 1938.

Jwalaprasad Mishra

Kāmandakīya Nītiśāra. Srivenkateshwar Stream Press, Bombay, 1874.

Jatindra Bhimal Chowdari

Viddhasālabhajñjika of Rājaśekharā. The Calcutta Oriental Press, Calcutta, 1943.

Kane, P.V.

The History of Sanskrit Poets as *Introduction* to *Sāhityadarpaṇa*. Nirnayasagara Press, Bombay, 1951.

Kālidāsa

Kumārasambhava. Ed. by Suryakant with Introduction by Radhakrishna. Sahitya Akademy, Delhi, 1962. *Raghuvaṁśa I & II*. (Text Tran. by Rāmachandra Sukla) Rāmanarayan Lal, Beni Madhava, Allahabad, 1960.

Kalhaṇa

Rājataraṅgiṇī. Hindipracarika Samsthana, Varanasi, 1967. Part II, Vishweshwaranand Vedic Research Institute, Hoshiarpur, 1965.

Krishnamachariar, M.

History of Classical Sanskrit Literature. Tirumala, Tirupati, 1937.

Krishnamacharya, T.R.

Vālmīkī Rāmāyaṇa. Vol. I & II. Srisatguru Publications, Delhi, 1982.

Macodonell, A.A.

History of Sanskrit Literature. Munshiram Manoharalal, Delhi, 1955.

Manjul Gupta

A Study of Abhinavabhāratī on Bharata's Nāṭyaśāstra, and Avaloka on Dhanañjaya's Daśarūpaka–Dramatical Principles. Jain Publishing House, Shantinagar, Delhi, 1987.

Misra, Mohanalal

Śṛṅgārarasa. Balachandra Rao Telang, Padmakar Anusandhan Shesa, Aurangabad, 1974.

Pandit Haragovind Sastri

Manusmṛti. Chowkhamba Sanskrit Series Office, Varanasi, 1979.

Raghavan

Śṛṅgāraprakāśa. Srikrishnapuram Street, Madras, 1963.

Rājaśekhara

Kāvyamīmāṁsā, Gaikwad Oriental Series, Baroda, 1966.

Rāmakrishnakavi, M.

Nāṭyaśāstra of Bharatamuni. Oriental Institute, Baroda, 1956.

Rāmaswami, K.S.

Kālidāsa. Vanivilasa Press, Srinagar, 1960.

Rudraṭa

Kāvyālaṅkāra. A–Treatise on Rhetoric of Rudraṭa with Sanskrit Comm. of Namisadhu. Ed. with Prakash Hindi Comm. Varanasi, 1966.

Sastri, J.L.

Upaniṣad-Saṅgraha. Motilal Banarasidass, Delhi, 1980.

Sri Goswami Damodar Sastri

Kāmaśāstra of Vāstsyāyana. The Chowkhamba Sanskrit Series Office, Varanasi, 1929.

Swami Chidbhavanand

Bhagavadgītā. Sriramakrishna Tapovanam (Publication Section), Tirupparaitturi, 1982.

Sukla (Rāmachandra)

Rasamīmāṁsā. Ed. by Visvanathaprasadamisra. Nagari Prakasan Sabha, Kasi, 1954.

Tarlekar, G.H.

Studies in the Nāṭyaśāstra. Motilal Banarasidass, Delhi, 1975.

Tiwari, R.S.

Critical Approach to Classical Indian Poetics. Chowkhamba Oriental Publications. Varanasi, 1984.

Winternitz, M.

History of Indian Literature. Vol. 1 & 2. Motilal Banarasidass, Delhi, 1963.

Vishwanath

Sāhityadarpaṇam. Ed. by Kaviraj Shivadatta. Published by Khamaraj Krishnadeva - Venkateswar Press, Bombay, 1917.

Vāchaspati Upadhyaya

Dharmaśāstra Saṅgraha. Navarang, New Delhi, 1982.

Vallabhadeva

The Subhāṣitāvali. Ed. Peterson and Durgaprasada. Bhandarkar Institute Press, Poona, 1961.

HISTORICAL WORKS IN ENGLISH

Basavaraj, K.R.

History and Culture of Karnataka. Karnatak University, Dharwad, 1984.

Desai, P.B.

A History of Karnataka. Kannada Research Institute, Dharwad, 1970.

Krishnaswami Iyengar

Sources of Vijayanagar History. Madras, 1919. South India and Her Mohammadan Invaders. S. Chand & Co. (Pvt.) Ltd., New Delhi, 1921.

Krishnaswamg

Tamil Country under Vijayanagar. Annamalai University, 1964.

Mahalingam, T.V.

Administration and Social Life under Vijayanagar. Madras, 1940.

South Indian Polity. Madras, 1955.

Mugali, R.S.

The Heritage of Karnataka. Bangalore, 1946.

Nilakaṇṭaśāstrī

Historical Method in relation to Problems of South Indian History. Madras, 1941.

Saletore, B.A.

Social and Political Life in Vijayanagar Empire. 2 Vols. Madras, 1934.

Sathianathaier, R.

History of the Nāyakas of Madura. Madras, 1924.

Studies in the Ancient History of Tondaimandalam. Madras, 1944.

Srinivasa Sastri and Harihar Sastri

Madhurāvijayaṁ by Gaṅgādevī. Trivandrum, 1924.

Thiruvenkatachari, S.

Madhurāvijayaṁ of Gaṅgādevī. Ed. with a Historical Introduction, Annamalai nagar, 1957.

Tiruvenkatachari, S.

Kampaṇa as Viceroy of Vijayanagar. Proceedings of the Indian Historical Records Commission, 1945.

Venkataramayya

The Early Muslim Expansion in the Deccan and South India. Madras, 1942.

JOURNALS AND REPORTS

Journals

1. Quarterly Journal of the Andhra Historical Research Society, Vol. II, Part 3 & 4.
2. Quarterly Journal of the Mythic Society, Vol. 45, 1954-55.
3. Quarterly Journal of the Mythic Society. Vol. 25, 1934-35. Daily Memorial Hall, Nratung Road, Bangalore.
4. Quarterly Journal of Mythic Society. Vol. 71, 1980.
5. The Adyar Library Bulletin. A.L.C. Research Centre, Adyar, Madras.
6. The Journal of the Bihar & Orissa Research Society, Bihar, Orissa.
7. Journal of the Royal Asiatic Society. Queen Anee Street, London.

Reports

1. Annual Reports of South India Epigraphy. Madras 1887 to 1951 referred to as Madras Epigraphical Reports.
2. Mysore Archaeological Reports, Bangalore, 1924-27.
3. Epigraphica India. Vols. 1 to 29. Calcutta, 1892 to 1954. Studies in Chola History and Administration, Madras, 1932.

Index

Abheda 117
Abhijāta 154, 155, 158
Abhisārikas 43
Abhyāsa 163
Adbhuta 189
Adil Shah 36
Ādikavi 76
Ādiśeṣa 51
Agaru fumes 83
Agastya 14, 47, 71, 174
Agastya star 124
Agnipurāṇa 106
Agrahāras 19, 35
Airāvata 41
Aja 63, 66, 69, 93
Alaṅkāras 105, 106, 110, 122, 141, 143
Alakā 43, 91
Ālambana Vibhāva 157
Ālīḍha posture 61
Allauddin Sikhandar Shah 36
Amarāvatī 15, 89
Anantarangachar N. 14
Ānandavardhana 105, 106
Āndhras 58, 148
Angry lovers 82
Anuṣṭub Metre 22
Anuṣṭup 178
Anubhāvas 145
Anumāna 140
Anuprāsa 107
Apacchandasika metre 22
Apahnuti 24, 110, 134, 189
Aprastutaprasaṁsā 140
Apsarās 92
Aquatic sports 93
Arabian traveller Albereine 12
Aravinda 179
Ardhachandra 55
Arirāya 30
Arjuna 57
Artha 28, 105, 166
Arthaśleṣa 109
Arthālaṅkāra 107
Arthāntaranyāsa 110
Arthāpatti 140
Asaṅgati 140
Astācala 176
Atharva Veda 50
Atiśayokti 24, 109, 110, 115, 116, 129, 132, 133, 189
Añjanā hill 172
Aujjvalya 190
Aśoka 89, 178

Aśoka tree 77, 172
Autumn season (Śarad Ṛtu) 18, 81, 82, 124
Aśvaghoṣa, 144
Avantisundarī 1
Ayodhyā 42, 70

Bībhatsa Rasa 23, 157
Bībhatsa sentiment 158
Bṛhatkathā 74
Bāṇa 8, 14
Bakulā 178
Balarāma 167
Battle scence 70
Battle-field 66
Battle-scenes 94
Beautiful ladies 84
Beautiful lakes 76
Beautiful palaces 89
Bhībhatsa 24
Bhīma 57
Bhalla 66
Bharata 70, 144
Bhatti 88
Bhavabhūti 9, 14, 154
Bhaya 155
Bhayānaka 23, 156
Bhayānaka Rasa 155, 156
Bhāgavata Purāṇa 167
Bhāmaha 105, 106, 143, 144
Bhoja princess 63
Bhojacarita 9
Bhramaṁ 130
Bhāratī 2
Bhāravi 14, 40, 73
Bhrānti 129
Bhrāntimān 24, 110, 121, 129, 131, 132, 133, 189
Bhujaṅgas 90
Bilhaṇa 8
Blooming lotuses 76
Blossoming flowers 76
Botany 164
Bow-men 55
Brahmā 68
Brahmapurāṇa 167
Brāhmaṇas 120
Buddhi 117
Bukka 15, 87, 89, 108, 111, 127, 134, 136, 139, 149, 165
Bukkarāja 41, 42
Bukkarāya 17, 29, 186, 187

Caṇḍīśa's ḍamaru 125
Caṇḍīśa's ḍamaru (drum) 49
Cakora birds 121
Cakravāka 92, 172, 179
Cakravāka birds 90, 127
Cakrācala mountains 89
Campaka 89, 178
Camparāja 94
Candana 179
Candratīrtha 177
Carcikābhiḥ 109
Champū 186
Champū Bhārata 94
Champarāja 17, 155
Chandas-śāstra 189
Chikka Kampaṇa 31
Chirping birds 76
Chola and Pāṇḍya regions 7
Cintāmaṇi 16, 179
Classical Sanskrit literature 187
Clestial kettle-drums 80
Clouds violently 80
Cola (s) 46, 48, 50, 58, 95, 145, 187
Cold season (Śiśira Ṛtu) 18, 83
Cooing-cuckoos 76
Cātaka 179
Cātaka birds 79, 80

Dīlipa 40, 60, 71
Dṛṣṭānta 24, 140
Daṇḍin 3, 14, 105, 106, 144
Ḍamaru of Śiva 125

Dance 164
Dancing peacocks 129
Daśakumāracaritaṁ 3
Daśarathī 43
Daśaratha 41, 70, 188
Dayāvīra 145, 146
Deity of War 54
Delhi Emperor 6
Delhi Empire 4
Devāyī 15, 30, 40, 41, 111, 112, 122, 147
Dhīrodātta 21, 23
Dharma 23, 28, 31, 46, 87, 166
Dharmaluptopamā 125
Dharmaśāstra 164, 165, 189
Dharmaśāstras 165
Dharmavīra 145
Dharmavīratā 147
Dhirodātta 146
Dilīpa 41, 69
Dānavīra 145
Dramiḍa 17
Dramila 17
Dravida 17
Draviḍa country 176
Dravyotprekṣā 114, 115
Drutavilambita 178
Dvārakā 88

Eastern and Western oceans 30
Eastern Region 138, 152
Ekaśilānagara 2
Elephant warfare 93
Elephant-fight 65
Epics 29

Fakhruddin Mubrak Shah 36, 37
Ferava 179
Full bloomed pāṭala flowers 84

Gūḍhokti 140
Gaṇapati 14
Gaṅgā 11
Gaṅgādevī 2, 9, 10, 11, 12, 13, 14, 15, 16, 19, 21, 24, 31, 32, 40, 41, 42, 70, 71, 74, 75, 76, 77, 78, 79, 82, 85, 86, 87, 88, 90, 91, 93, 94, 96, 107, 108, 113, 117, 121, 123, 125, 126, 140, 141, 146, 150, 151, 152, 155, 156, 157, 158, 163, 169, 170, 173, 174, 175, 177, 178, 179, 186, 187, 188, 189, 190
Gaṅgādhara 13, 14
Gaja 179
Gamyotprekṣā 110
Gandaraguli Mārayya 33
Garbhalakṣaṇa 40, 41
Garuḍa 167
Gauḍa 17
Gaurambikā 187
Geography 164
God Gaṇapati 22
God of Love 66
God Virūpākṣa (Śiva) 91
God Śiva 46, 68
Goddess of fight 53
Goddess of Madhurā 152
Goddess of sky 80, 115
Goddess of Valour 50, 70
Goddess of Victory 49, 50, 58
Goddess Pārvatī 16, 124
Goddess Sarasvatī 14
Golden cymbals 131
Gopinath Rao 30
Gopinatha Rao T.A. 31
Guṇaparama maheśvara 8
Guṇas 143
Gurus 127

Harṣa 3
Harṣacaritaṁ 3
Hari Hara Rāya 7, 187
Harihara 186
Hemanta Ṛtu 82

Hetūtprekṣā 112
Hetumān 24
Himavān 87
Himālayas 5
Hindu chronicles 36
Hindu culture 8
Hindu gods 175
Hindu nāyakas 6
Hindu Religions 7, 8
Hindu society 11
Hindus 12
Historical evidence 9
Hoyisala 4
Hoyisala kingdom 5
Hāsya 144, 154, 189
Hāsyarasa 155
Humming bees 76

Indian scholars 12
Indra 48, 60, 62, 175
Indravajrā metres 22
Indumati 63

Jagannātha 143
Jamunā 165
Japākusuma 179
Jayanh Rāmayyapantulu 9
Jāta-karma 16, 41
Jātakarma Caulakarma 175
Jugupsā 157
Jyotsnā 118

Kṣīrataraṅgiṇī 34
Kṣatriya 21, 30, 61
Kūṭaja 81
Kṛpāṇa 171
Kaṁsa 47, 175
Kadalī 178
Kadamba 78, 80
Kadamba trees 129
Kaiṭabha 175
Kalaṅka 90
Kalahaṁśa 179
Kalhaṇa 3
Kali age 59, 87
Kalpa 108
Kalpavṛkṣa 112, 147
Kalāśāstra 164, 168, 189
Kamala 179
Kampaṇa 8, 9, 10, 11, 12, 13, 14, 15, 16, 17, 19, 20, 23, 29, 30, 31, 33, 45, 48, 51, 52, 53, 54, 55, 58, 59, 69, 70, 71, 75, 78, 80, 82, 83, 87, 88, 93, 95, 108, 112, 114, 115, 118, 120, 121, 123, 125, 128, 129, 131, 134, 135, 136, 138, 139, 145, 146, 147, 148, 149, 150, 151, 153, 154, 155, 156, 157, 165, 166, 168, 171, 175, 187, 188
Kamparāja 10, 11, 41
Kamparāya 60
Kampila Deśa 6
Kampila kingdom 5
Kampilarāya 6
Kampile kingdoms 4
Kampilirāya 5
Kannada Kāvyamīmāmsā 2
Karnāṭa race 59
Karnatak 4
Karnāta forces 53, 155
Karnātak forces 156
Karpūra 178
Karuṇa 21, 24, 76, 144, 189
Karuṇa Rasa 153
Kastūri-hariṇa 179
Katas 48
Kathāvastu 41
Kādambarī 88
Keṭaka flowers 81
Keṭaka trees 80
Kerala 17, 48, 145
Kesara 89, 178
Ketaka 78, 179
Khadgi 179
Khaga 85, 167

Khilji dynasty 4
Kiṁśuka trees 77
King Achutadevarāya 2
Kirātārjunīya 21, 73, 92
Kālidāsa 9, 14, 40, 74, 75, 79, 92, 117, 144, 154, 166
Kāma 18, 28, 78, 166
Kāmadeva 175
Krauñca mountain 57
Krishna and Godavari regions 7
Krishnaswami A. 33
Krishnamachariar M. 9
Kriyotprekṣā 114
Kriyāśakti 14, 116
Kārya form 133
Kāryakāraṇabhāva 126
Kuṁkuma 179
Kāśas 82
Kubera 149
Kāñcī 2, 16, 17, 19, 32, 34, 55, 71, 146, 147, 148
Kumada 179
Kumāra 61
Kumāra Kampaṇa 31, 33, 34, 35, 37
Kumāra Kampaṇadu 187
Kumārasambhava 21, 74, 88, 152, 154
Kumudvatī 139, 152
Kunda 179
Kuntala ladies 77
Kuravaka 179
Kurubaka 77
Kuśa 42
Kuñjara 179
Kuvalaya 179
Kāverī 19, 35, 45, 48, 153
Kāvya 23, 71, 93, 96, 97, 124, 126, 149, 151, 174, 175, 187, 189
Kāvyaliṅga 110, 121, 125, 127, 128, 129, 132, 189

Lakṣmī 62, 89, 137, 138
Lakṣmaṇa 70
Lakshminarayan, N. 13
Lakshminarayan Rao N. 10
Lodra 179
Lord Śiva 14, 40, 86, 90, 167
Lord Śrī Kṛṣṇa 88
Lotuses blossom 114
Luptopamā 122, 125

Mīnākṣī shrine 13
Mīnākṣī temple 13
Mṛdaṅga 173
Mṛdaṅga drums 45, 79, 153
Mṛdaṅgams 19, 35
Mṛdaṅgas (drums) 172
Maṇināga 167
Madhu 175
Madhurā 21, 32, 35, 37, 45, 47
Madhurāvijayaṁ 2, 3, 10, 11, 13, 14, 15, 16, 21, 22, 23, 24, 29, 30, 31, 32, 35, 41, 42, 45, 48, 69, 70, 71, 76, 77, 81, 84, 89, 94, 95, 108, 110, 113, 114, 116, 121, 125, 126, 130, 134, 141, 144, 145, 148, 150, 152, 154, 157, 158, 163, 166, 168, 173, 175 178, 185, 186, 188, 190
Magadha 17
Mahā-maṇḍaleśa 30
Mahābhārata 74, 109, 144
Mahilā 109
Mahākāvya 2, 21, 22, 24, 39, 40, 73, 74, 75, 94, 144, 145, 158, 165, 178
Mahāmaṇḍaleśvara 31
Mahāpradhāni Somappa Udaiya 34
Mahāpralaya 52
Malabharini 178
Mallikā 179
Malvāyilu 176

Mammaṭa 163
Mandara 48
Manmatha 121
Mantraśāstra 164, 169, 189
Manu 111
Maraca 179
Maratakanagaral 17
Mādhūrya 190
Mādhavīya Dhātuvṛtti 29
Mādhava Mantri 187
Mādhavācārya 187
Meghadūta 76
Merciful teacher 81
Māgha 40, 73, 75, 92
Mākanda 178
Mālatī 179
Mālatī flowers 129
Mālava 17
Mālopamā 24
Mohammad-Bin-Tuglak 5
Mohanāṅgī 2
Mokṣa 28
Mārtaṇḍa 175
Mātalī 63
Mugali R.S. 10
Mulbagal region 7
Mulbāgal 48
Music 164
Musical instrument (s) 82, 173
Musical notes 81
Muslim armies 6
Muslim occupation 152
Muslim rulers 7
Muslims 20, 23, 35, 45
Mutual conversation 92

Nāṭyaśāstra 143
Naiṣadhīyacarita 21, 73
Naiṣadha 88
Nala 88
Nature 75
Navacampaka 179
Navalavaṅga 179
Nāga 89
Nāgakesara 178
Nāgānandam of Harṣa 3
Nicula 179
Nidarśana 136
Nimba 178
Nipa 179
Nipuṇatā 163
Nirukti 140
Nāma 140
Nārada 57
Nārikela 179
Nārāśaṁsis 28
Nāyaka 33

Pūrṇopamā 124
Paṇḍits 2
Padaividu 48
Padmarāga gems 90
Paḍaividu 137, 188
Pāṇḍavas 135, 136
Pāṇḍya (s) 4, 46, 47, 48, 51, 58, 95, 145, 176, 187
Pallavas 176
Palmistry 164
Pampā 174, 176
Pampapathi temple 6
Paramaparita 120
Paraddi, M.B. 11
Paraśurāma 57
Parikara 115, 139, 140
Parisaṅkhyā 24
Paryāyokta 140
Pañcama notes 77
Persian 46
Phalotprekṣā 112, 113
Philosophy 164
Physical Science 164
Poetic charm 140
Poetic work 123
Political Science 164, 168
Prabandha 40, 188
Prabhudevī 9

Prasāda Śleṣa 190
Pratīpa 24
Pratināyaka 145
Prativastūpamā 140
Pratāpa Rudradeva 13
Prauḍhokti· 140
Preya 140
Pārijāta 16, 179
Prince 69
Priyamvadā 66
Prof. M. Hiriyanna 143
Pārvatī 40, 125, 175
Pātala 179
Puṣpitāgrā metre 22
Puṣpitāgra 178
Puṁsavana Saṁskāra 16
Purāṇas 29, 164, 166
Puruṣottama 61
Puruṣārthas 166
Putanas 48

Rūpaka 24, 109, 110, 117, 118, 119, 120, 121, 129, 172, 189
Rīti 106
Rītis 143
Raṅganātha inscription 177
Raghu 48, 67
Raghu-nāthārāya 2
Raghuvaṁśa 21, 40, 41, 42, 60, 67, 69, 70, 74, 91, 92, 93
Raghavacharya, K. 9
Raghavan, V. 13
Rainbow 115
Rainy season (Varṣā-Ṛtu) 18, 79, 81
Rajas 166
Ramā 11
Rasa (s) 74, 106, 107, 141, 143, 144
Rasa delineation 96
Rasa theory 143
Rasātala 114
Ratikrīḍā 151
Raudra 189
Red sandhyaka flowers 86
Religion 164
Rāhu 175
Rāja Parameśvara 30
Rājagambhīra 54, 95
Rājagambhīramalai 33, 48
Rājagambhīrarājya 34
Rājanītiśāstra 189
Rājanārāyaṇa Śambuvarāya 33
Rājataraṅgiṇī 3
Rājaśekhara 1, 8, 9
Rājādhirāja 30
Rājyalakṣmī 59
Rākṣasa (s) 56, 157
Rākṣasis 53
Rāma 32, 42, 48, 57, 67, 68, 69, 70, 71, 188
Rāmabhadrāmbā 2
Rāmachandra Deva 4
Rāmananda 31
Rāmāyaṇa 40, 70, 74, 75, 88, 93, 144
Rohiṇī 40, 122, 123, 175
Row B.S. 29
Royal ladies 83
Ṛtusaṁhāra 76, 79
Ṛturāja 76
Rāvaṇā 42
Rāvaṇa 48, 67, 68, 69, 70, 71

Sūratrāṇa 20, 148
Sītā 9, 68, 71
Śṛṅgāra 21, 23, 24, 76, 96, 144, 149, 154, 165, 189
Śṛṅgāra Rasa 150, 151, 158
Śṛṅgārarasa 84
Saṅgīta-Sahityarnava 8
Saṅgītai-kanidhi 8
Saṅgītaśāstra-Nṛtyaśāstra 189
Saṅgama 16, 29, 30
Sacrificial fire 55
Safarā 179

Sahṛdayas 2, 14, 15, 23, 126, 143, 153, 163
Sahṛdayāhlādi 109
Sahakāra 179
Sahokti 140
Saletore B.A. 11
Sairibha 179
Śārṅgin 11
Samatā 190
Sambuvarāya ruler 17
Samādhi 190
Samrāja 20
Samāsokti 140
Sandeha 132
Sanskrit drama 2
Sanskrit kāvya (s) 9, 10
Sanskrit literature 1, 2, 9, 21, 75, 88, 92
Sanskrit Mahākāvyas 29
Sanskrit poets 76, 79, 87
Sanskrit scholar Nacha-mamba 2
Sanskrit scholars 1, 8, 9
Śānta 21, 144
Sarasvatī 117, 118
Sarasvatī's anklets 17
Sarvamaṅgala (Pārvatī) 116
Sasandeha 140
Satī 11
Satakratu 61
Sattva 166
Sañcārībhāvas 153, 157
Saukumārya Arthavyakti 190
Sādhāraṇadharma 122, 123, 125
Śaṅkara 175
Śabda 105
Śabdaśleṣa 109
Śabdālaṅkāra 107, 108
Śaivism 174
Śakti 163
Śākra 11
Śambhu 11
Śambuvarāya 32, 33, 34, 48, 52, 55, 69, 71, 93, 94, 128, 132, 145, 146, 147, 157, 168, 171, 188
Śambuvarāya territory 125, 130, 173
Śatrughna 70
Serpent Kaliya 60
Sevuna 17
Śeṣa 49, 68, 87, 114, 132, 133, 147, 149
Siṁha 179
Siṁhaḷa 17
Śiśupālavadha 21, 40, 73, 88, 89, 92, 94
Siddhārthī 187
Śirīṣa 84, 179
Śiva 16, 42, 61, 131, 167
Sāmrājya (Supremacy) 95, 148
Soma Deva 6
Śoṇa 64
Śleṣa 107, 110
Sphuṭaṁ 115
Spring festival ladies 18
Spring Season (Vasanta Ṛtu) 18, 77
Sri Lanka 177
Srirangam 45
Śrī Kṛṣṇa 47, 165, 167
Śrī Mahā Viṣṇu 188
Śrīharṣa 73, 75, 154
Śrīkṛṣṇā 86
Śṛgāla 179
Sthāyībhāva 157
Subhadrā 9
Subrahmaṇya 16, 124, 125
Sudakṣiṇā 40, 63
Śūkara 179
Sumeru 87, 90, 135
Summer Season (Grīṣmaṛtu) 18, 84
Sundarapāṇḍya 177
Suratrāṇa 30, 58, 59, 95

Suratrāṇa (Sultan) 36
Svabhāvokti 140
Svarūpotprekṣā 112, 113
Svargaloka 89
Śvetāśvatara 166
Swinging creepers 76
Sāyaṇācārya 187

Tadgunaṅkāra 140
Tamas 166
Tamāla 85, 179
Tamraparṇī 20
Taraṣku 179
Telagu-Rāmāyaṇa 2
Thunder murmurings 80
Tikkayya 14
Tirumalāmbā 2
Tāmraparṇī 15, 35, 46, 57, 91, 158
Tondaimaṇḍalam '176
Trilocana (Śiva) 116
Tuṅgabhadrā 3, 15, 16, 52, 89, 91
Tugalak Rāj 4
Tuglak empire 4
Turīya 82
Turaṣka 48, 59, 95, 156
Turaṣka king 20
Turaṣkas 45, 46, 47, 153
Turaṁga 179
Turuṣka forces 57, 69
Turuṣka Samrājya 36, 59

Udayagirirāja 29
Udayarāga 169
Udātta 138
Ullekha 140
Upajāti 22, 178
Upamā 24, 105, 109, 115, 117, 121, 122, 189
Upamā Pratipādaka 122
Upameya 110, 116, 122, 129, 130, 131, 132, 135, 136, 137
Upameyas 118, 119, 120, 124
Upamāna (s) 111, 115, 118, 119, 120, 121, 124, 129, 130, 131, 134, 135, 137
Upamāpratipādaka śabda 124
Upmeya 117
Utprekṣā 24, 110, 111, 112, 113, 114, 116, 117, 121, 172, 189
Utsāha 145

Vīṇā 173
Vīra 21, 24, 144, 145, 165
Vīra Ballāla 95
Vīra Kamparaya Caritaṁ 11
Vīra Kumāra Kampaṇa 10
Vīra Rasa 23, 149, 150, 189
Vīrabukkarāya Kampaṇa 31
Vīrakampaṇa 12
Vīrarasa 144
Vṛtra 20, 58, 95, 175
Vṛttyanuprāsa 108
Vaṁśastha 178
Vaṁśastha metre 22
Vaidarbhī style 190
Vanninyas 32
Vanya kingdom 58
Varṣārtu 128
Varadāmbikā 2
Varadāmbikāpariṇaya 2
Vasanta 123
Vastūtprekṣā 114, 115
Vastudhvani 110, 140
Vedas 45, 153, 164
Vedic Dharma 8
Vedic mantras 174
Venrumankonda Śambuvarāya 33
Vernal (vasanta) season 77
Viṣṇu 35, 44, 82, 85, 87, 137, 147, 149, 167
Viṣṇupāda 167
Vibhāda 30

Vibhāvanā 132, 140
Vibhāvas 74
Vidūṣaka 154
Vijayanagar empire 7
Vijjanaka 9
Vijjhatā 2
Vikṭanitambī 9
Virūpākṣa 15, 174
Virinchipuram 48
Virodhābhāsa 110, 137, 138, 189
Viśvanātha 13, 14
Viyogabhāva 127
Viyoginī 178
Viyoginī metre 22
Vākyārtha 126
Vālmīki 14, 40, 70, 71, 76, 79, 188
Vāmana 105, 106, 147
Vow of chastity 86
Vāritābhiḥ 109
Vāruṇāstra of Kāmadeva 92
Vyatireka 24, 110, 134, 189
Vyāsa 14, 109
War-drums 48
War-music (war-drums) 50
Western Ocean 131
Western oceans 29
Western sanskrit scholar 12
Winter Season (Hemanta Ṛtu) 18
Whitney, W.D. 12
Winternitz, M. 10

Yūthikā 78
Yadava Rāmachandra 4
Yamaka 24, 107, 108
Yamunā 60, 167
Yathāsāṅkhya 140
Yatudhanas 48
Yavana (s) 20, 46, 47, 58, 95, 148
Yavana king 59
Yellow-rice (akṣata) 59
Yāgadhūma 19
Yogic sleep 137
Yuddhaśāstra 189
Yuddhavīra (s) 145, 146, 149
Yuddhavīratā 147
Yuvarāja 186